Entrepreneurship in Developing and Emerging Economies

Entrepreneurship in Developing and Emerging Economies

Maleehah Gull

SOCIETY Publishing

www.societypublishing.com

Entrepreneurship In Developing And Emerging Economies

Maleehah Gull

Society Publishing
224 Shoreacres Road
Burlington, ON L7L 2H2
Canada
www.societypublishing.com
Email: orders@arclereducation.com

ISBN: 978-1-77407-716-0 (Hardcover)

ABOUT THE AUTHOR

Maleehah Gull obtained her Masters in Business Administration in Management Information System and Master of Science Degree in Project Management from University of Malaya. She served as lecturer for two years and Currently, pursuing her PhD in Management Science from Universiti Teknologi Malaysia.

TABLE OF CONTENTS

LIST OF ABBREVIATIONS

BIPIK	Pembinaan dan Pengembangan Industri Kecil
BRIC	Brazil, Russia, India, and China
CI	conservation international
CVC	corporate VC
DMFs	developed advertise firms
EMFs	emerging business sector firms
EU	European Union
FDI	Foreign Direct Investment
FINEP	Financing Agency for Projects and Studies
GEM	Global Entrepreneurship Monitor
GIIN	Global Impact Investing Network
GNP	gross national product
ICTs	information and communication technologies
IMF	International Monetary Fund
IPO	initial public offering
IRIS	impact reporting investing standards
IRP	integrated resource plan
NGOs	non-governmental organizations
NSB	National Science Board
OECD	Organization for Economic Co-operation and Development
RBV	resource-based view
SEZs	special economic zones
SMEs	small and medium-sized enterprises
TEA	total entrepreneurial activity
UNIDO	United Countries Industrial Development Organization

VC	venture capital
VCs	venture capitalists

PREFACE

It has always been challenging for entrepreneurs to operate in developing and emerging economies. These challenges could include unsteady practices and insecure monetary conditions. Such entrepreneurship has been highly influenced by the globalization, technology revolution, and environmental concerns. This book sheds light on the macro-level entrepreneurship in emerging economies. It further explains the concept of developing and emerging economies.

In today's era of technology, one cannot ignore the significance of the technology revolution which has impacted the business world and has hanged the meanings of entrepreneurship. Therefore, this book explores the technological aspects of digital world which has greatly contributed to the emerging economies.

As for the entrepreneurs in developed economies, the fiscal matters and environmental concerns are also discussed for the developing economies as well. Furthermore, opportunities for the new and old entrepreneurs are also included in this book. The book has covered the geographical aspect mainly to focus on the countries having developing and emerging economies.

Chapter 1

GLOBAL ENTREPRENEURSHIP

The financial advancement of a nation relies today upon qualified incorporation into the world economy. Before, internationalization would in general be confined to huge organizations. Today, small and medium-sized enterprises (SMEs) have gotten associated with the worldwide market in an assortment of ways. The developing internationalization of the small and medium-size firms has animated the formation of a field of studies planned for understanding this new marvel, the alleged "universal new pursuits," "brought into the world worldwide," "worldwide new companies" or "global entrepreneurship." The internationalization of these organizations depends on particular highlights: their tasks and systems are not equivalent to the huge firms, as they are not equivalent to the organizations that stay on the home market. Internationalization requires small and medium-size firms to activate various types of assets (monetary and social) that particularly force more noteworthy degrees of risks and indeterminacy. Previously, small and medium-size firms would in general be viewed as unfortunate casualties; at present, they are viewed as 'players in the game.'

Universal entrepreneurship is definitely not another marvel, yet today is absolutely more noteworthy than it was a few decades prior. Components that have added to small and medium-size firms inclusion in universal business are, among others, the expanding utilization of data and correspondence advancements (ICTs: information and communication technologies), development of information escalated enterprises, decreased expenses of transportation and coordination, exchange progression and expanding rivalry, more noteworthy familiarity with global financial opportunities, the need to impart information and expenses to accomplices and the absence of qualified HR on the home markets.

In reality, because of movements in innovation assembling and information concentrated administrations, an overall rebuilding is occurring. This can be shown by looking at information on world exchange for the periods spreading over 1980–1993 and 1994–2008. Information shows a noteworthy increment in the yearly normal of worldwide fare from 3.6–7.8% just as an adjustment in the sort of merchandise and enterprises sent out: there has been expressive development of high mechanical products and information escalated administrations while work concentrated products have endured a decrease.

A move in the transition of world exchange can likewise be watched, with fare of medium and progressive products and enterprises expanding at higher rates in the emerging economies (coming about basically from Chinese and Korean exhibitions) than in the developed economies. The idea of worldwide tasks has additionally changed: notwithstanding export or potentially business exercises, these activities currently incorporate organizations and agreements with different ventures for assembling or collection forms, for appropriation, upkeep, after-deal support, and for brand move and establishments abroad. These progressions can, to an enormous degree, be viewed because of the idea of advancement, innovation move encouraged by worldwide corporate interests in R&D, just as the expanding volume of outside direct interests in emerging economies and to wrap things up, the spread of science and mechanical limit far and wide. In fact, explore ventures are developing all the more quickly outside the focuses that recently overwhelmed world R&D North America, Europe, and Japan.

The development of information serious entrepreneurship in emerging economies might be related with overall decentralization of R&D, made conceivable, as it were, by ICTs, Information from the Science and Engineering Indicators, 2010, of the National Science Board (NSB), USA, uncover another guide of R&D in 2007, North America and European Union (EU) were liable for 63% of the world's US$ 1,10 trillion put resources into this territory, when contrasted with 71% in 1996. The Asian Pacific's (basically China, Japan, and Korea) commitment rose from 24% to 31%. Latin America stayed a minor player with a simple 2.6% of the aggregate. Regardless of the area's low execution, Brazil rises as its pioneer in R&D, showing development that has repercussions for advancement and innovative entrepreneurship.

Since the finish of the 1990s, progressive Brazilian organizations have put forth critical attempts to animate the internationalization of the Brazilian firms, through a scope of motivating forces which have included SMEs. The Productive Development Policy gave in 2008, planned for expanding private interests in R&D so as to make conditions for the nation's certified coordination (counting SMEs) into worldwide exchange. The Brazilian Research and Innovation Enterprise (EMBRAPII) were made, in association with the German Institute Fraunhofer. It targets advancing development in modern and administration divisions, in light of the standards of the effective Brazilian Enterprise of Agricultural Research (EMBRAPA), which works 90 research habitats all through the nation. EMBRAPII tries to extend the arrangement of development principally inside SMEs.

Internationalization is a general idea that incorporates an assortment of exercises, for example, exportation of merchandise and ventures or foundation of joint enterprises and auxiliaries abroad, planned for setting up agreements and associations among enterprises for the improvement of R&D exercises. Right now, utilize the idea "internationalization" in its general sense, that is, the transition to convey monetary and profitable exercises past fringes; as it were, exercises that are not confined to business activity. Internationalization is constantly viewed as here with an attention on mechanical development.

There is some agreement in the writing that internationalization positively affects firm execution. Internationalization infers more prominent exchange costs than would be brought about inside home markets, in this manner requiring the improvement of firm execution. Hence, a procedure of corresponding impact is set off: internationalization favors the improvement of a company's innovative limit which, thus, benefits its seriousness. Firms may likewise profit by trades that are set up with universal research places, some of which are known for their greatness. Moreover, the chance of setting up organizations with different firms for joint improvements of products and enterprises, planned for getting to new markets, is opened.

The presence of solid relationship between exportation, advancement (R&D) and increment in efficiency are considered as well. That relationship would be particularly evident while considering SMEs in emerging countries, which profit by the association with outside enterprises through the exchange of innovative, administrative, and advertise information. There is additionally proof that shows a positive relationship between trading firms and improved HR the executives (for example, higher wages and interest in preparing). Firms that depend essentially on trading what they produce have 3.6 occasions more likelihood of delivering radical advancement than firms depending on nearby or local markets; firms that take an interest in agreeable courses of action with different associations for the improvement of development have multiple times a greater number of odds of creating radical development than firms that are not engaged with participation with different associations.

Information based firms will in general utilize increasingly complex procedures in planning another item, an improved formation strategy or progressively proficient assistance conveyance. For example, in the Bio-mechanical area, a firm may create forms that include some kind of control of human qualities. These organizations may appreciate the chance of internationalizing to the extent that they will in general hold a serious practical bit of leeway which might be popular in different countries. The inventive internationalized firms pay better wages, utilize qualified individuals consume relatively more assets in preparing, which improves the laborers' capability.

New highlights of monetary improvement set apart by information based ventures, internationalization, and advancement speak to a noteworthy test for an emerging economy like Brazil. The Brazilian industrialization process depended on an import-substitution model, intended for the home market and supported by solid state protectionism. This attempted to forestall the development of a culture of advancement, to the extent that the prevailing concern turned into the formation of merchandise that had recently been imported. However, in the course of the most recent two decades, stood up to by new monetary elements, Brazil has been put forth an enormous attempt to defeat the lacunas that were the inheritance of the "old culture." Since the finish of the 1990s, the nation has been executing arrangements targeting invigorating development, helped by private interest in R&D and trying to make the nation famous as a pertinent player in the universal advancement situation. Motivations likewise target smaller scale and small progressive organizations.

Despite government motivators, creative small and medium size organizations in Brazil show low execution in export exercises. In addition, this is especially valid as to the main divisions of the "new economy"-ICTs and the Life Sciences area. Solitary 11.2% of the respondents announced repetitive fare action, while 22.4% revealed that they traded sometimes. In any case, 30.7% of these organizations pronounced a goal to partake on the planet showcase inside the following two years. Enterprises are being made to conquer low execution: in the territory of Biotechnology, BrBiotec, a Technical Network in Biotechnology and Health, was as of late made, to reinforce the character and execution of Brazilian firms on a world scale.

Regardless of low execution in the fare of innovative merchandise and ventures, Brazil's fare structure has experienced change. On account of products delivered with lower levels of innovation (materials, calfskin, shoes, wood, paper, and cellulose), a diminishing from 43%, in 1996, to 36%, in 2007, can be watched; in any case, this was trailed by a later increment that brought the collection up again to past rates, arriving at 42% in 2009. Items requiring medium-high and medium-low mechanical force kept up a generally adjusted example, with some minor variance, over the period. The world emergency clarifies drops in the medium-high collection (vehicles and capital merchandise, refined oil and different fills) and the medium-low collection (elastic, plastic items, refined oil and different energizes; other mineral items) in 2008–2009.

The innovative collection (planes and aviation gear/administrations, pharmaceuticals, data, and correspondence advances, clinical, and optical hardware) has expanded its interest from 5%, in 1996, to 15%, in 2000, because of planes and wireless fare. From 2003 on, trades right now tumbled to 9%, fundamentally because of the drop in phone sends out; in any case, when contrasted with 1996, a huge increment gets clear. There is an inclination to sum up firms' internationalization direction as a continuum that moves from neighborhood to around the world, with territorial nearness as a transitional stage.

This inclination runs on the supposition that the lower the degree of social contrasts and lands separation, the quicker, and progressively fruitful the course to internationalization. However, the legitimacy of this supposition might be addressed, since in the time of simple correspondence, an association's direction is probably going to be identified with the monetary dynamism of an area or market, paying little heed to land or social separations (a contention that we will be grow later on).

In looking at the internationalization of small and medium-size firms, momentum writing will in general feature the purported auxiliary viewpoints or empowering powers: quicker and lower cost transportation that have empowered individuals and products (the containerization of cargo) to move effectively among countries and improved correspondence (on line correspondence through computerized innovation as well as offices for abroad travel). Be that as it may, it is likewise recognized that all together for auxiliary variables to be compelling, persuading powers must be set into movement. Concerning the internationalization of little firms, a few viewpoints might be recognized as inspiring drives: decrease of taxes in target countries; motivating forces gave by the nation of origin government; the impact of universal disapproved of the executives; sharing of information and research costs through key collusions and joint effort; great deals and benefit opportunities in remote markets; new markets; willful requests from outside purchasers; outside skill to improve household seriousness; attainable approaches to transport to outside business sectors; unused gainful limit; unfriendly local economic situations; looser item guidelines in target countries; good cash trade values; remote contenders' passageway into the residential market and access to human and money related assets.

Past goal and empowering factors, a few investigators additionally underline the capacity of specific people to see important opportunities, which they call "opportunity acknowledgment." This is viewed as a focal quality of entrepreneurial conduct, the hidden emotional part of the wonder: how entrepreneurial entertainers decipher or intervene the opportunities that are made by empowering and rousing powers. The manner by which an entrepreneur watches and deciphers opportunities to empower internationalization is viewed as unexpected, to enormous degree, on close to home encounters and attributes (e.g., earlier universal encounters) and mental characteristics.

Different experts challenge the emotional point of view by attesting that opportunities must be perceived by people with specific capacities. Surely, the impression of opportunities requires a decent variety of data. The significance of the systems and their expansion, just as taking in procured from before employments or other expert encounters are on the whole notable components. Research discoveries feature the outright pertinence of such factors. In any case, they might be viewed as an essential yet not adequate condition, since among numerous individuals in comparable individual and social circumstances; just a couple decide to establish a firm.

To put it plainly, a few methodologies stress the entrepreneur's capacity to see opportunities and settle on choices dependent on his/her qualities and mentalities; others feature the job of organizations and the general financial conditions preferring or compelling entertainers' choices and dynamic. To seclude just one of these points of view would prompt too short-sighted a situation; as Thornton attests; entrepreneurship is a powerful wonder, changing as indicated by social-financial and innovative changes. Individual or financial or social elements might be liable for the rise of the marvel in one period yet not in another, since the idea of entrepreneurship and the necessities for beginning a business additionally change. This is by all accounts an increasingly sufficient methodology for breaking down universal entrepreneurship too, since little firms' internationalization results from a blend of elements made by foundations, condition, the nature of the business and on-screen characters' abilities.

Various firms have taken various ways towards internationalization, in this way restricting conceivable outcomes for speculation. This thusly represents a few issues for points of view that expect firms move, bit by bit, from shorter to longer separations, regardless of whether in land or potentially social terms. The directions of the organizations depict different situations. Following the customer, this is the situation of firm A, made during the 1990s and work being developed of programming for the shoe business (in southern Brazil). It was established by a scholastic that deserted scholarly exercises because of the troubles he had in joining them with business. These challenges were increased by internationalization itself, with its attendant promise to travel and long remains abroad.

Right now, internationalization process started in 2004, following in the wake of a customer-a Brazilian shoe organization which had started formation tasks in China. Around 80% of the firm salary is developed from trade (a past 90%). As we see here, the procedure of internationalization came about because of a backhanded factor: the fundamental customer moved formation to China, trying to confront the test of Chinese challenge. Truth be told, this is not a strange type of internationalization; it has happened inside the cowhide business with certain organizations moving to Spain and China. Albeit "following a customer" may appear to be a simpler method to internationalize since obviously, the weighty work has been completed by the customer-as a general rule the procedure requests noteworthy changes for the product provider. Backing and upkeep administrations, require extensive alteration, for example, workers' serious preparing; this has remembered assembling aptitudes for oral and composed correspondence in English, not frequently required for Brazilian representatives, not even in the product business. The requirement for visit travel to inaccessible spots is referred to by workers as another issue, requesting the capacity to conform to various or irregular circumstances.

The firm utilizes 30 individuals, of whom 70% hold undergrad and advanced educations. The staying 30% are right now going to college classes. The organization's organizer communicated worry over the current circumstance: as indicated by him, since 2004, PC experts' wages have expanded 80%, while the business' pay was diminished significantly because of the de-valuation of US cash trades rate. Additionally, high staff turnover should be considered, a sign of shortage of work force, which endangers firm interests in preparing.

The firm continues a cozy relationship with the college, through joint improvement of research ventures with scholastics, just as giving preparing to understudies. Key coalitions with universal accomplices-this is the situation of firm B-one of the most creative little firms in the field of Biotechnology in Brazil. It is a run of the mill information-serious firm, contributing 60% of its yearly salary in look into exercises. Its author is an ideal case of "researcher entrepreneur," saving the characteristics of a genuine researcher which he melds with the useful perspective on an entrepreneur. There, he was presented to another kind of experience: his scholarly preparing was joined by specialized preparing inside a biotech firm situated inside the college mechanical park. This experience gave him ability in specialized parts of the field. As opposed to what happens in Brazil, the age of information was thought about there as a potential tradable item. His arrival to Brazil, in 1999, harmonized with the government approach that made an arrangement of help for Science, Technology, and Innovation, ensuring account assets for R&D focused on the advancement of research and development in the private part too-something that had been beforehand nearly inexistent.

Development systems include interest in important advancement, so as to create new information at the worldwide level, instead of just adding enhancements to an item previously existing abroad. This sort of development increases the value of the item. The firm develops and brings in cash not by just misusing the company's assets, however, by increasing the value of the items. This organization has accomplices in Canada, Germany, and Brazil, through exchange understandings (dispersion and portrayal), joint enterprises (through common innovation move) and through contracting. The collaboration understanding marked with a Canadian firm, from Toronto, looks to build up an antibody for prostate malignant growth. The Brazilian firm is planning to go to open contributions (IPO: initial public offering), at the Toronto stock exchange.

Brought into the world Worldwide-Firm C began in 2003, trading electronic games (for family amusement focuses), first, to Spain, through the assistance of an affiliate. The firm had the option to extend to other European markets: it has traded to in excess of 30 countries in Europe, Asia, Africa, and

Middle East and has dispersion contracts with 17 worldwide firms. Toward the start, markets were opened through the assistance of individual informal organizations. Development to different markets was to a great extent helped out through the association's essence in fairs and through contacts by means of Internet. Up to this point, it sent out up to 60% of its formation. In 2010, sends out dropped to 20%, because of the fall of universal interest and the concurrent development of the home market, basically because of up and coming worldwide occasions, for example, World Cup and Olympic Games, which will require electronic gear developed by the firm.

The firm likewise creates casting a ballot machines utilized in a few state parliaments in Brazil. The association's entrepreneur considers sends out significant basically in light of the estimation of criticism from abroad-which he sees as contributing with new thoughts that help to improve the items and to tax reductions, thought about a method for making up for the high tax assessment from the home market. The company's objective is to export 50% of its complete formation. One of its originators, as of now the minor accomplice, is a college specialist in Computer Science. The significant accomplice has a foundation as a staff part at a firm which made games. The mix of the two sorts of expertise has permitted them to turn out to be fruitful, through development in electronic hardware and games.

The company's R&D has around 30 representatives (33% of the complete number of workers). The significant piece of firm C speculations originates from its own assets, in spite of the fact that it has as of late taken an advance from an open bank so as to construct new establishments. In spite of the straightforwardness with which credit (at lower rates) can be acquired (particularly since the firm was granted a prize for its creative presentation), the proprietor is wary about taking advances; he fears erratic moves in the market.

Sub-contracting in China-Firm D decided to subcontract out to China so as to profit by lower work costs in creating the bureau for one thing in its telecom gear. In any case, it kept its imaginative research area at home. Delivering in China is likewise an approach to manage Chinese challenge. It includes a procedure of innovation move from the Brazilian firm to the makers in that nation, so as to ensure consistence with quality principles and utilization of tests to guarantee the quality benchmarks required. Besides, the pieces delivered in China experience careful testing for consistence with gauges at home. The firm has 90 representatives, 33% of whom work in R&D. The firm likewise contracts out R&D benefits and keeps up an organization with a college to do two research ventures. Previously, these assets originated from the company's own assets. At present, some portion of this cash originates from a government gift: the firm and a college have gotten assets to create inquire about enterprises mutually. The emphasis on R&D is additionally identified with the association's anxiety for expanding its item portfolio so as to diminish showcase helplessness.

Firm E is a little firm which centers around R&D. It was made in 2001 by a collection of specialists from two notable colleges in the South of Brazil who were roused by a call from a government program to back information concentrated firms. Its present proprietors are three people holding PhDs in Biotechnology, two of whom work in the scholastic region and a third, gave to the board exercises. The products and ventures the firm offers depend on present day Biotechnology and Bio data.

Firm exercises are focused on R&D, concentrating on biopharmaceutical inquire about. They do take part in business exercises yet depend on affiliates for pressing and offering the items to different firms. Firm E utilizes 22 gifted staff individuals. For around four years, firm pay was produced by the stock of biopharmaceuticals to bigger residential firms. These organizations, be that as it may, were purchased by other bigger organizations, a solidification procedure normal for what goes on in the business around the world. Beforehand marked agreements were broken, creating punishments that permitted Firm E to proceed in the business. The biotech firm depended intensely on government financing. To supplement its financial limit, the firm does administrations for bigger firms. Its salary is completely depleted on maintaining the business and proprietors are not as of now accepting installment; their pay originates from their scholastic work at the college.

This firm delineates of the principle highlights of the new worldview very well, that is, the cozy connection between scholarly life and business. Its internationalization started through a remote request coming about because of a scholarly paper composed by one of its authors which were gotten to on line. The American backup of a German global communicated enthusiasm for a potential item and asked the organization whether it would be keen on delivering and sending out it. The American firm at that point helped the Brazilian firm with the techniques to get the fare procedure going an unwieldy procedure for sure, since they are managing organic material that requires severe confirmation rules. The connection between the organizations worked well overall, until the 2008 monetary emergency which decreased and in the end ended interest.

Firms have an assortment of attributes: a few items and administrations, for example, the ones identified with life sciences and Biotechnology are increasingly mind boggling and harder to work with than others. Biotechnology is one of the key segments in the "new economy" draws in billions of dollars in capital on an overall scale, yet should adapt to outrageous risk and vulnerability. Advancement in Biotechnology requests a long procedure and relies upon time-concentrated R&D work. In any case, the existence sciences, and Biotechnology industry in Brazil is developing, especially in wellbeing biotechnology (fundamentally in the regions of antibodies and diagnostics). The nation has procured a solid specialized situation in various pivotal empowering territories, for example, foundational microorganism inquires about, genomic contemplates, plant Biotechnology and immunizations. Around 75% of the part is made up by little firms. Despite the significant governmental job in supporting R&D inside life sciences organizations, focusing on internationalization (64.1% of the aggregate sum of US$ 95.8 million put resources into 2008), the area's global accomplishment despite everything stays exceptionally low.

In the hardware business, where rivalry is brutal and items have a short life, internationalization is viewed as a type of enduring, through fare, as well as by setting up key coalitions and subcontracting. In all, terms, internationalization was seen by our interviewees as a method for improving organization intensity, since in the worldwide period-where access to the business sectors is as far as anyone knows simpler-products and enterprises must have universal quality and costs, whether or not developed for home or outside business sectors.

In spite of sectorial contrasts and the unmistakable ways to internationalization that describe the cases we have investigated, the entirety of our interviewees professed to have been profited by ease in correspondences, especially electronic correspondence. Now and again, it has been completely essential for business rise and extension. Dependence on electronic correspondence is especially valid on account of Brazil, where work laws make it for all intents and purposes unthinkable for a little firm to keep up representatives abroad. Web was viewed as a considerable device for getting data of various types identified with firm execution. Access to fairs and shows was additionally observed as a significant opportunity to take part in worldwide business.

Internationalization experience positively affects firm execution. Imperatives originating from necessities and affirmations which are now and then very severe were viewed as an opportunity to learn and to improve the nature of the items and administrations. Imperatives were recognized as emerging fundamentally from local issues. A typical protest was identified with the absence of gifted work force expected to manage inventive research connected to advertise requests. It was noticed that individuals holding college degrees are set up for the scholastic world yet not for creating advancement. The absence of talented staff produces overwhelming challenge over HR inside information concentrated firms. Different issues that entrepreneurs highlighted were the abundance of bureaucratic methods forced by Brazilian establishments and money trade rates that devaluate the US dollar versus other national monetary forms, along these lines preferring imports over fares.

The world financial emergency was viewed as an issue acting to diminish request. Regardless, the nation's financial development and ideal economic situations ensure the extension of the home market, without the vulnerabilities and challenges of exchanging across fringes. In this way, little new companies which have been included just sporadically inside the world market become less propelled to internationalize. The organizations we examined have had various directions, execution results, and way reliance, showing the risks of speculations about creative information escalated entrepreneurship. Their affinities can be distinguished as a mutual spotlight on development.

The two firms that come nearest to what could be classified "radical development" are in the Biotechnology field. One of them (Firm E) is still subject to government support while the other one (Firm B) depended vigorously on government support previously. It had the option to combine its direction through key global coalitions and it is presently getting ready to go to IPO, in Canada. The two different firms which are at present experiencing procedures of development (Firms C and D) depend primarily on their own assets and can be viewed as dependent on gradual advancement. At present, they are diverting the significant piece of their formation to the home market, due to conjuncture conditions. Firm A, concentrated on programming advancement, was additionally the one which answered to have been most brutally influenced by the negative effect of the present money trade circumstance.

At the full scale level, the alleged information economy and globalization invigorated by ICT achievability have would in general kindness monetary decentralization of formation and of R, D &I, which may encourage disclosure of promising business sector specialties and business opportunities. The accessibility of a national/provincial arrangement of advancement, anyway early, will in general kindness the development of innovative entrepreneurship in eminent economies. In the Brazilian case, despite horrible social and institutional highlights, government enactment since the finish of the 1990s has been a solid factor in invigorating entrepreneurship.

At the smaller scale level, it has been demonstrated that entrepreneurs have a specific perspective on the possibilities of some economic situations, adding to the quest for their objectives, even contrary to what would be expected of transcendent social and social originations. In that sense, their nonconformist point of view appears to assume a job. Singular contrasts in economic wellbeing did not compare to contrasts in the "opportunity acknowledgment," a capacity that depends to a huge degree on data yet in addition on a capacity to utilize it through creating information.

Singular presentation to numerous social and social impacts (regardless of whether at work, in school or through different methods for data, locally or abroad) is essential in supporting the choice to be an entrepreneur, especially when this does not appear to establish a level-headed decision. The reliance of fruitful entrepreneurial enterprises and financial exercises on inserted and thickly associated system of social entertainers was illustrated, just as the significance of system broadening permitting firms to distinguish and get to novel data and the assets required for supported advancement and improved execution. For the situation in point, rising social orders, the enunciation of instructive and logical foundations, understudies, teachers, government, different enterprises, among others social entertainers, uncover connections that are not appropriately installed inside social settings but instead gained from a specially appointed circumstance. To adapt to troubles, firms need to expand their systems past the shut logical hover, so as to arrive at various outer accomplices: the fund business and driving financial specialists, managerial experts in zones identified with law, assessments, and showcasing, nearby specialists, clients, outside accomplices and contenders.

Progressive firms can assemble various techniques that permit them to confront rivalry from contenders who are better-situated in efficient and mechanical terms. A key distinction between firms was recognized: a) those delivering steady developments (enhancements in effectively existing items—new to the national and to the Latin American markets), depended on their R&D offices, on pertinent data generally looked for abroad and on imported gear; b) those organizations whose advancement can be described as radical development or something like it, (new to the world market) uncover a higher degree in originators' degree of logical preparing. This might be vital factor in clarifying the distinction we have recognized.

The internationalized information based firms we have inquired about here spotlight on R&D exercises, since advancement is the primary technique they utilize to contend in the worldwide market. All the organizations we considered had their own R&D division, which as a rule represented 33% of absolute staff. This component shows another pattern among firms, since in Brazil—an enduring outcome of the import-substitution model of industrialization-even huge organizations will in general have little enthusiasm for keeping up a R&D division. A portion of the creative firms we contemplated would in general benefit the R in drawback of D. Now and again, firms follow the hierarchical standards of the new division of work, which will in general separate R&D from formation, which, thusly, is re-appropriated. Two firms in our examination fell in that classification.

The attention on R&D has made motivations for the improvement of connections among firms and colleges. The organizations we examined all referenced a relationship with the colleges. The two firms in the Biotechnology part have a closer relationship to scholastic life albeit both have their own R, D&I divisions. Nonetheless, development, the making of merchandise and ventures focusing available-was practiced at the firm itself while colleges contributed with information formation and the preparation of gifted work force. The college job has not been an applicable wellspring of development for the organizations, however, keeps up an auxiliary job, basically identified with work force enrolment, consultancy, and research associations. One instance of joint improvement of research ventures was watched, uncovering a closer connection between the firm and scholastics in which the scholastics were additionally the proprietors of the organization.

To encourage internationalization, advancement must be joined by showcase possibilities and information on correspondence channels. Data advances are a priceless commitment in facilitating the weights of correspondence that have, before, presented limitations on the SME internationalization. For our respondents, another pivotal methodology alludes to keeping up participation at displays and fairs, so as to get mindful of oddities, distinguish the courses that huge firms are clearing and quest for worldwide purchasers and associations.

As we have referenced, the cases we considered did not affirm the theory that one of the significant motivating forces for firms to participate in universal business is identified with purported "clairvoyant separation," that is, the better information they have about business opportunities in their quick environment, empowering the procedure of internationalization to follow a slow way from territorial to worldwide. Our discoveries, in actuality, show that the unequivocal factor in regards to decision of a business fate is not identified with "mystic separation," however, to monetary dynamism. On the off chance that a unique economy is found in an inaccessible as opposed to neighborhood area, social, and geological separation may not be determinant. Among the organizations we considered, universal systems were not situated in Latin America. It appears that simpler types of correspondence, for example, those gave by the Internet, just as the more prominent recognition of remote societies and achievability of covering long separations, have added to make social and topographical separations less significant than they used to be.

These conditions affirm the significance of what a few examiners call social capital-access to special data through associations (organize) gave before any financial exchange. There is a stamped requirement for the author to be implanted not just in a logical system (framed by senior specialists) yet additionally inside a system previously situated toward imagining age of information as a potential tradable business item. In that sense, we likewise feature the pertinence of cross-authoritative systems and entrepreneurs' capacity to move experience acquired abroad in utilizing the exhibition of their enterprises.

The riches and neediness of developing countries has been connected in present day times to the entrepreneurial nature of their economies. Where it has existed in bounty, entrepreneurship has assumed a significant job in financial development, advancement, and seriousness, and it might likewise assume a job after some time in neediness lightening. However, entrepreneurship in developing countries is apparently the least concentrated critical financial and social marvel on the planet today. More than 400 million people in developing countries are proprietors or directors of new firms. Of these, more than 200 million are found in China and India alone, contrasted, and only 18 million entrepreneurs in the United States. However, in extraordinary compared to other general books on the condition of research on entrepreneurship, China is referenced on two pages and India is not referenced by any means.

Entrepreneurship was generally the equivalent the world over driven by similar driving forces that played on home economics all over. Research in conduct financial matters and money has propelled our comprehension about the breaking points of discernment in portraying financial conduct, for example, entrepreneurship. Specifically, the intellectual inclination of over-optimism has helped us to comprehend why entrepreneurs start businesses notwithstanding chances of firm endurance that would contend something else. Corresponding to developing countries, the most compensating future research exertion right now be to break down the contrasts in vagueness repugnance, poise, defenselessness to surrounding thus play an urgent job in the development and advancement of businesses. How these distinctions may change across countries, and the fundamental drivers of these distinctions, may assist us with gaining a better comprehension of why a few countries have more effective entrepreneurs than others.

Entrepreneurship is certifiably not an all-around developed segment of current monetary hypothesis. Numerous neoclassical market analysts think that it is hard to accommodate the prerequisites of balanced dynamic with the capacities credited to entrepreneurship coordination, exchange, development, and vulnerability bearing. Entrepreneurs have been depicted differently as bearers of risk, specialists that unite the elements of formation, or coordinators of advancement. However, none of these scholars recognized entrepreneurs working in various business conditions or considered contrasts between entrepreneurship in well off and poor countries at different stages in monetary history. Four sorts of entrepreneurial firms have been distinguished in developing countries: recently settled, set up by not developing, set up, however, developing gradually, and graduates to a bigger size.

More liberated, increasingly serious, poor countries are not associated in a factually critical manner with more elevated levels of chance entrepreneurs. Ongoing monetary development in a poor nation is not connected in a measurably huge manner with more elevated levels of chance entrepreneurship, and; Insurance of property rights and levels of defilement do not appear to make a difference either. Some particular qualities of entrepreneurship in developing countries seem to improve the likelihood of achievement for development arranged firms, while others seem to keep down these organizations.

Opportunities for entrepreneurs in developing countries are more extensive in scope than in developed markets, permitting firms to seek after a portfolio way to deal with procedure that can productively deal with the more elevated levels of business and market chance. Entrepreneurs in developing countries face an alternate situation than their partners in developed economies. These contrasts are established in the fundamental economies in which they work. Developing markets come up short on a stable of develop markets and the consistency that such markets offer. Thusly, the open door for entrepreneurship in developing markets is inescapable. While Western entrepreneurs work at the edges of the economy, developing business sector entrepreneur's work nearer deeply, the necessities and openings are progressively across the board.

While the serious risk to these entrepreneurs from settled officeholders is decreased, the risks presented by financial, political, and administrative vulnerability is increased regularly exceeding direct serious risks. The reasonable, however, strange, reaction (particularly for those prepared in Western business technique) is for entrepreneurs in developing countries to spread assets over a few separate yet related businesses so as to moderate deliberate risk. As a result, the entrepreneur working in fragmented markets (a component of numerous developing countries) regularly assumes a surrogate job as a money related financial specialist who oversees risk through portfolio broadening. He oversees portfolio risk by working a few different businesses in lieu of financial specialists who may some way or another do likewise. Lacking elective sources of financing, the effective entrepreneur may utilize inside developed income from one business to finance his different businesses. The keiretsu framework in Japan and Chaebol in Korea are models of exceptionally developed aggregates with interlocking possessions and business associations that developed right now. Notwithstanding risk alleviation and a wellspring of financing, interlocking businesses give a wellspring of casual data stream, access to a more extensive pool of abilities and assets, and, when all around executed, a brand name that can be utilized over all businesses.

In the event that interlocking business combinations are normal in developing markets, how would they start? Lacking access to capital and divided retail and appropriation regularly expect entrepreneurs to start businesses downstream with direct access to the end customer. Beginning downstream businesses decreases beginning capital necessities as working capital is greatly diminished and allows access to customers and data stream that is as often as possible lacking. Access to such data is frequently disregarded as a key achievement factor. Absence of access to the end customer is an essential explanation behind the disappointment of South American businesses to move past product markets into higher worth included exercises. Having made progress in retail what's more, conveyance, effective entrepreneurs regularly influence the area experience, data stream, and income produced to vertically incorporate and move into upstream businesses.

While entrepreneurial opportunities are more extensive and resultant techniques are normally self-hedging in developing countries, constrained individual and family reserve funds and a nonattendance of monetary advancement seriously restricts the development possibilities of promising new companies in developing countries. The idea of entrepreneurial opportunities in developing countries assumes a basic job in the showcase for entrepreneurial fund in these countries. To a more prominent degree than in developed countries, incipient entrepreneurs must answer the accompanying central monetary inquiries: if the chances of another undertaking enduring its initial five years are under half, is it objective for an entrepreneur to submit money related assets to another firm? If not, by what method can we comprehend the constant propensity of entrepreneurs to begin new businesses? What's more, by what means can we understand financing businesses whose chances of progress are regularly not as much as that of a coin tosses?

Mirroring the unpromising chances of entrepreneurial achievement, interior money involves the greater part of financing for SMEs in most developing countries. Entrepreneurs in developing markets depend intensely on casual sources of money to begin their businesses; these sources gave somewhere in the range of 87% and 100% of the outside capital raised by entrepreneurs. Different sources of financing commonly focused by advancement fund establishments keen on improving access to back in the developing markets bank loaning and funding assume an extremely constrained job at present in financing entrepreneurs; at least in the start-up organize. Next to no is comprehended about the systems by which potential entrepreneurs in developing countries assemble the capital important to begin a business. How do entrepreneurs' spare assets from their own sources of pay so as to begin a business? Start-up capital necessities could be very unobtrusive in developing countries. There are two issues here: sources of pay, and suitable vaults for reserve funds until the new business is begun. Sources of salary can incorporate held income from a past business, frequently in the retail or circulation segment. In countries where generously compensated government positions are as yet accessible, for example, the Middle East, some potential entrepreneurs can spare beginning up capital from their pay rates.

Countries that have encountered monetary shakiness are bound to have higher paces of private sparing, kept up as a protection instrument. Emergency speaks to circumstance, at any rate similarly as framing the pools of private capital fundamental for start-up account is concerned. Additionally, while effective entrepreneurship is related with urbanization, urbanization likewise brings about an expansion in singular utilization furthermore, an attending decline in private investment funds. Subsequently, fruitful entrepreneurs are probably going to discover approaches to get to the more noteworthy pools of private sparing in the wide open so as to begin their businesses.

This features the conceivable significance of very much grew family organizes that range both urban and provincial regions. How such private provincial investment funds are intermediated into urban entrepreneurship is not at present surely known and very likely will change by nation. In principle, microenterprises could likewise assume a job in making a pool of reserve funds from which a bigger, progressively refined endeavor may be propelled. Be that as it may, a lack of alluring reserve funds systems (counting negative genuine loan fees on bank stores) in the formal and casual money related areas and the troubles related with putting resources into land or land as an investment funds vehicle (counting land residency issues) have seriously restricted reserve funds. Different types of de facto investment funds, for example, stock collection, are likewise constrained by the nonappearance of secure premises. These are a portion of the numerous reasons why microenterprises have not by and large filled in as take-off platforms for development arranged entrepreneurship in developing countries.

At long last, a significant, however, ignored and undocumented, improvement is the inexorably consumerist nature of developing nation economies, which has caused individual investment funds rates to fall and individual purchaser related obligation to develop. Episodic proof from districts such as the Middle East and North Africa propose that wrong degrees of individual obligation may seriously compel an entrepreneur's eagerness and capacity to begin another firm. When built up, new firms utilize a wide assortment of capricious procedures and systems to acquire account. Given the immature idea of budgetary markets in many developing countries, bootstrap financing may have become the transcendent type of beginning time financing in these countries. For instance, little scope Chinese entrepreneurs have structured a wide assortment of systems and establishments to give casual account. Why have outside, formal sources of financing, especially types of risk capital fund required by development situated entrepreneurs in developing markets, neglected to emerge in considerable amounts? One significant reason is that the macroeconomic conditions in many developing markets militate against the high IRRs that financial specialists require so as to remunerate them for their risk.

Thus, while there are no industry-wide measurements on private value putting resources into developing markets, it is assessed that acknowledged IRRs are generally breakeven for the first age of such assets (those began in the mid-1990s). It's a given that such returns are deficient to pull in a lot of new speculation into the up and coming age of risk capital vehicles. Risk capital fund is especially significant for development situated entrepreneurs in the developing world, since it adjusts the impetuses of entrepreneurs and outside financial specialists. Each is appropriately propelled to augment monetary estimation of the endeavor, as opposed to playing lose-lose games intended to profit to the detriment of the other. Such lose-lose situations are normal of business bank loaning to entrepreneurs in developing countries. Moreover, appropriately structured and staffed finance the executives' associations can include considerable post-speculation value to the development arranged entrepreneurial venture. Loan specialists do not have impetuses to give such post-venture help. Post-venture value formation is regularly a key to the improvement of development ready entrepreneurial enterprises.

While risk capital account has been a significant part of the entrepreneurial procedure in various developed countries, it has not understood its guarantee in the developing scene. The American model of investment has had constrained material in these business sectors, however, has frequently been the primary methodology taken by support chiefs concentrated on developing countries. Adventure capital (VC) assets can work with just little quantities of organizations, constraining their advancement sway. Investment and private value reserves have been not able to exit a considerable lot of their ventures, because of the illiquidity of nearby financial exchanges in developing countries. Effective investors have moderately uncommon aptitudes that can for the most part be obtained uniquely through experience, instead of through instruction and preparing, in this manner constraining the quantity of risk capital associations that can be sorted out. Current types of risk capital fund require the arrangement of new establishments (typically both a reserve and a store the board organization) before beginning of speculation tasks, along these lines easing back the venture procedure and making reserves contribute as well late in the speculation cycle by and large.

By what method may a portion of these obstacles be survived? Shockingly, notwithstanding the upset in fund that has moved through evolved capital markets in the course of recent years, minimal money related advancement has advanced toward entrepreneurial firms in developing countries. As one model, salary connected (advances, the reimbursement of which is attached to a borrower's future pay) were first acquainted with money advanced education in the United States, yet could be applied to different classes of borrowers, remembering entrepreneurial firms for developing countries. Loan specialists (business banks, non-bank budgetary establishments, finance directors, and others) could offer long-term (10 years or more) credits to entrepreneurial borrowers. The reimbursement terms of these credits would be attached to both the company's future pay and some file of total wages. This record of total livelihoods may incorporate borrowers from a similar area all through a locale (for instance, all article of clothing producers in Indonesia), corporate borrowers from any area, however, in the equivalent geographic district (for instance, every corporate borrower in Brazil), or a blend of the two.

Specialized, industry-explicit preparing is a significant segment in the production of universally serious firms. These organizations regularly structure into geologically engaged modern groups. Without a doubt, we have seen this as an incredible model that can be reached out to the rise of all-inclusive serious enterprises in developing countries. The product bunch in India, the liveliness re-appropriating group in the Philippines, and the remote market in China each fit in with differing degrees with the determination of grouping. In any case, the grouping model is of constrained an incentive for by far most of entrepreneurial openings and those associated with open strategy in business sectors where fundamental preconditions do not yet exist and may not be understood. It is not certain that grouping is a precondition for the production of all-inclusive serious firms in developing countries. What's more, what could possibly be done businesses in which the market size is national and sub-national and business conditions are basically homogenous? How does one work in developing markets without the ordinary roads of readiness and mentorship?

What does one do when in mal-developed or degenerate economies where driving organizations do not essentially fill in as the best aides for new businesses? How do businesses accomplish scale in the nonattendance of certain ranges of abilities locally, for example, budgetary administration? Entrepreneurship is a forlorn calling rendered progressively troublesome without the advantage of mentorship and apprenticeship. Driving hotspots of development, for example, Silicon Valley have a wide pool of all around prepared ability, a culture that energizes development and new businesses, and marquee organizations that fill in as casual completing schools for entrepreneurs. Indeed, even in the nonappearance of these perfect circumstances, apprenticeship, and entrepreneurship might be developed in pair. At the simplest level, smaller scale loaning associations have discovered that reimbursement furthermore, business achievement rates increment particularly with even the most essential business preparing and neighborhood bolster collections of similarly invested entrepreneurs. Sadly, not many of these enterprises scale to locally serious levels, not to mention national or worldwide levels. At a more significant level, multinationals have assumed a main job as preparing justification for planned entrepreneurs. Given that outside direct speculation by multinationals is regularly legitimately identified with the general business condition, and that apprenticeship in these organizations can be a significant street to entrepreneurship, we will need to accommodate these perceptions with the absence of relationship of levels of entrepreneurship with the general business condition. In those markets where entrepreneurship has prospered, effective nearby businessmen may fill in as tutors and outside guides. As a business extends, corporate administration overrides mentorship as essential direction and oversight; a blend of clever nearby businessmen and industry specialists, regardless of whether pulled in from abroad, assume a significant job during this development arrange.

Developing markets require progressive change, however, have scarcely any individuals with the essential abilities also, experience to impact such change. High potential businesses in developed economies gather official groups with basic encounters yet various, integral abilities. Potential partners search for astutely chosen, total groups that incorporate experienced administrators in deals, showcasing, money, and activities. In developing markets, these abilities are similarly substantial, however, frequently hard to come by. Accordingly, entrepreneurs search for different attributes that are relevant to the neighborhood advertise condition, including the capacity to see through the mist of governmental issues and financial matters in emergency inclined developing countries. Trust is much more exceptionally respected in these circumstances than in developed markets where careful distance transactions are well set up. Family claimed and worked businesses are even more common in emerging markets than in Western economies.

Chapter 2

EMERGING ECONOMIES

Any conversation of new markets must incorporate emerging markets. The expression emerging markets regularly alludes to outside countries where the economy is developing, or prospects favor development later on. The economies are estimated as far as gross national product (GNP). GNP is the complete estimation of the nation's formation and administrations locally and abroad through the span of one year. Presently, China, and India are the two biggest emerging markets, and the main four are regularly alluded to as BRIC (Brazil, Russia, India, and China). Emerging economies are appealing ventures since they will in general become quickly bringing about better yields for the financial specialist. That potential prize, in any case, is joined by more serious risks. Geopolitical vulnerabilities, farming appropriations, moving money values, framework issues, and fluctuating organic market all can impact costs in emerging markets.

In an inexorably worldwide and serious scene, entrepreneurial aptitudes are as significant as ever for some progressive agrarian businesses. Capital and work are the fundamental information elements of enormous scope formation that overwhelmed the business world in present day developed economies until the late 1980s. The expanding level of exchange costs brought about in enormous scope formation directed expanding firm size after some time. Without a doubt, factual proof focuses towards an expanding job of enormous enterprises in the economy right now. This improvement towards enormous scope movement was noticeable in most present day developed economies. Right now, the significance of independent work furthermore, private venture appeared to be melting away.

All the more as of late, with knowledge being perceived as an essential factor in endogenous development models numerous researchers further anticipated this would render independent work and little firms considerably increasingly purposeless. How might they produce the means and experiences to abuse R&D exercises, to utilize exceptionally prepared information laborers and to carry their enterprises to the patent or even the business organizes? Fundamentally, researchers reason that with the appearance of information as a formation factor the universe of business gets commanded by trading mammoth firms. This is the universe of worldwide markets, worldwide items, and worldwide players. Little firms were believed to be at a weakness opposite bigger firms in light of the fixed expenses of finding out about outside conditions, conveying at long separations and haggling with national governments.

Combination appears to have become a law of nature, while the quantity of worldwide players decreases ceaselessly. Notwithstanding these powers, little, and youthful firms have returned as the motor of monetary and social improvement in profoundly developed economies. This arrival required a sensational monetary switch. The model of the overseen economy is the political, social, and financial reaction to an economy directed by the powers of huge scope formation, reflecting the prevalence of the formation elements of capital and (generally untalented) work as the sources of upper hand. On the other hand, the model of the entrepreneurial economy is the political, social furthermore, financial reaction to an economy progressively overwhelmed by information as the formation factor, yet additionally by an alternate, yet integral, factor that had been disregarded: entrepreneurship capital or the ability to take part in and produce entrepreneurial movement.

Without new and youthful firms, it is not clear that information or R&D consistently overflows to a domain where it prompts substantial items. In developing what's more, emerging economies matters are convoluted on the grounds that the two components of the managed and entrepreneurial economies are regularly found one next to the other. The job of entrepreneurship in the blended managed entrepreneurial model of emerging economies is an under-explored wonder, not just in light of the fact that the job of entrepreneurship for financial improvement is mind boggling and in a blended economy even all the more along these lines, yet in addition in light of the fact that a common model of blended emerging economies does not exist. Rise or non-development has numerous faces that way of progress (East Asia and Eastern Europe) and that of fizzled or delicate states (Africa).

Developing countries and emerging markets have significant entrepreneurship exercises to show increasingly well-off districts. Projects inside Chile, India, and Brazil, for instance, have empowered monetary development and entrepreneurship. These equivalent enterprises and standards could be applied to propel the United States considerably further. Government activities in emerging markets have assumed an essential job in permitting entrepreneurs to prosper, regardless of whether those creative daring people are home-developed or attracted from abroad. This state help has taken different structures. In 2010, Chile made the primary freely financed start up quickening agent on the planet. Start-Up Chile draws in sprouting business trailblazers by offering $30,000 USD in value free financing and a one-year impermanent visa alongside opportunities for tutoring and instructing. Until now, the venture has helped in excess of 1,400 new companies and 4,000 entrepreneurs from 79 distinct countries.

Other South American countries have properly observed. Start-up Brazil echoes the Chilean model. It offers a government speculation of as much as 200,000 Brazilian genuine (generally $60,000 USD) just as tutoring for youngster firms chose to take an interest. Maybe U.S. offices could consider a motivation of this sort to help Silicon Valley's incredibly famous tech biological system and keep it on top. Governments in the developing scene additionally have perceived the need to help little scope entrepreneurship to battle social hardship. India is utilizing computerized innovation to handle rustic destitution by advancing agro-industry new businesses. The government propelled ASPIRE, a system of tech focuses and hatcheries to quicken entrepreneurship in provincial zones. American government officials long have lauded the temperance of tech entrepreneurship as a monetary improvement apparatus in cursed urban regions. Maybe a comparative model could be applied to America's underserved country areas, as well.

Albeit in excess of 9,000,000 U.S. firms are female-claimed, American lady's entrepreneurs despite everything face numerous hindrances, including making sure about speculations and discovering mentorship. NextGen female entrepreneurs start their youngster adventures with 50% less capital than their male companions. Moreover, a source at Morgan Stanley reports that lone 10% of funding is at present allowed to women or ethnic minorities. Such insights speak to botched chances. These contrarily sway people, society, and the economy all in all. Given the more conventional perspectives towards gender orientation in the developing scene, it's anything but difficult to envision women attempting to dispatch businesses there would face much more prominent difficulties than their American companions. The insights present a more nuanced picture. In Turkey, where 29.5% of workers are women, females despite everything hold 12% of official positions. That is multiple times the level of those running the best 500 organizations in the U.S.

In certain emerging markets-including Vietnam, Indonesia, and Peru-women' entrepreneurs effectively approach or dwarf their male partners. Less wealthy countries, for example, Bangladesh, and Uganda have the absolute most noteworthy paces of female entrepreneurship overall since women go into business adventures out of need. Shockingly, social acknowledgment in a few of these countries is high, as indicated by MasterCard's 2017 Index of Women Entrepreneurs Report. Solid help from associations, for example, Enterprise Uganda and Uganda Women Entrepreneurs Association incorporates business-warning and credit-assistance administrations. These, as well, assume essential jobs in shutting the gender hole.

In the U.S., African-American women are the quickest developing collection of entrepreneurs. The quantity of dark female business proprietors has developed by a dumbfounding 322% since 1997 (Dana and Ratten, 2017). To get their fantasies off the ground, these women need bolster that is custom fitted toward network enterprises just as sparkling tech new businesses. The Build Institute in Detroit fills in for instance. The little charitable runs eight-week-long business courses focused on minorities. One alumni, Danielle Smith, propelled the cleaning administration Detroit Maid. Subsequent to accepting guidance on promoting and marking, Smith scored her first large customer in quite a while.

Directed help of this sort need not break the government bank. On the off chance that the U.S. government was, set up to give such projects as opposed to depending on charities to do as such, the general financial advantages could be considerable. While government support for monetary activities through focused financing, good enactment and foundation improvement all are critical to making a start-up accommodating condition, individuals despite everything stay a business' most significant asset. Effectively reassuring those from non-traditional foundations will achieve more than help monetary development-it will make a more grounded, increasingly different society in general.

Since the rush of consideration on BRICs, the conversations on emerging and developing economies have gotten progressively polyphonic, the importance of specific districts has gotten increasingly perceived and investigate plans have been presented for global entrepreneurship. For instance, Sub-Saharan Africa or the megacities of the southern side of the equator, similar to Dhaka, Jakarta, Lagos, are increasing expanding consideration as business sectors (World Bank, 2019).

There are various difficulties from institutional condition to showcasing tasks that produce bottlenecks and obstructions for global entrepreneurship, framing diverse underpinnings for business. In any case, the populace improvement of many developing settings gives particular and totally different opportunities for business and entrepreneurship than maturing developed countries. Countries like Bangladesh, Pakistan, Indonesia, and Nigeria with enormous and youthful populaces are drawing entrepreneurial movement towards their potential nearby with different on-screen characters in worldwide formation systems.

The Bottom-of-the-Pyramid idea, the new wilderness economies-point of view and related research, particularly in worldwide showcasing, has additionally underlined the significance of these business sectors later on. The opportunities identifying with neighborhood market interest star groupings are frequently ignored while the formation and cost-driven perspectives ruled by MNEs have been the focal point of many research areas. Be that as it may, clever entrepreneurs are progressively putting and working in countries where some PESTEL examination could keep more risk touchy firms out, even multinationals (Rana and Elo, 2017). Regularly, global enterprises grumble about the troubles and risks in working in developing setting.

In earlier research, the job of global entrepreneurs in molding the business scene and biological systems has been discovered powerful and even focal, demonstrating internationalization the two different ways. Thusly, it is exceptionally intriguing to investigate and comprehend the vital job of SMEs and entrepreneurs in developing and forming the business in and from these requesting settings (Ado, Chrysostome, and Su, 2016). For instance, there is motivation to expect that the commitment of transnational Diaspora and transient entrepreneurs who length the limits of at least two markets is advantageous for monetary advancement and worldwide business (Elo and Minto-Coy, 2018).

Throughout the years, those in the scholarly community and financial analysts have pursued seething skirmishes of semantics in an offer to grapple with what globalization is, the thing that it is not, who it benefits and who it does not. It is a subject of developing contention, and there is by all accounts no accord on the thought. The world is combining socially, strategically, and financially. Subsequently, globalization could be characterized dependent on social, political, and financial intrigue exemplified monetarily as access to new markets, decrease in exchange rules and guidelines and the nearness of exchange rivalry (Nwokah and Adiele, 2015).

The idea of globalization is not any more a novel to financial analysts and business administrators. What's going on and appealing are the energy with which it has been grasped of late and the profundity of importance which it has accepted in present day private enterprise. Globalization since its presentation has progressively picked up money as a key instrument for countries' advancement and for developing world economy. In particular, it has assumed a gigantic job in breaking the hindrances which until now have comprised bottlenecks to universal mix and free progression of products and assets. At origin, globalization was confined to huge enterprises yet this has changed in the last not many a long time. It has now pervaded all structures and sizes of businesses with the goal that it is not simply huge partnerships that have worldwide concentration yet in addition, littler firms are progressively going worldwide. There are various ideas of globalization, however, basically, it envelops the possibility of the incorporation of national monetary, budgetary, and showcase exercises.

Globalization moreover wraps the interconnection of social and social parts of necessary social orders, and their ensuing political association, which at last will bring about their common progression of exchange, innovative improvement and later changes in exchange arrangements at the governmental level (Nwokah and Adiele, 2015). Globalization is the procedure of association and coordination between individuals, organizations, furthermore, governments around the world. Globalization has become because of advances in transportation and correspondence innovation. With expanded worldwide communications comes the development of global exchange, thoughts, and culture. Globalization is fundamentally a monetary procedure of communication and combination that is related with social and social perspectives.

The marvel of globalization is a complex and vague term which influences practically all parts of public activity, e.g., correspondence (free relocation), media communications (Internet), economy, and accounts, strategy (political relationship of states coming about because of financial combination), new advancements, mass culture (lessening the job of custom and social factors inside the social plane, a cosmopolitan worldwide culture, environmental, and social wellbeing. The view that globalization speaks to the worldwide reconciliation of universal exchange, speculation, data innovation and societies. Government arrangements intended to open economies locally and globally to help improvement in more unfortunate countries and raise ways of life for their kin are what drive globalization. Be that as it may, these strategies have made a global free market that has mostly profited worldwide enterprises in the Western world to the impairment of littler businesses, societies, and everyday citizens. Through globalization, partnerships can increase an upper hand from lower working expenses, and access to new crude materials and extra markets. Likewise, global companies can production, purchase, and sell merchandise around the world. For instance, a Japan-based vehicle producer can make car parts in a few developing countries, transport the parts to another nation for collection, and offer the completed autos to any country. Open approach and innovation are the two fundamental driving elements behind the current globalization blast. In the course of recent years, governments worldwide have incorporated a free advertise monetary framework through financial strategies and exchange understandings. This advancement of monetary frameworks has expanded industrialization and budgetary opportunities abroad. Governments currently center around evacuating boundaries to exchange and advancing global trade. Globalization influences numerous parts of mankind mechanical, political, affordable, biological, philosophical, social, social, standardizing, and so forth because of the escalated increment of global exchange, data trade, and remote venture. Globalization is a system of connections impacting the relations between the state, transnational, and integrative forms and the various territories of human action.

Globalization is a procedure of continuous change from autonomous national economies into one financial creature a worldwide market of merchandise and administrations. It is a procedure of expanding combination and connection between states, associations also, transnational foundations that work all inclusive (Anifowoshe, 2016). While giving greater advancement opportunities to developing countries, the globalization process is additionally presenting gigantic risks. Globalization has put some developing countries in risk of confronting ominous outside components. Right now, entrepreneurship is anything but an exact solution for financial improvement of developing countries, it can help monetary advancement when polished helpfully.

The entrepreneur is envisioned as starting change and creating new opportunities. By and large, different variables have been seen as upgrading the globalization belief system, one of such is the improvement of the entrepreneurial part. Be that as it may, because of the underdevelopment of the entrepreneurial area in most developing countries like Nigeria, the globalization belief system has endured mishaps in spite of the accessibility of various opportunities that would have been until now used to put the nation at vantage point in the worldwide request. The observational proof obviously demonstrated that the firm-size dispersion in developed countries started to move away from bigger organizations and toward entrepreneurial action.

One dynamic and essential power in contemporary globalization process is monetary progression, which has been grasped by for all intents and purposes all countries and significant universal establishments inside the worldwide framework. Financial progression alludes to the way toward accomplishing unhampered financial exercises. Unhampered here suggests free markets (access to business sectors), organized commerce (exchange deregulation) and rivalry. It looks to expel all deterrents to exchange, formation, and speculation; stresses opportunity of financial exercises and predominance of private ventures; and points at last at the separation of the state from the economy.

At the worldwide level, financial advancement enterprises to make all economies completely open for free interpenetration and interstate access. Issues identifying with the powers of financial advancement are commonly more confused than and not as evident as in innovation. In quest for monetary advancement, the worldwide framework is captivated into different collections. In one collection are the industrialized (G8) countries that work personally with the world money related (IMF, World Bank) and Trade (WTO) establishments, and seek after an expansive and goal-oriented plan that endeavor to construct universal free enterprise on the establishments of open world exchange and capital streams, privatization, adjusted spending plan, opening up of trade controls and comparable deregulation and progression measures.

In another collection are the 'Asian-Tigers' who have, through financial progression process, accomplished phenomenal development in their delicate economies. These countries, moreover to advancement, have utilized other strategy instruments to grow Foreign Direct Investment (FDI) what's more, accomplish higher monetary development. These incorporate developing a solid supervisory crew, formation base; opening up of new venture territories; just as structuring and actualizing sound macroeconomic arrangements. They have likewise made a decent atmosphere and stable political and financial condition to pull in outside speculations. These arrangement measures have improved the extension of FDI in the countries and prompted their quick development and improvement.

Different collections of countries that have accomplished ground-breaking accomplishment because of financial progression incorporate the change economies of the Eastern Europe just as the Latin American countries. Likewise included are the African States the greater part of which has endured immensely from extraordinary neediness and absence of approach center. In this manner, clearly financial progression is currently a typical component among country states. It can, in this way, be appropriately inferred that no nation in the contemporary world can truly be an island unto itself, either because of its dynamic financial quality, e.g., the United States or in light of the fact that it chooses to close its ways to the outside world like China effectively did previously. The basic message of globalization right now that in the current snapshot of mix of worldwide markets, Nigeria, and other developing countries have minimal decision yet to attempt to join the globalization train in spite of their distraught situation simultaneously.

Entrepreneurship improvement is worried about the investigation of entrepreneurial conduct, the elements of business set-up, improvement, and development of the endeavor. Entrepreneurship improvement likewise alludes to the way toward upgrading entrepreneurial aptitudes and information. It fundamentally means to grow the base of entrepreneurs so as to rush the pace at which new adventures are made. This quickens work age and monetary improvement (Gebel and Giesecke, 2016). Entrepreneurship improvement centers around the person who wishes to begin or grow a business. It likewise centers around developing the endeavor. Along these lines, this idea of entrepreneurship advancement has two viewpoints or levels.

The primary level arrangements with the advancement of entrepreneurial character abilities, inspiration, qualities, and conduct of a person that will empower him/her play out the entrepreneurial job or assignment. Entrepreneurship advancement as the bestowing or working in the real entrepreneurs, potential characteristics and social attributes, the essential abilities and capabilities to make them compelling and better-carried on people in their entrepreneurial jobs. The subsequent viewpoint bargains with pulling together of assets to frame a beneficial and working endeavor. As such, it is the formation and activity of a business adventure. It includes the real venture of money related assets, time, and exertion, and completing administrative capacities to guarantee the achievement of the venture for example to guarantee that its benefit making objective is figured it out. Right now, entrepreneurship improvement is worried about the responsibility of assets to a business adventure. Just, it is the procedure of business possession and activity.

Entrepreneurship improvement centers around the person who wishes to begin or grow a business, then again, it likewise centers around developing the undertaking, regardless of whether it utilizes or is driven by people who can be viewed as entrepreneurial. Besides, entrepreneurship improvement focuses more on development potential and advancement. In any case, a significant number of the exercises gained from encounters in both kinds of improvement are comparative. Entrepreneurship is elevated to help ease the joblessness issue, to beat the issue of stagnation and to build the intensity and development of business and enterprises. Different enterprises have been made to advance and create entrepreneurship; by giving explicit help to improve the ability of the entrepreneur and his endeavor in order to improve his entrepreneurial goals and suit more individuals to become entrepreneurs also.

There is an inescapable propensity to compare entrepreneurship improvement with independent work. Numerous independently employed people are in reality entrepreneurs, yet the lion's share is not. Their businesses are essentially microenterprises in the casual part, with little development potential. The advancement of independent work is an advantageous goal, yet it ought not to be mistaken for entrepreneurship improvement (Yusuf, 2016). Entrepreneurship improvement centers around the accompanying components to accomplish process headway: developing a constructive individual demeanor, developing entrepreneurial aptitudes, Activity, opportunity chasing and acknowledgment, determination, constancy, flexibility, data furthermore, information-looking for, enthusiasm for quality and productivity, great risk craving, objective setting and objective getting, responsibility, precise arranging and observing, influence, and systems administration, autonomy, and self-assurance, increment in independent work mindfulness, making entrepreneurship the vocation decision, business aptitudes for independent work, business improvement abilities, imaginative, and inventive aptitudes, promoting aptitudes, serious aptitudes, CEO aptitudes (Gianesini et al., 2018).

Entrepreneurship is regularly identified with the formation of new businesses. Be that as it may, entrepreneurship, and entrepreneurial elements is as pertinent to the making of not-revenue driven activities. It is tied in with creating thoughts, sorting out and hands-on activity that can have a wide range of impacts. Entrepreneurship can assemble individuals, assets, and creative practices and are key to the manners in which we compose social orders. Right now is placed with regards to developing countries. Both prudent parts of business based entrepreneurship, social parts of common society based entrepreneurship, and parts of joining affordable/social points in a manageable improvement are expounded on right now.

The setting of developing countries welcomes an attention on issues identified with low financial improvement and neediness lightening, economies on the move and emerging markets just as advancement of both social and political foundation past what normally is expounded on in western ruled entrepreneurship talk. In this manner, it is likewise fundamental to basically examine entrepreneurship exercises, the guarantees it represents and the potential results. In economies that are marginally behind their progressive modern partners, entrepreneurship is regularly seen as a significant segment in invigorating financial development, advancement, intensity, and in any event, mitigating destitution for these countries. In any case, before that is practiced, there are a few interesting highlights that influence entrepreneurship in developing countries. While a portion of the unmistakable parts of developing countries hinder entrepreneurship, others empower entrepreneurial exercises and permit new companies to be effective in spite of incredible chances.

The first and maybe clearest consider influencing entrepreneurship developing countries is the absence of capital and money related advancement. Numerous individuals in these countries have restricted individual reserve funds and come up short on the important cash-flow to go into business. Entrepreneurs should then go to outer financing where they are charged high loan fees because of the unsafe idea of new business ventures. With immature monetary markets and costly obtaining rates, entrepreneurs in emerging economies regularly utilize casual sources of fund to begin their businesses and create salary from numerous occupations or businesses.

All things considered, this is the place a preferred position of developing countries becomes possibly the most important factor. Having various occupations and maintaining a few new companies one after another gives an extraordinary preferred position to entrepreneurs in developing countries. For instance, an entrepreneur may have a cultivating business while simultaneously be engaged with carpentry, development, or product businesses to create salary for his cultivating business. This wide-extending business nature is regular in developing countries and permits entrepreneurs to effectively kill significant levels of various market risks as they follow an enhanced portfolio system.

Alongside this expansion impact, the requirements and opportunities are increasingly across the board in developing countries which means new businesses can seek after benefits in various markets of need. In developed countries, development arranged firms normally center around one specialty showcase as there are less needs and significant markets are packed with different businesses. Interlocking businesses in a few markets of need likewise permit entrepreneurs in developing countries to build up a more extensive pool of aptitudes, fabricate assorted client relations, and if effective, make a brand name that can be utilized over a few markets.

Last is the social part of developing countries that influences entrepreneurial practices. An educator from the University of Utah has directed research that anxieties the significance of culture interaction in understanding entrepreneurship in various countries. Socially based convictions and various perspectives influence how entrepreneurs work their businesses. Understanding these distinctions and turning out to be socially mindful are basic parts in completely fathoming the entrepreneurial exercises of developing countries. While entrepreneurs in emerging economies face numerous difficulties in beginning businesses, their enterprises, and devotion to making new thoughts, give a promising future to their individual countries.

An economy is known as an emerging economy or an emerging business sector when it is seen through the entrepreneurial idea of the economy. In the previous decade, developed countries have developed minutely. A few developing economies have extended at remarkable rates. As developing countries are huge piece of the world's monetary yield many driving market analyst have anticipated them as emerging economies and the worldwide upper hand is likewise moving from developed to developing countries. Entrepreneurship assumed a noteworthy job in monetary development, advancement, and lightening neediness. Also, mindfulness in regards to entrepreneurship is required. In a large number of the developing countries is tentatively the least contemplated.

Entrepreneurship may influence monetary development in different manners. They may present significant developments by entering markets with new items or formation forms. They may support effectiveness by mounting rivalry. They may improve our insight into what is actually reasonable and what buyers lean toward by presenting varieties of existing items and administrations in the market. The coming about learning process accelerates the revelation of the prevailing structure for item showcase blends. Information overflows assume a significant job right now. Lastly, they might be inclined to strenuous working hours as their pay is noticeably connected to their working exertion.

Right now endeavor to discover that what are the forthcoming or effectively installed difficulties and opportunities for entrepreneurs particularly youthful in the emerging economies particularly BRIC countries and how with condition they ought to support continuing achievement. Numerous speculators, entrepreneurs, and business pioneers are as yet battling with it as a guide for future venture and business opportunities. The four BRIC countries are recognized from a collection of other promising emerging markets by their segment and monetary potential to rank among the world's biggest and most critical economies in the 21st century.

Together, the four unique BRIC countries include more than 2.8 billion individuals or 40% of the total populace, spread in excess of a fourth of the world's property territory more than three main lands, and record for additional than 25% of worldwide GDP. The BRICs are significant drivers of financial development and that is the reason they are considered as emerging economies. Basically, there are three drivers of monetary development land, work, and capital which are otherwise called the components of formations. A nation's populace also, segment conditions are one of those components that could influence the potential size of the economy and furthermore demonstrates its skill to work as steam motor of monetary development. China and India China and India would turn into the first and third biggest economies by 2050, with Brazil and Russia catching the fifth and 6th spots.

These BRIC countries and their advancement markers are indicating the relative preferred position of gazing new pursuits lie more in these emerging economies that is the manner by which we are seeing that China had the most noteworthy GDP and is developing as the quickest economy so speculators from the developed countries are likewise wanting to make interest in these economies by opening new adventures and further we would see that how entrepreneurship could be all the more compensating for entrepreneurs by examining nation shrewd the difficulties and opportunities. Brazil is a nation which is rich with ample assets like minerals, wares, oil, and gas, soybean, rainforest, and had satisfactory measure of water. Brazil is likewise being renowned for what it's worth the biggest exporter of sugar, coffer, squeezed orange and poultry. This nation is rich with a few assets and for entrepreneurs there are numerous immaculate opportunities as these assets as it were.

Brazil is considered by numerous financial experts one of the expensive economies, even the eateries which arranged in Sao Paulo is valued higher than of Europe. Hair styles cost more than of London; bicycle rentals are additionally costly as contrast with Amsterdam. The nearby costs right now economy is high and when a guest originates from an affluent country to this nation, they felt that there is nation is not developing. Brazil is the main exporter of huge numbers of the crude materials and furthermore a main accomplice with U.S. in 2009. It is the nation with a costly cash and high loan fees. Brazil had per capita salary of $12,000 multiple seasons of china. Brazil is wealthy in one of the asset what's more, it is oil, and it is currently expected to have world's tenth biggest saves and is called as straightaway Saudi Arabia that is incredible sign for its development. The youthful populace is one of the best favorable circumstances for this economy which brings extraordinary interest for western style clothing types, buyer merchandise.

Be that as it may, seeing these realities the brazilin economy is attempting to develop as a portion of the advancements are in process and some have been done. According to specific investigations led by the nearby Brazilian office, it had been seen that youthful business assumes critical job in nation's development and advancement. Small and medium-sized enterprises (SMEs) are capable for 96% of the employments in Brazil and involve 98% of all organizations in the nation. As indicated by the OECD, Brazil detailed countless high-development ventures in 2006. The government's Financing Agency for Projects and Studies (FINEP) has propelled a noteworthy task to help new companies, PRIME, which will dispense around $65,000 to new businesses concentrated on development. FINEP hopes to help 10,000 imaginative organizations more than four years, also, along these lines produce 10 new openings for each every one legitimately developed by another organization.

In 2005, the Inter-American Development Bank and SEBRAE occupied with a $1.5 million specialized collaboration program to help Brazilians getting back from Japan with the objective of beginning new businesses. In 2004, for example, the government passed a law that permits administrative college educators impermanent leave to make a beginning up. Notwithstanding, there is a ton of opportunity to get better in the arrangement domain. Brazil's Ease of Doing Business rank in the World Bank's Doing Business venture is 129 out of 183 economies. Beginning a business there takes 120 days, twofold the normal for Latin American and Caribbean countries and far more awful than the normal 13 days for OECD countries.

The duty framework right now the greatest weight for the new pursuits and the new entrepreneurs, the taxation rate now right now for 38%of GDP that is the most noteworthy in the emerging economies, there is overwhelming heap of individual and corporate duty which is hampering up the venture from the corporate. The poor framework could be another test for the emerging entrepreneurs as the government here contributes less on streets and on foundation advancement. In the event that the inventory chain would be influenced by the poor vehicle framework, the interest cannot be maintained and it leads to rising costs. The traffic framework is poor to such an extent that businesses there had built up another option transport framework like landing cushions on rooftop tops. The low speculation on the instruction and ability advancement make aptitude deficiency, schools are underfunded. Despite the fact that the joblessness rate has fallen in 10 years to low as 6% be that as it may, the business as they required labor they must choose the option to employ these unfit candidates.

The significant expense of work and transport in Brazil is immediate aftereffect of putting less in it. The venture rate in Brazil is only 19% from numerous years which is least in the emerging economies. Brazil pioneers are attempting to oversee and balance out trade rates, loan fees and the stream of outside cash all through the nation. The brazilin are fundamentally perplexed all things considered hard for them to take care of the issue of growth as expansion hampers higher monetary development, so they are expanding the financing costs, however, it is again pushing up the estimation of cash. This economy quite greater speculation, low loan costs, and modest cash. Brazil is one of the sultriest securities exchange in the emerging scene. Be that as it may, what the Brazilian economy needs is the way which causes it to be out of low financial development, straightforward expense systems, evacuation of exchange boundaries and minimal effort of borrowings, great sparing propensities.

Russia is one of the main economies and is the biggest exporter of wheat. It is the world capital of larger than usual recently rich individuals and incomparable for its conspicuousness. It is the nation which has the biggest shopper class, which develops as entrepreneurial opportunities for some. Entrepreneurship and private ventures began to show up in the Soviet Union after the financial reproduction that occurred in the late 1980s and toward the start of the 1990s. The adjustments in the Soviet framework prompted the privatization of government-claimed organizations and made new potential outcomes for people to dispatch entrepreneurial exercises. Certain reality about the rising emerging class shows that Russia is rich with tycoons.

As indicated by the 2011 Forbes review of tycoons, Moscow has progressively tycoons (79) than some other city on the planet (the nearest is New York with 58) and Russia represents 33% of Europe's 300 very rich people, and 15 of the world's 100 most extravagant individuals. Of course, retail deals in Moscow currently surpass Paris and London, and by 2025 the customer showcase in Russia, which is presently approx. 142 m, is relied upon to be bigger than Germany's, perhaps the biggest market. Vladimir Putin when became president in 2000 he attempted to get numerous changes the Russian economy like merging banks, slicing the formality required to begin organizations, diminishing individual personal assessment to simply 13%, this all assistance the Russian economy to bring customer blast.

There are sure divisions in the Russian economy which made it extremely appealing for the entrepreneurs like nourishment, drinks, agriculture division. Nourishment and drink speaks to 45% of Russia's absolute retail exchange and is developing at over 19% every year (contrasted with approx. 12% for non-nourishment shares). Similarly, as with ascend in the per capita salary Russians become progressively prosperous, they are requesting more excellent, confided in brands and more noteworthy assortment which speaks to extraordinary opportunities for new contestants, especially in meat, dairy, fruit, and vegetables. The normal Russian has higher extra cash than their Western partners; the average Russian has presently more than one cell phone while only 70% of Chinese claim just one. For an entire range of authentic, social, and monetary reasons, in addition to a 13% level expense rate, high home proprietorship with no obligation (an inheritance from the post-Soviet period wherein most Russians were given their homes at no cost) Russians be slanted to go through their cash, as opposed to sparing it, and this is invigorating a retail blast which is presently spreading to their Eastern European neighbors and boosting the economy for the entire area.

At the point when the worldwide emergency in 2008 hit a significant number of the economies, Russia was one of the hardest hit countries on the planet. The economy got shrunk by 10%. The government took certain measures to assimilate stuns of that emergency. Growth is one of the issues for the Russian economy and for the emerging entrepreneurs additionally for as long as two years it is arrived at the midpoint of at 7.8% which ought to be 4.5% for an emerging business sector. Russia is additionally putting less in foundation like in streets, plant, and types of gear that laborers there are getting less beneficial, Russia need institutional quality and political readiness to actualize genuine changes that help to support development.

One more issue or challenge emerge right now the center is gone off to some faraway place that is the extent of little and medium venture are lower in Russia as contrast with some other emerging economy. The grouping of riches and monetary influence is seen in just a single city that is Moscow. It is missing adjusted local improvement; the greater part of the extremely rich people is dwelling in Moscow itself. The Russian economy is likewise ailing in banking framework as there are no such current banks in Russia and the financing costs are high about 15% to 20% on business advances which is a major obstacle for the entrepreneurs. The net outside direct contribute was negative for example $9.5 billion out of 2010 importance Russians were putting more in processing plants and business abroad, however, the outsiders were putting less in Russia. Another significant test for entrepreneurs here could be the working age populace which fall by around 870,000 individuals for each year between 2010 what's more, 2015 that is the loss of close to 1% of populace every year. With these troubles, it is seen that the Russian economy is getting less well-disposed for business.

After the changes of 1991, India took a fresh start and began its excursion to become one the developing and emerging economy. India has numerous valid justifications which come to be viewed as each man of emerging countries, an encapsulation that catches the best and nastiest stunts of all the liveliest youthful economies. There is incredible decent variety in the nation in which youth still have the alternatives between world class designing schools and Maoist revolt, yet the huge order of English among elites can make it profoundly uniform and effectively available to the outside world. India is opening entryways for a considerable lot of the entrepreneurial opportunities and in the earlier year's realities have indicated that there is part of entrepreneurial improvement in our economy. The developing youthful populace is turning into a serious edge, and a driver of monetary development. By 2020, the normal Chines will be 37 years of age, the normal Indian will be 29. This information makes an expectation that china will get old before it gets rich and India will come to the center pay class status while still they are youthful. India had various opportunities in the field of land, IT, and correspondences, retail, instruction, and the rundown is long.

China is one of the main emerging economies; in the previous not many years, we have perceived how china had contacted the mind blowing apex of development and innovative advancement. Around 1.2 billion individuals in the economy it is developing with twofold digit pace development. The Chinese have made an exceptional advancement regarding foundation and innovation. In the twelfth multiyear plan by the government had made certain opportunities for entrepreneurs like lashing speculation seaward and in genuine corporate resources for expand their introduction to US treasuries, to secure assets and items yet additionally to redesign their administration division (the travel industry, instruction, medicinal services, innovation, money related administrations and so on.). This move will make opportunities for remote organizations just as entrepreneurs.

The Chinese utilization has been developing and this give numerous opportunities to the entrepreneurs and one of the zone is natural nourishment with expanding urbanization the extent of present day general stores has expanded the Chinese are moreover particularly careful with respect to sanitation, wellbeing, and diet which expanded opportunities in natural nourishment industry. Also, the Chinese buyer spending has expanded at normal early pace of 9%; it is one of the main markets and had supplanted Europe and US. This information itself shows that there are extraordinary opportunities for the entrepreneurs. A few realities appear that china previously had 25% offers in the worldwide extravagance showcase. The Chinese men have begun re-evaluating themselves have their way towards being sleek the offers of healthy skin items developed at 40% in mid-2011.

China is currently very nearly typical break; the sign has begun showing up. To become 10%, the nation needs to continue this development. The development drivers which had pushed the economy are presently coming to a different position, the pool of surplus labor disappears, and manufacturing plant business arrives at most extreme limit. Demographically china is hindering the provincial class gradually evaporating endlessly as they improve paid employments in the urban areas. The modest work which was the quality of Chinese economy is never again being there as the urban wages are as of now rising strongly. Also, the Chinese are losing the youthful work power as after the foundation of one youngster strategy in 1979 this positive advance had negative affect that now we are finding in the long run. Thus, that lone 5,000,000 between ages of 35 and 44 will join the china's center work powers this decade and 90 million in the earlier decade, which is a significant obstacle for the entrepreneurs.

This issue is making one more test that is the pay driven expansion. In late 2011, the normal wages were increasing at a normal pace of 15% and the costs were ascending at pace of more than 5%. The circumstance is that the businesses paying to get return their laborers busy working. The developing need had just emerged given to laborers which shows the expanding refutation intensity of laborers, as strikes and walkouts. Every one of the BRIC nation is offering different opportunities for the entrepreneurs, however, the present circumstance need not be ignored as these difficulties would assist the entrepreneurs with sustaining accomplishment through developing methodologies.

Discussing manageability, it requests for living and completing business so that monetary profit and financial development do not move toward at the expense of spoiling the earth or make defenseless expectations for everyday comforts and social prosperity. The entrepreneurs need to plan their business models likewise to the economies points of interest and inconveniences. The entrepreneurs so as to continue their prosperity ought to concentrate on these BRIC as well as other breakout countries like turkey, Saudi Arabia, Indonesia, and so forth. Making the positive conditions for quick development is more workmanship than science, whimsical polices are required to advance a greater amount of entrepreneurial culture.

Since the time the opening up of the worldwide economy during the 1990s, a few up to these point Third World countries in Asia and Africa started to change and coordinate themselves into the worldwide financial framework. This implied there were more possibilities for entrepreneurs in these countries and from abroad to prosper due to the business well-disposed arrangements sought after by the governments in these countries. This additionally had the impact of prodding speculation and brooding new pursuits either because of funding ventures from the West or due to inside produced or sourced roads for venture. While the previous was helped by the opening up of the budgetary markets of countries, for example, India to outside capital, the last was helped by the quickening monetary development in these countries which opened up capital of the business houses that would then be able to save some cash for financing new companies and new pursuits.

Having said that, it should likewise be noticed that in spite of the progression and the free enterprise approach taken by these countries, a few deterrents stayed in the method for entrepreneurs when they wandered into the business world. For example, however, India saw a start-up blast in the most recent decade, as of not long ago, entrepreneurs needed to fight with managing formality and administration which implied that as a rule, they needed to confront delays in tying down endorsements and licenses to begin their enterprises. In addition, in the underlying hurry to open new pursuits, numerous entrepreneurs in the emerging economies in Asia, for example, Indonesia, Thailand, and India turned to "colleague private enterprise" which implied that they succeeded not on the grounds that they had a game changing thought or on the grounds that their business models were unrivalled, but since they had the correct contacts and the correct associations which made it simpler for them to make sure about licenses, subsidizing, and different perspectives.

In this manner, these enterprises regularly began with a blast and finished with a cry once the anticipated incomes did not appear because of the inadequacy in their business model or because of the way that a large portion of the stratospheric projections that they made to make sure about subsidizing depended on wobbly and ridiculous development and income desires. Matters were likewise not helped by the worldwide monetary emergency of 2008 which saw numerous such enterprises falling due to the financing that evaporated just as because of the way that a considerable lot of these enterprises depended on questionable business rehearses. Also, the controllers who at this point knew about these dirty tricks immediately began to look further into these enterprises which implied that they couldn't depend on their associations alone to support themselves. Further, the common society and the activists battling such practices turned out to be progressively mindful and increasingly aware of these practices which brought about more prominent investigation.

Obviously, this does not imply that every new pursuit propelled during the financial blast was essentially founded on imperfect and degenerate practices. For example, there are numerous Asian organizations that not just became pioneers in their picked business territory yet additionally took their brands worldwide and prevailing with regards to winning in the worldwide commercial center. In fact, the way that Asian brands were presently perceived for their value and intrinsic worth creating capacities is exemplified in the achievement of the Indian IT Industry, the accomplishment of the Chinese organizations, for example, Alibaba Group and the fabulous development of Latin American and African organizations. Nonetheless, the reality remains that in the repercussions of the bust of 2008, numerous Western financial speculators were careful about subsidizing emerging business sector new companies without due tirelessness and began to demand "indicating them the cash" or to have powerful business models.

At long last, the circumstance as it stands currently is that ecommerce organizations, for example, Flipkart, Snapdeal, and Myntra in India have pulled in billions of dollars in financing as of late. While one cannot paint them with a similar brush and infer that their business models are suspect, the reality remains that the majority of these ecommerce organizations including Uber base their income development projections and gauges on future business just as gross deals which in the wake of limiting cannot be said to return much in benefits. To be sure, the way that few inquiries are being raised about the supportability of these organizations should without a doubt alert financial specialists and industry examiners regarding whether these organizations would not meet the destiny of the Dotcom ones that crumbled during the blasting of the tech bubble and different new businesses that fallen in the repercussions of the 2008 emergency.

Hopeful entrepreneurs around the globe have a few opportunities both inside their countries just as in abroad goals. With the opening up of numerous Asian economies, western entrepreneurs would now be able to put resources into countries, for example, China, and India alongside Indonesia and Thailand notwithstanding the most recent participants Vietnam and Cambodia. In fact, every one of these economies has been developing at a quicker rate than the ones in Latin America and Eastern Europe. Having said that, it must be noticed that in spite of the governments in these countries being business benevolent and open to outside speculation, the ground truths are with the end goal that entrepreneurs may locate the going intense because of various reasons.

To start with, the formality and the administration in these countries implies that except if the entrepreneur is all around associated locally, the individual would confront leaps in land securing, licenses, and different endorsements. Likewise, the lawful framework in a considerable lot of these countries is moderate moving and obsolete implying that regarding of agreements and discretion if there should be an occurrence of lawful debates would take quite a while and all the more critically, would be liable to age old laws and guidelines. Second, in spite of the energy at the national level, entrepreneurs would need to manage the state and common governments in these countries which have their own arrangement of approaches administering business and directing trade.

Third, the framework in these countries is in some cases not up to worldwide and western measures implying that terrible streets, inconsistent and poor force supply, sporadic water, and urban blockage imply that the entrepreneurs need to manage these difficulties also. Fourth, social soundness and distress are large risk factors just like the part of security of women which implies that except if the entrepreneur is intending to have an arrangement with insignificant staff, the individual would need to battle with every one of these issues too. Notwithstanding, the image is not as desolate as it sounds since there are still some brilliant spots in these countries that offer entrepreneurs the opportunity to realize their fantasies. For one, the emerging white collar classes in these countries are a wellspring of rich workforce which implies that there is a promptly accessible base for the entrepreneurs to contract. Second, the wages are low by western norms and this implies any endeavor in these countries can be done at significantly low expenses than in the west. Third, the buying intensity of the individuals in these countries is developing implying that there is a prepared and undiscovered market for buyer merchandise and durables.

In this way, it is obvious that while there are difficulties there are opportunities too and the other way around and henceforth, discovering balance is up to the entrepreneurs with the goal that their businesses or adventures can succeed. There are various manners by which the entrepreneurs can guarantee achievement of their enterprises and this is in finding imaginative and inventive answers for the issues. For example, both Shanghai in China and Bangalore in India have developed as advancement hotspots where new companies and adventures are succeeding. Furthermore, Ho Chi Minh City in Vietnam and Laos in Cambodia have developed as practical contenders to these countries, however, they are still a long way behind. The point that we are attempting to make is that these countries offer the truly necessary laborer and buying power capacities notwithstanding having desert gardens of business hatcheries in the midst of the bedlam. To be sure, on the off chance that one takes a gander at the quantity of tech new companies in Bangalore over the most recent two years and the quantity of biotech and elective vitality adventures in Shanghai, there is a particular inclination that the entrepreneurial vitality is being released after a respite following the 2008 worldwide financial emergency.

The achievement of the ecommerce adventures in China and India wherein organizations, for example, Alibaba, and Flipkart have been developing exponentially implies that there are sufficient opportunities for development in these countries. This is the motivation behind why many financial speculators and heavenly attendant speculators have been emptying cash into these segments notwithstanding worldwide monsters, for example, Amazon setting up their provincial bases. At long last, every one of these countries are putting forth attempts to tackle the intensity of the entrepreneurs since the governments just as the individuals have understood that except if they develop and keep on developing, guaranteeing that the youthful land positions and completing dependability for the individuals would be troublesome prompting mayhem and turmoil. Thusly, the case these countries do not have the advantage of trusting that development will occur and rather, they need to get it going and this is something that entrepreneurs can cheer up from.

Entrepreneurs need subsidizing and investors and agents need emerging businesses with extraordinary potential for speculations. Along these lines, there is a harmonious relationship with entrepreneurs and the agents wherein each need the other for common addition. While the entrepreneurs would utilize the capital contributed by the agents to develop and extend their businesses just as the more significant part of returning benefits on the speculation, the lenders would profit by the benefits since their ventures are producing returns. Having said that, it is positively not the case that agents put resources into pretty much every new business without doing their due industriousness. For sure, one of the key perspectives about entrepreneurship and entrepreneurs is that they have to have convincing business thought and a strong business model that would persuade the agents to put resources into their organizations. This is one reason why entrepreneurs think that it is difficult to raise reserves particularly during monetary downturns since the agents would demand vigorous and benefit making business models which not all entrepreneurs can concoct.

Going to how agents finance during monetary blasts, when cash is bounty and capital is inexhaustible, the lenders would be more than willing in siphon in a lot of cash in what they regard to be strong enterprises. Presently, when does capital become bottomless and when does it become rare? As referenced before the previous is when there is a blast wherein "hot cash" is looking for wise speculations and the last is while during financial downturns when capital is difficult to find. Lately, the Western world has seen the ascent of numerous lenders who have profited by the ultra-free money related approaches and the way that financing costs in the West are near zero. This is a motivation for them to search for roads to channel their capital.

For sure, this is what is alluded to as "hot cash" wherein there is such a great amount of liquidity in the framework that the lenders would put even in unremarkable new companies that guarantee humble returns. As can be seen from the focuses made up until this point, at whatever point there is hot cash looking for speculations, there will in general be a blast in the ascent of the new companies wherein even those entrepreneurs who have prior not liked their odds become cheerful of speculations into their enterprises.

Having said that, there should be a note of alert here particularly when such hot cash streams bring about "bubbles" being made. An air pocket in financial terms is when there is a fake expansion or increment in the estimation of a benefit or an element which is not upheld by basics. As it were, state you have a house which merits a million dollars. When there is income sans work streaming in the framework, a similar house can be sold for in excess of a million dollars since there are more purchasers ready to dish out more cash. This is on the grounds that the purchasers are flush with assets because of simple financing, expanded pay rates, or even the developing economy due to which they feel that they can contribute more since the costs would go up later on.

Such air pockets can be seen in a significant number of the ongoing yield of new businesses particularly in the Indian ecommerce segment. This is on the grounds that there are numerous Western lenders who wind up with plentiful capital and subsequently, need to contribute such capital some place. Taking into account that most resource classes in the West are not creating the sort of profits that the financial specialists need, they are searching for greener fields in Asia which they feel would legitimize their speculations. Further, with the future projections for the Indian economy being estimate as brilliant, these financial specialists feel that they would be more than getting their foreseen returns.

This has prompted a circumstance in the Indian ecommerce segment wherein even organizations that have not developed any profits or benefits are the subject of billion dollar speculations and valuations so high that one marvels whether there is another air pocket really taking shape here. In fact, the circumstance right now suggestive of the Dotcom bubble during the 2000s wherein financial specialists were eager to put pretty much in any endeavor with a.com addition since capital was bounteous to such an extent that it required roads for ventures. Obviously, the speculators are not tricks now or and, after it is all said and done since whenever there's any hint of the air pocket blasting, they would pull back their subsidizing and "exit" from the enterprises similarly as they did when the dotcom bubble burst. Thusly, entrepreneurs must be aware of this reality and not offer too much when everything they can convey are unassuming reruns from their businesses. What's more, the individual speculators in the supplies of these organizations must continue with alert particularly when they put resources into IPOs (Initial Public Offerings) of these organizations.

At last, it is in every case better to remember that what goes up needs to descend in the end. It implies that in spite of all the publicity and advertising just as opportunity over the possibilities of the new companies, except if the business essentials are firm, there is an inclination for amendment at some point or another and subsequently. Every entrepreneur must be conscious of the nuts and bolts of financial aspects. At the point when the progressions of "hot cash" die down in the long run as the financing costs in the West are ready to be climbed in the coming months, the organizations and businesses of entrepreneurs that have the business models dependent on sound monetary and the executives' standards would be the ones that would stay in conflict.

The term pioneer is regularly used to allude to somebody who should change their positions and stand contingent upon the conditions. In reality, when somebody says that another person is a go-getter, it is as a rule in the adverse sense wherein the other individual is being sorted as a person who cannot be trusted. Be that as it may, most definitely, they have to hold onto opportunities and change with the occasions just as benefit from the business opportunities as they emerge and influence on changing business sector patterns and shopper conduct. For sure, there is nothing amiss with an entrepreneur being a shark since the person is relied upon to bring in cash for their financial specialists just as themselves.

Further, it is likewise the situation that entrepreneurs must be "chameleon" like implying that they should have the option to change with changing business sector drifts and guarantee that their enterprises stay serious. Moreover, entrepreneurs must have the option to "arrive early" and "sense the future" implying that they should be consistently vigilant for new opportunities to develop their businesses and make feed while the sun sparkles. Arriving early implies that entrepreneurs need to keep themselves side by side of changes in the outer commercial center and situate their business methodologies as needs be. In addition, contending with others implies that upper hand is increased just when entrepreneurs can detect showcase inclines and intuit the progressions superior to their companions and adversaries.

Consequently, entrepreneurs should without a doubt gain by the emerging opportunities and subsequently, they should be deft and nimble not to forget about armada footed as they endeavor to keep up their seriousness and improve their business worth. For every one of these reasons, we feel that entrepreneurs must be sharks who can contend by arriving early. Additionally, entrepreneurs must have the option to be responsible for their future implying that "Dark Swans" and other high effect and low likelihood occasions must not shake them or their businesses. The term Black Swans has been begat by the popular master on future detecting and probabilistic arranging, to allude to abrupt disengagements and unforeseen occasions that can possibly overwhelm everybody and cause greatest harm.

For example, when market crashes or market moving geopolitical and socio-political occasions occur out of nowhere, entrepreneurs must not be overwhelmed and rather, be in a situation to "brave the tempest" or far superior, ready to detect that the "ground is shaking under their feet" and get ready and strategize likewise. Likewise, they should likewise have the option to "ride the rushes of things to come" by peering into the skyline and detecting when the waves would hit the shore. We live during a time of disturbance when the normal period of organizations as far as their life span has tumbled from around 50 years after the Second World War to 18 years right now.

Additionally, exponential mechanical change implies that organizations, for example, Blackberry, and Nokia which were the market heads only a couple of years prior are no place in the retribution now. Aside from this, with globalization and the arrangement of a "global city" where disseminating communications is as easy as it seems (with little or no effort). Everybody from anywhere contends with anybody from around the world implies that entrepreneurs need to build up the talent of thinking worldwide and performing locally. So that, worldwide changes do not wipe them away and local interruptions do not cause disengagements and disappearing of their enterprises.

As can be seen from the focuses made up until now, entrepreneurs ought to without a doubt be global in their methodology just as have the option to take advantage of lucky breaks and influence on the quickly changing business sector patterns. The progressive rushes of Entrepreneurship that started with the underlying business people when countries were industrializing, and afterward proceeded with the coming of the Digital Age, has now arrived at a phase where ecommerce organizations and Smartphone App based aggregators and businesses are the main types of entrepreneurship.

Right now, is advantageous to take note of that the organizations, for example, Uber, AirBnB, and Alibaba in the United States and China, Flipkart, and Zomato in India, and Amazon overall speak to the most recent rush of entrepreneurial new businesses that have proceeded to get well known and pull in billion-dollar financing. Undoubtedly, it would not be a distortion to express that the Entrepreneurs behind these enterprises and new companies have actually shaken the current market models deeply and disturbed the manner in which business is done both in the developed and developing world.

The media is brimming with stories and inclusion about these "New Age" adventures that have risen up out of no place and have pulled in billion dollar valuations and financing from profound stashed holy messenger speculators and investors. In fact, the media has authored a term for the most sweltering of these new businesses by naming them Unicorns after the Mythical animal that could fly and do no off-base. Further, the eye popping financing and the high and soak valuations must imply that going ahead there would be more entrepreneurs who might want to imitate and follow the examples of overcoming adversity as good examples.

Having said that, it should likewise be noticed that this "silly abundance" that is being seen now is suggestive of the late 1990s and the mid-2000s when the Dotcom boom was at its pinnacle where it was flippantly said that anybody with a site and a fundamental business model could pull in subsidizing from VCs and Angel Investors. Hence, one should in reality be vigilant while assessing whether the estimated stratospheric valuations are for sure secured. Another thing to consider is that they deal with the venture of surplus flowing cash because of the ultra-free financial arrangements of the Central Banks of the world in the decades which instigated the 2008 crisis and in succeeding years. It was believed that the best way to bring development is by drawing off cash into the account.

At the end of the day, since the Federal Reserve has held rates at or close to Zero almost all the recent decade, this has brought about more cash being accessible in the account. While not minimizing the sound business models of Unicorns, for example, Uber that have well and genuinely disturbed the state of affairs, the case one must adjust these parts of simple liquidity with that of whether the Unicorns and those enterprises that are being driven by entrepreneurs with "overwhelming joy in their heart" are in fact worth the ventures.

Another point that should be made is that for some new ecommerce companies in emerging economies, for example, India, their present technique is to take part in a value war with their rivals in showcasing. Business practice wherein a lot of these enterprises are "photocopying cash" implying that they are losing cash just to pull in new clients and hold existing clients by offering at a very low rate. To be sure, any individual who has shopped on the web or on portable over the most recent couple of months in China, India, and somewhat the United States would have seen the rebate during occasion periods and seasons that reach out to half or more which as any businessperson would let you know are basically not feasible.

The thought behind these limiting wars is to develop a reliable and wide client base that would continue coming and returning for all the more once they are "snared on" and afterward increment the costs with the goal that the piece of the pie that has been developed cannot be dissolved in any event, when costs are raised. Without a doubt, this is the methodology that has been trailed by the "perfect case" of the Unicorns, Uber that has guaranteed that once it picks up piece of the overall industry, at that point it would participate in valuing that is progressively practical and dependent on business basics. Thought this seems like a decent business methodology, one needs to recall that there can be other new participants who flush with financing can likewise take part in value wars so that at this point set up Unicorns are given a "run for their cash."

At the risk of sounding skeptical, all that we are stating is that there must be progressively reasonable appraisals and assessments from this "new age and new age" entrepreneurs and their funders with the goal that a rehash of the Dotcom bust that happened 10 years and half prior is not rehashed. To finish up this article, it should be repeated that while some really problematic Unicorns are changing the guidelines of business, there are an equivalent number of them that are essentially reveling in the sunlight of good fortune along these lines raising the chance of them colliding with the ground once the happiness fades away. As such, businesses must bring in cash and benefits and financial specialists must get returns on their capital and speculations sooner or later in time and thus, as any business the board hypothesis would let us know, just organizations with sound basics "make the cut" eventually and this is something that applies to the Unicorns too.

For what reason do businesses in Europe and the United States flourish when contrasted with the ones in Asia and Africa? For what reason do businesspersons think that it's simpler to work together in the West when contrasted with the countries in the East? Aside from characteristic topographical preferences and accessibility of assets, is there something different that guarantees that businesses think that it's simpler to work in certain countries while they neglect to do as such in different countries? The response to this halfway can be found in the manner the West works under the standard of law and agreements while the East works through fixing and gaming the framework? At the end of the day, businesspersons need to escape laws and guidelines in numerous Asian and African countries though in the West they can be guaranteed that legally bound commitments would be respected. If there should be an occurrence of disasters, the courts and the political basis even detached from the Policymakers would give them a quick and reasonable hearing and trail. To clarify this further, consider a worldwide organization that works worldwide and has a broad system of providers, clients, and merchants separated from representatives and different partners everywhere throughout the world. In the event that for example, a provider reneges on their guarantee to convey; this organization can sue the provider and guarantee that misfortunes are recouped. Nonetheless, if such legal disputes and lawful cures take years or decades and additionally are loaded with vulnerabilities, at that point the organization would essentially need to investigate extra-legal techniques to recuperate its misfortunes. Then again, if the courts and the legal framework alongside the law requirement offices help the organization recoups from its misfortunes with the providers in a rapid and time bound way, and afterward the organization would no doubt work in a nation or a district that ensures these advantages.

This is the vital contrast between the West and the East as far as maintaining and implementing the standard of law that guarantees smooth tasks for businesses. Surely, this is the motivation behind why numerous multinationals are hesitant to enter countries, for example, India where the sclerotic and the late and lazy legal and law authorization framework cannot ensure security against extortion and misbehavior. In addition, they likewise need to offer incentives and go through tremendous measures of cash just to lead their business that makes extra expenses just as brings more layers into their effectively perplexing method of tasks.

Further, this is likewise the motivation behind why numerous multinationals that work in India like to have Singapore as the discretion place in the event of legitimate and business debates. To be sure, the way that Singapore offers quick and time bound removal of contest goals instruments has frequently been referred to as one reason why worldwide enterprises demand taking their debates in Asian countries to the city state. The instance of China is unique in relation to India since, however, it additionally has an old equity and legal framework, in any case, the political and the bureaucratic framework offers the business insurance and ensures that their cases would be taken care of and settled in a speedy way. As it were, the standard of law is upheld particularly where it concerns businesses since China needs increasingly more multinationals to work in its nation.

Having said that, it must be noticed that issues, for example, piracy, and copyright infringement despite everything force costs on Western businesses when they work in China and this is something that remaining parts a staying point. Obviously, it is not necessarily the case that Western businesses in China do not offer incentives or kickbacks. Simply that they stand a superior possibility in issues relating to the standard of the law when contrasted with India. Going to the point that the standard of law is totally important for businesses to work, we can perceive any reason why this is the situation by taking another case of an organization that has numerous partners. For example, on the off chance that a representative is found abusing the sets of principles, at that point the organization is well inside its privileges to fire the person in question.

In any case, if the organization does not do as such out of dread of culpable some segment or interests that help the representative, at that point it very well may be said that the organization is liking to go without instead of observing the law. For another situation, if the organization finds that there are visit strikes and work agitation wherein despite the fact that it has observed the law, it despite everything is being irritated, at that point unquestionably it would look to migrate to another state or nation where its inclinations are secured. In addition, the standard of law is likewise important for businesses to ensure the wellbeing of their representatives particularly on the off chance that they have night moves and transport their workers from their homes to the work environment.

Without a doubt, in all the cases talked about up until now, no business might want to work in a state or a nation where rebellion wins and they need to reward their way at each level just to proceed with their tasks. There is nothing more critical to businesses than countries where the standard of law is implemented and maintained completely and thoroughly as something else, their activities would be hit and their business would endure. Surely, who needs to work in countries where there are visit shutdowns and irregular demonstrations of brutality and disorder that lead to disturbances to the business tasks? At whatever point we think about the terms, entrepreneurship, and entrepreneurs, there are a few pictures that are summoned in the psyche.

For example, the most widely recognized inclination is an individual or a lot of people meeting up to dispatch another business with overwhelming joy in their heart and brimming with enthusiasm.

Next, we consider how such entrepreneur's can in fact become enormous businesspersons given they have a convincing thought or an inventive item notwithstanding gobs of difficult work and responsibility. Added to this is the accentuation as of late about the alleged new businesses driving the following influx of development and entrepreneurs changing the world with their brightness, responsibility, and enthusiasm with liberal assistance from financial specialists and the governments. For sure, given the way that the Unicorns or the new businesses that have accumulated billion dollar valuations have taken the inside stage in the news, we can be excused when imagining that entrepreneurship is exciting and tempting.

In any case, is it the case that entrepreneurship is about new businesses and the style and fabulousness of turning into the following Mark Zuckerberg or propelling the following Uber? Likely, not as any businessperson with a thought and some financing can be thought of as an entrepreneur. This implies while not all businesses proceed to become Facebook, Uber, and Google, their commitment to monetary development and improvement is as significant as the Biggies among the entrepreneurs. Surely, the way that in many developing countries, for example, India, we rely upon the business aptitudes of the little entrepreneurs to prop our lives up and our reality very much oiled implies that little entrepreneurs are as significant as the huge names that succeed.

This is the explanation that this article puts forth the defines for all conceivable assistance to be reached out to the little entrepreneurs as opposed to propelling plans and fitting arrangements to serve just the individuals who are in the tech or related fields. As a general rule, countries, for example, India function in view of the business trade between the individuals and the little entrepreneurs for example, the paper delivery merchants, the milkmen, the local food merchants, the vegetable sellers, the shipment organizations, and in particular, little businesspersons (e.g. the administration offices who handle everything from plumbing to electrical fixes to the individuals who have some expertise in organizing deliveries of goods and services).

Be that as it may, while developing countries, for example, India has customarily offered governmental help and backing to the SMEs (Small and Medium Enterprises), generally, there has been a propensity to take into account those with high spending plans. In reality, the way that it is anything but difficult to become mixed up in the media publicity just as capitulate to the impulse to spoil the spectacular and the captivating implies that numerous Third World countries are seeking after arrangements that advantage a few entrepreneurs and not all entrepreneurs. Having said that, it is not completely the situation that little entrepreneurs have been disregarded. Plans, for example, Microcredit, and Small Business advance arrangements have implied that even the entrepreneurs who are little and juvenile are offered some help to maintain their businesses.

Nonetheless, given the way that it has gotten popular to celebrate the Unicorns and disregard the others requires a genuine rectification toward the path that the governments in Third World countries are taking and requests a move in their needs back to the days during the 1980s and the 1990s when little entrepreneurs were energized. This does not imply that governments should again go to welfare and free advances to the little businesspersons. In reality, this is something that must be stayed away from no matter what since such welfare perspectives just advance Moral Risk where the inclination to hold the benefits and give the misfortunes to others would land us wrecked that some state catalyzed the move from communism to private enterprise.

Consequently, we are stating that while it is okay for speculators and governmental organizations to spoil the big deal among the entrepreneurs, it is additionally occupant upon them to hand hold and brood the little entrepreneurs also. Consider how troublesome it would be if the classes of little businesspersons referenced before were to skip work or close their enterprises because of absence of help and sustenance. Research has indicated that such little entrepreneurs over all need financing on an everyday or week after week or month-to-month premise which converts into shorter term liquidity and working capital prerequisites.

In reality, while little entrepreneurs probably would not need millions in subsidizing, they are additionally people who are frequently helpless before credit sharks and usurious banks for their everyday financing needs. This implies the government can help such entrepreneurs without incredible expenses and controls that make it simpler to get to financing from banks, a few sponsorships to counterbalance their costs, expedient endorsements and quicker clearances of their applications. It is needed from such little entrepreneurs to utilize innovation so they can scale up advantage from the collaborations and the efficiencies of the economies of scale.

More than anything, little entrepreneurs must not be irritated basically for the explanation that they do not have significant associations or the capacity to display their thoughts in a media benevolent way. All in all, unmistakably developing countries on development directions ought to have both full scale and smaller scale empowering agents of development and the little entrepreneurs who fall under the last classification are as significant as the marquee names. Have you at any point asked why entrepreneurs and new businesses will in general bunch around specific topographical areas? What is so exceptional about the spots referenced over that, entrepreneurs' rush to certain land areas for propelling their enterprises and most of the new businesses will in general group in those spots?

While a few specialists accept that it is the climate and the way that current new businesses are as of now in those places and successively, it is simpler for new companies to just follow old companies lead. There are other people who point to the exceptionally fundamental certainty that these places will in general have entrepreneurial environments that empower development and cultivate a culture of entrepreneurship. What is this tricky thing called entrepreneurial biological system and for what reason does it make a difference? First of all, entrepreneurs need access to quality ability or the HR who are imaginative, inventive, dedicated, or more all have an enthusiasm for making something new and all the more critically, transforming their thoughts into solid businesses.

This implies places, for example, Silicon Valley, Bangalore, and Shenzhen are appealing on the grounds that they will in general have enormous representative pools that the new companies can tap to staff their enterprises. Having said that, this is likewise the situation with different spots and urban areas on the planet where there are sufficient assets that can take care of business. Anyway, for what reason would they say they are not the beginning up capitals of the world? The response to this inquiry can be found in the "Intelligence of Crowds" clarification wherein individuals will in general follow whatever the group is doing in the supposition that the group recognizes what it is doing. In this way, when Bangalore turned into the IT capital of India, there was no thinking back as a large number of graduates and specialists discovered their way to the spot looking for work.

Besides, the way that entrepreneurs like to base their new companies in places that brood other new businesses implies that spots, for example, the Silicon Valley that is as of now home to numerous acclaimed and emerging new companies has a flourishing biological system set up that pulls in ability as well as different entrepreneurs who can get to the hatcheries fortress their enterprises. The hatcheries here allude to the mix of VCs or venture capitalists (VCs), Angel Investors, and money related establishments that can give the genuinely necessary seed capital for the entrepreneurs. Hence, while access to quality ability is the principal determinant, access to back and financing is the subsequent determinant.

Taken together, these two components guarantee that new entrepreneurs might want to base their new companies in places where acclaimed business characters live with the expectation that they can profit by their recommendation just as any subsidizing from them. In reality, it is very normal for entrepreneurs in Silicon Valley and Bangalore to hobnob with prior age entrepreneurs in social occasions and expert body collections where they can profit by the counsel of those characters. We have talked about access to ability and hatcheries being two factors that figure out where the new businesses are found. Similarly, significant is the job of the governments right now entrepreneurs need a government that works for them and not against them by passing laws that "throttle" inventiveness and smother entrepreneurship.

This implies either the government helps and energizes the new businesses or essentially escapes their way as opposed to setting obstructions on the way of the entrepreneurs. Right now, is to be sure the way that most beginning up capitals on the planet has governments that either effectively supports them or just let them be how they are. This discloses to an enormous degree why Silicon Valley and Shenzhen have risen as of late to become advancements center points while Bangalore which for quite a while had progressive governments that supported entrepreneurs is presently losing the race to Hyderabad and different urban communities where Apple, Amazon, Google, Facebook have reported that they would find their activities there.

The purpose behind this is again the "intensity of motivations" grinding away. Entrepreneurs will in general go any place they feel welcome and any place the foundation and the governmental strategies are steady. In this manner, right now world, these essentials for development are the reasons why a few urban areas raise as advancement hotspots though others lose the race. Having said that, it is additionally the situation that the emerging beginning up blast on the planet is likewise spreading to more current spots and countries. For example, Israel, Ireland, and the Midwest in the United States are presently contending with the huge names, for example, Silicon Valley, Shenzhen, and Bangalore. Likewise, some European urban communities are additionally endeavoring to join the group of development center points. Along these lines, neither the entrepreneurs nor the governments can underestimate anything or anybody when a lot is on the line and consequently, each must supplement the other as far as administrations conveyed and returns developed to guarantee that they stay serious constantly.

This is the message that VCs and Angel Investors have been telling all partners that while the group tends to rush at specific spots, it additionally will in general relocate to different spots if the conditions fall apart in the previous and are empowering in the last mentioned. To finish up, entrepreneurs need environments to flourish and consequently, they will in general run to any place such frameworks are set up. Underneath all the charm and glamour of new businesses that rise millions and billions of dollars in financing lies difficult work, assurance, and devotion of their originators. In fact, Entrepreneurship is as much about lumpy tirelessness for what it's worth about having a smart thought and taking shape the thought without hesitation with the assistance of a submitted group. It is not generally the situation that entrepreneurs would have it simple and discover sponsor and funders ready to bankroll their enterprises.

For each Flipkart that raises billions falsehood a hundred other new companies that drop out of the race at various stages in the beginning up lifecycle. This implies any potential entrepreneur must consider a few angles or traps to stay away from on the off chance that they are to appreciate proceeded with accomplishment in the commercial center and on the off chance that they are to guarantee that their enterprises become beneficial and transform into fruitful organizations. First among the entanglements is to choose when to look for subsidizing from the VCs and the angel investors. The initial phases in the life of an entrepreneur are generally the ideation organizes and the brooding stages wherein entrepreneurs start with an activity intend to change their thought and afterward dispatch their dares to hatch their thoughts and change them into useful businesses and items.

In these stages, it is prudent to guarantee that entrepreneurs invest, however, much energy as could be expected thoroughly considering the different issues and the entanglements that they may experience as far as timing. As there is nothing, for example, too soon, there is likewise nothing, for example, past the point of no return implying that looking for the first round of subsidizing from Investors and afterward utilizing them reasonably to spread the assets across different stages must be painstakingly arranged and overseen. For sure, even before the Investors discharge the assets, the entrepreneurs must be careful about the terms and conditions that the

Investors are proposing as uncalled for and extreme terms can undoubtedly lead the entrepreneurs to surrender command over their enterprises when they "strike gold."

The purported "fine print" named so in light of the fact that a great part of the significance of the terms and conditions is typically covered inside the agreements and in inside pages implies that entrepreneurs better have their very own legal advisor or look for legitimate assistance before they sign the agreement with their financial specialists. Aside from the way that such a significant number of Twenty Something's are propelling enterprises which implies that some of them scarcely comprehend the legalese and the complexities, the other viewpoint has to do with "getting overjoyed" in the "elation" of "raising subsidizing" and consenting to all the terms and conditions set forward by the Investors. Along these lines, it is suggested that Entrepreneurs practice bounteous alert before they invest in outer collections. Going to the inquiry about What Next once the Entrepreneur gets fruitful and consequently, needs to settle on a decision between taking the organization open or turning it off and beginning another endeavor, a few traps here are the possibility of antagonistic takeovers from set up businesses and industry veterans who "know the game" superior to numerous and thus, are skilled at such methodologies. While a considerable lot of you who are perusing this probably would not have known about who was a serious sensation during the 1990s for surprising the world with Hotmail, those of you who were in school around then would definitely perceive the name and all the more critically, would likewise recollect how he was "outmaneuvered" into surrendering control of Hotmail.

While the case Bhatia brought in enough cash on the arrangement, it is additionally the situation that such a game changing thought couldn't convert into preceded with progress after the deal wherein the present age knows Gmail yet not Hotmail. The exercise from this for entrepreneurs who strike it huge is that be cautious in "playing your cards" and go to your inward voice for direction in the event that a "crossroads" shows up and you need to settle on similarly appealing alternatives. While the above is in the event of effective enterprises, the opposite side of the coin in particular what happens when adventures do not meet the desires for their financial specialists, authors, and the market must be considered also. In situations where adventures fall flat or are fizzling, it is an intense requires the entrepreneurs to choose when to get together and proceed onward.

While there may be enthusiastic reasons just as truth based reasons in "staying and sticking around" to "tide over the extreme occasions" and trust in "the promising end to present circumstances," it is likewise the situation that the choice to end the endeavor, anyway difficult it is must be taken sooner or later or the other. In reality, if such a choice is not taken, the entrepreneurs risk being "submerged along" with their enterprises and subsequently, the trap to maintain a strategic distance from here is about how soon to throw in the towel and how to exit without a lot of misfortunes for all partners. Therefore, there are numerous entanglements that Entrepreneurs must be careful about and we have shrouded some of them right now. While it is enticing to luxuriate in the greatness of fruitful enterprises, Entrepreneurs must understand that there are exciting bends in the road in each business and adventure just as recollect that achievement one day can without much of a stretch be trailed by disappointment the following day.

The expression "start-up" and the environment encompassing it is a moderately late formation! Despite the fact that the specialized definition includes any business that has as of late set up for business, the working definition alludes to investment financed associations. Right now, will take a gander at past new businesses. The "mother and pop stores" that have a high disappointment pace of 90%. We have to comprehend that the issues looked by these new businesses and the assets that they have accessible are totally not the same as the million dollar new businesses. It is thus that warrants a different investigation for these associations.

The main purpose for the disappointment of mother and pop stores is the absence of core interest. Businesses will in general flourish when they are experts. Clients have an obvious recognition about them. Additionally, they can fabricate ability that will permit them to manufacture a strong notoriety. Notoriety is the main resource on which mother and pop stores endure. Consequently, lost center methods suicide with regards to these small scale associations. Be it clothing or a basic food item shop or a video rental store, the accomplishment of the mother and pop stores lies in understanding the socioeconomics superior to the outstanding organization. The super organization may beat them on cost, however, it cannot contend most definitely.

New companies tend to possessed, managed, and run by a solitary individual. This, much the same as the absence of center, is a significant impediment to their prosperity. In spite of the fact that, mother, and pop stores cannot stand to enlist a multitude of supervisors and pros, they should in any case follow the major rule of division of work. The entrepreneur must utilize his insight to perform key enterprises. Ordinary errands that can be assigned must be designated. A near sighted perspective on expanded costs must not stop the mother and pop stores from redistributing paltry enterprises. Legitimate division of time must be done to guarantee that operational, strategic, and key capacity of business is completely focused on.

In progressive business, robotization is the name of the game. It does not make a difference whether super partnerships contend of whether mother and pop stores do the ones that computerize live one more day. By and by, mother, and pop stores do not have the spending limit for mechanical procedure mechanization. In the event that they had that sort of spending plan, they would not be called mother and pop stores! Be that as it may, a great deal of robotization is currently accessible economically or in any event, for nothing. A few ERP's give cloud-based "pay more only as costs arise" choices that fit into the pockets of these miniaturized scale associations well overall. These applications spare occasions from unremarkable errands like bookkeeping and duty documenting. Mother and pop stores should likewise make an endeavor to work in productivity.

Mother and pop stores will as a matter of course is an item that has an excellent valuing. Super partnerships have economies of scale attempting to further their potential benefit. They can purchase from providers in mass and pass the advantages to the purchasers. The mother and pop stores cannot contend on value. Rather, these stores must contend on customized administration. Clients would not pay a premium since they like "mother and pop stores" and are feeling beneficent towards them! Clients pay all the more simply because they show signs of improvement administration. Mother and pop stores must put vigorously in client relationship the executives. All workers must be situated towards having a help outlook.

Mother and pop stores are additionally intensely subordinate upon their area. Their center competency is administration, and they lose while contending on cost. Henceforth they should work in upper white collar class neighborhoods. Individuals in these areas will in general have working companions. Henceforth, neither has the opportunity and families will in general value the customized administration gave and are happy to take care of it. Actually, most mother and pop hides away up in low class neighborhoods in light of the fact that the rentals are lower. Low class neighborhoods have individuals with part of leisure time, however, less of cash. They do not value customized administrations. In such cases, the association is probably going to come up short due to poor comprehension of socioeconomics.

The core of the mother and pop stores is client relationship the executives. They should live by the adage that the client is above all else and cannot in any way, shape or form do any off-base! What really happens is that mother and pop stores are overseen by individuals that do not have a help mentality. Rather, they attempt to downy clients. Since the clients are eye to eye with the proprietor, they regularly express their disappointment. The proprietors frequently neglect this disappointment. This is an enormous mix-up. Adaptability is at the center of the independent company. They should focus on the assessments of their clients and adjust rapidly.

There are various opportunities to bring in cash on the web and there are a similarly huge portion of experts, specialists, remain at home people, resigned staff, and understudies competing for these opportunities. For sure, a basic Google look for bringing in cash online would hurl a large number of results with the outcomes indicating everything from straightforward undertaking based occupations to convoluted and complex exchanging and research employments. All in all, how can one approach choosing and figuring out which opportunities to seek after and which plans to evade just as situating oneself and taking advantage of such opportunities?

The responses to such inquiries rely upon the sort of opportunity that you might want to seek after dependent on your range of abilities, chance taking capacities, the time you can dedicate to the employments, or more all, your mentality and disposition that are maybe the most significant determinant in producing cash on the web. To be sure, demeanor, and mentality are basic and vital in any activity and particularly so while seeking after opportunities where you are all alone and where the most significant point is that achievement and disappointment are controlled by your character and the entire arrangement of convictions, contemplations, sentiments, and perspectives that you bring to the table.

To begin with, let us look at the instance of an expert who has stopped their corporate activity to seek after opportunities on the web. Such experts by prudence of having worked in an all-day work know the significance of time the board, inspiration, the estimation of difficult work, and the aptitudes that are required for various occupations. Having said that, this without anyone else does not ensure accomplishment as they would need to make the "outlook change" from working for an association to working for a business that does not have any commitment towards them. For example, experts in all day occupations can pace their work and hope to be held in the activity regardless of whether their presentation plunges during a quarter or a year. In fact, most corporates place the non-entertainers on watch, and in the wake of allowing them to improve their presentation, they at that point make a move if there should be an occurrence of no indications of progress.

Notwithstanding, the circumstance when outsourcing or bringing in cash online is subjectively extraordinary as the sites and firms that work online do not convey any such commitments towards their representatives. This implies experts need to make the "switch" from full-time attitudes where they are guaranteed and consoled to a model where they must be constantly alert and vigilant. Surely, the sort of changes that anyone who is endeavoring outsourcing and bringing in cash online lies in tolerance, difficult work, separating themselves from the challenge, the capacity to spend extended periods of time going after positions and not anticipating moment reactions, or more each of the, an assurance to prevail regardless of the chances.

In addition, while seeking after opportunities on the web, one must watch out for the sort of opportunities and whether one's abilities and mastery matches such opportunities. There is no reason for going after positions essentially in light of the fact that everything necessary is a tick of a mouse as one must "fit" the ideal profile that is being publicized. Another mentality change, particularly for those beginning, is the need to manufacture a system of contacts that would be convenient for sending resumes, looking for input, and for proficient references. While organizing is the way to achievement in any activity as all the understudies who have moved on from Management Institutes would have more than once been told during their instruction, there is a principal distinction from physical systems administration to virtual systems administration where the last is for the most part fabricating associations with individuals you would not have met face-to-face.

In conclusion, the key mentality change here is that one must progress from a physical mode to a virtual mode where each connection, each installment, each criticism, each bit of work or undertaking you convey, and each contact occurs in the internet and where Skype and Phones supplant face-to-face collections. On the off chance that you feel that you can make this mentality change, at that point welcome to the universe of online work that is as exhausting as it is energizing, as monotonous as it is fulfilling, and where you have the opportunity to set your own hours and figure out which work to acknowledge. At long last, you ought to likewise recall that regardless of how the earlier day/week/month/year went; you should find a good pace up and not surrender.

Nowadays, entrepreneurs are all over the place. From Silicon Valley to Sao Palo in Brazil, and from Boston to Bangalore, going into business is in fact the wrath among the youthful and the anxious. Besides, since the time the Great Recession of 2008, all day employments have gotten rare and what's more, with the ascent of temps and the gig Economy (the term used to portray the outsourcing and the low maintenance work model), most experts are truly and allegorically "all alone." Aside from this, with the mechanical advances fashioned about and realized by the mobile computing and the smartphone revolution, Entrepreneurship is the true decision for any individual who needs to ride the peak of the "Fourth Industrial Revolution." Having said that, it is not generally the situation that Entrepreneurship is simple or compensating absent a lot of difficult work or even possibility and unadulterated coarseness. Without a doubt, comprehensively, just a few out of ten new pursuits have a possibility of accomplishment and even among them, just a couple really proceeds to turn into the market heads. Much the same as during the 1980s and 1990s, for each Bill Gates or Steve Jobs, there are hundreds and thousands of other people who have "failed miserably" and along these lines, in the 21st Century, for each Mark Zuckerberg, there are incalculable other people who are either bankrupt monetarily or have deserted their mission.

To address these inquiries, we have to dive into history just as companion into the future and simultaneously, keep ourselves concentrated solidly on the present. Because "income sans work" because of Ultra Low Interest Rates by Central Banks is discovering its way into Entrepreneurship does not imply this would keep on being the circumstance going ahead. For sure, with the Federal Reserve in the United States "flagging" its goal to raise rates, it is in no way, shape or form sure that financial specialists would keep on emptying cash into new businesses. Simultaneously, with exponentially quickening innovation, the "time span of usability of thoughts" and items are getting absurdly shorter and compacted implying that what is presently a hot App or Software would rapidly be overwhelmed by the following huge thing.

If nothing, these two patterns are sufficient to make the eventual entrepreneurs anxious and reconsider before they see overwhelming joy in their heart. In spite of the fact that this does not imply that would be entrepreneurs should surrender their fantasies, what this surely implies is that their feet must be solidly on the ground. Aside from this, the globalized world economy has without a doubt "contracted" separation and anybody anyplace and everybody wherever are basically rivaling one another. For example, with data transfer capacity and consistent and dependable foundation being the determinants of the biological system notwithstanding simple human asset accessibility and access to subsidizing, plainly worldwide the start-up capitals, for example, the Silicon Valley and Bangalore are in direct challenge with other start-up capitals around the globe.

In any case, with rising protectionism and the risk of retreat of globalization, the fate of entrepreneurship would likewise be nearby or a blend of worldwide and neighborhood or Glocal (the term proposed by the well-known creator and reporter, Thomas Friedman) to portray the adjustment of the worldwide to the nearby so one advantages from worldwide patterns and simultaneously, do not dismiss the absolutely neighborhood on the ground conditions. This can appear as more privately engaged and driven new businesses, for example, the different nourishment and basic food item adventures in India to the ecommerce and transport parts in China.

Furthermore, with outsourcing turning into the standard as opposed to the special case, in future, entrepreneurs anyplace on the planet need not be obliged by national limits and can take advantage of the plenteous multitudes of consultants around the globe. Further, with cell phones and Smartphones getting omnipresent, it is additionally the situation that future entrepreneurs should consolidate innovation easily of utilization of their items so that even the layman would profit by this merger. Aside from this, another pattern which is recognizable (particularly as of late) is that new businesses and their originators need to guarantee that they stay on the correct side of controllers and do not defy the guidelines or spurn standards as they continued looking for piece of the pie.

To be sure, the commended organizer of the ride hailing application, Uber, which is a worldwide example of overcoming adversity, presently ends up out of his post (however, this may be for a couple of months) for the most part due to the approach which he embraced towards everything from managing controllers to treating his representatives and particularly managing instances of inappropriate behavior and segregation. Therefore, it is obvious from the first conversation that while the future may be rough for entrepreneurs, it is likewise ruddy for those ready to be front line and simultaneously, not lose of antiquated qualities, for example, morals, and a consistent and stable way to deal with business.

Without a doubt, if there is one single take away from this article, it is that one ought to be controlled by innovation and front line items; one should likewise be driven by unadulterated business sense and a comprehension of financial aspects which has served past ages of entrepreneurs well. To close, being an entrepreneur can imply that one looks in reverse just as forward without losing one's present feet on the ground balance. Maintaining a business is not simple. Over 90% of the businesses set up every year fail inside the initial three years. Fewer than 10% keep on living throughout the years. The main explanation behind new businesses failing is the absence of money. This carries us to the inquiry, how do new companies go through their money? Do they have an approach to organize spending?

Tech new companies are generally subject to the representatives that work in them. Therefore, they need to boost capable workers to leave their comfortable well-paying occupations at global partnerships. In their offer to do as such, they regularly go over the edge. Authors will in general go through an excessive measure of cash attempting to have the coolest office around. It might be important to give workers a protected and secure condition. Be that as it may, it is not important to give them boundless food and beverages. The facts demonstrate that organizations like Google have such workplaces. Be that as it may, it would be better for a start-up to initially construct a hearty business model and at exactly that point spend too much on a costly office.

This is another region where a great deal of new businesses will in general squander valuable resources. As of late, organizations have begun a pattern of procuring piece of the overall industry before they become productive. This regularly drives new companies to give their items or administrations at a disposable cost. In a large portion of these cases, the association makes a misfortune from these deals and is in an ideal situation not selling. In any case, it is regularly expressed that this misfortune ought to be viewed as an interest in client obtaining. The thought is that clients will get snared on an item and will inevitably begin paying for it. Numerous new companies have taken in the most difficult way possible this is not in every case genuine. Much of the time, such arrangements just pull in freeloaders. These clients rush to forsake the organization once they are approached to pay for the item or administration. New businesses should, consequently, concentrate on getting certified clients instead of limiting their items to freeloaders.

New companies frequently need to contend with corporate mammoths. Henceforth they will in general purchase similar apparatuses that these goliaths do. For some new businesses, this may not be a monetarily feasible procedure. It would not be judicious to put hard earned money in getting licenses for email and calendaring programming. Correspondingly, organizations will in general spend an extreme measure of cash on bookkeeping and installment preparing programming. This is the place new companies need to use the advantages of present day innovation. A ton of these administrations are accessible in the cloud. They can be gotten by paying a small amount of what huge specialist co-ops like Google and Microsoft would request. New companies should initially recognize that their activities are little and consequently the devices utilized by super enterprises may simply be costly and monetarily unviable undoubtedly.

Organizers will in general have an enthusiastic connection to the organizations that they work for. Frequently they want to develop this association into the following enormous partnership. The headcount of an association is a significant pointer of its development. It is hence that numerous new businesses will in general scale up quicker on the headcount that they preferably should. Representatives are a perpetual cost that numerous new businesses just cannot manage. Rather, they should initially re-appropriate a portion of this work to different organizations. Just once their incomes have become strong should perpetual representatives be remembered for the group. Additionally, the way toward enlisting new individuals in the group ought to be examined to guarantee that lone representatives that will increase the value of the firm ought to be remembered for the group.

Marking is for large businesses. This is on the grounds that marking prompts a ton of interest in the previous stages. The advantages of marking are not so much quantifiable at the beginning times. By definition, marking is a long-term game. The issue with new companies is that they are uncertain about whether they will endure the long-term or not. Subsequently burning through cash on printing logos on caps, shirts, and flyers is not generally a supported cost. These costs would contradict the lean business model that new companies are relied upon to follow.

It is fundamental that new companies must approach solid lawful guidance. This is the main cost that gets disregarded. Lawful guidance is not as charming as showcasing. Be that as it may, it is unquestionably just as significant as promoting may be. New businesses go into a great deal of unchartered regions during their initial years. It is conceivable that the organization may run into lawful difficulty in some cases. It is in this way significant for the organizations to look for legitimate guidance and keep away from these snares. Claims can be costly in any event, for huge firms. Most definitely, one frightful claim can end the life of a promising start-up.

To summarize it, acquiring fund is a troublesome assignment for a start-up adventure. Be that as it may, the trouble does not end there. Organizers need to guarantee that they burn through cash on the correct things.

Organizations will in general work by and large. Thoughts will in general come to people inside the association. Notwithstanding, they should be spread over the association. Any change possibly happens if a few people in key positions accept that the thought is adequate. This is the place a business case proves to be useful. Administrators from all offices in all association need to make a business case in some structure. It is fundamental that officials comprehend the subtleties and delicate aptitudes utilized simultaneously. There are odds of a thought being dismissed or being taken by another associate if an appropriate business case is not made for the equivalent.

It is fundamental first to offer the presence of an issue to the crowd. This is on the grounds that individuals do not purchase an answer except if they accept that there is an issue first. The key is to make the issue look convincing and guaranteeing that the administration imparts your insight that prompt activity is required to fathom the issue. Additionally, by starting with the issue, one regards the authority of the administration. It is presumptuous to straightaway show up at a choice yourself. Top administration for the most part accepts that choices taken by one individual may not generally be precise. They like to include a great deal of partners and assemble data before showing up at a choice. Thus, the desire to legitimately jump to the end must be maintained a strategic distance from. This puts the administration on the back foot as they presently accept that you as of now have a plan that you are attempting to actualize.

At the initial barely any collections, it is significant just to make reference to the business need just as how you found it. For instance, was it found during a yearly survey or is it something that you watched while following the business procedure. When the administration has been persuaded, there is a need, and that move should be made quickly, the change the board procedure starts. Associations have made balanced governance to guarantee that choices are not taken by one individual alone. Henceforth, all things considered, a few people will survey the business need and your recommendations inside the association. So as to successfully exhibit your business case, it is critical to know the partners. As a rule, this incorporates your chief, your supervisor's manager just as senior pioneers in the association. When you know who your crowd is, you can tailor your introduction and message as needs be.

exercises, if acknowledged; they incorporate goals identified with development and business development.

At long last, entrepreneurial action commonly alludes to new pursuit formation. These three components of entrepreneurship are caught through the GEM. The GEM information has basically filled the hole that existed regarding characterizing entrepreneurship also, giving a measure proper to investigation. This amendment suggests that a more extensive perspective on entrepreneurship ought to be utilized. A multi-faceted way to deal with examining the effect of entrepreneurship on financial development, while representing a nation's degree of improvement, is received here. The center moves past entrepreneurial action just; it joins mentalities and desires too.

Entrepreneurship is the fundamental vehicle of financial advancement or the motor of financial development. Entrepreneurship can influence monetary development in various manners. These can incorporate information overflows, expanded challenge, and expanded decent variety as far as the item and administration offering accessible. Further components incorporate the making of occupations, the presentation of new advancements and profitability improvements. Entrepreneurs have a task to carry out in improving information with respect to the reasonability of new advancements just as helping with recognizing customer inclinations by bring new assortments of existing items and administrations to the market. There are few further systems through which entrepreneurship can emphatically influence financial development. Entrepreneurs can (i) power productivity after existing businesses through challenging existing business sector positions, (ii) quicken the pace of innovative decimation, whereby new firms drive modern change by supplanting existing businesses, (iii) invigorate the pace of development in enterprises bringing about the opening of new markets, and (iv) give a more noteworthy assortment of new items, administrations what's more, forms than would be accessible from existing firms.

The effect of entrepreneurship on an economy's development shifts as indicated by its phase of financial improvement (Ferreira, Fayolle, Fernandes, and Raposo, 2017). The impact of entrepreneurship on monetary development may not be predictable in developing and developed countries. The significance of entrepreneurship relies upon a nation's phase of monetary improvement. In any case, the experimental proof does not present definitive proof. The impact of entrepreneurial movement on monetary development is sure or more prominent in exceptionally developed countries contrasted with developing economies, others find that entrepreneurship does not straightforwardly influence monetary development in high-pay countries, however, does in poor countries.

Entrepreneurial mentalities are noteworthy and positive for high-pay economies, however, inconsequential in clarifying financial development in center/low-salary economies. Entrepreneurs in high-pay economies might be progressively inventive, internationalized, and development centered than entrepreneurs in center/low-pay economies. Undoubtedly, existing writing right now the expanded rate of need entrepreneurship in developing economies contrasted with developed economies. Need entrepreneurship, regularly borne from an absence of elective work alternatives, is pervasive in center/low-pay countries which might be coming through in the outcomes here. On the off chance that this is, in fact, the case at that point there is a need to figure approach in developing countries to endeavor to support entrepreneurship to be more than essentially need or subsistence entrepreneurship.

In most high income countries, noteworthy help is given to entrepreneurs as business advancement courses through colleges and other preparing frameworks, government awards and strategies which advance and bolster entrepreneurship and furthermore through built up instincts which can give subsidizing, for example, banks, and investment reserves. These preparation offices, awards, and foundations are regularly ailing in center/low-pay countries, which may adversely affect on entrepreneurial perspectives. Where in center/low-pay countries entrepreneurs may try to benefit in developing countries entrepreneurs may basically try to help families through need of an absence of other openings for work. Beating these distinctions in mentalities is not clear given the approach, monetary, and institutional imperatives present in developing countries; in any case, the proof here recommends that it is a fundamental test to embrace.

Entrepreneurial action, all by itself, is not adequate to advance monetary development. Positive entrepreneurial perspectives and yearnings in a nation are progressively significant. Run of the mill strategies and projects, planned for advancing entrepreneurial action centering explicitly on new firm arrangement, and may not be adequate to advance development. The arrangement concentrates needs to move from expanding the amount of entrepreneurs to concentrating on the perspectives and quality (e.g., development goals) of people and existing entrepreneurs.

More nuanced arrangements, which teach people all in about the significance of entrepreneurship and develop a constructive perspective on entrepreneurship, are required. This could likewise incorporate arrangements that mean to expand presentation to entrepreneurial good examples (e.g., organizing) and decrease the outcomes of entrepreneurial disappointment (e.g., through liquidation law). Universal advancement associations need to give more noteworthy consideration to the job of both entrepreneurship and training, including showing entrepreneurial abilities for instance. These approaches, in any case, may set aside more effort to encourage inspirational mentalities to entrepreneurship.

Infrastructure facilities are important to drive financial improvement in the economy and framework offices incorporate foundation of dams and force stations to meet the vitality needs of industry; transportation framework to move assets and completed items to wanted goal and correspondence framework to encourage business activities, among others. Facilities spread wellbeing, instruction, and social government assistance for reasonable monetary development. Infrastructure changes are basic to financial advancement. Nobody size change fits all; it relies upon monetary and political structures in every nation.

Changes are known to be fundamental, if not actualized would hose the soul of the individuals. The business subsystem as a major aspect of the bigger framework called the culture is displayed by the condition. The earth is typically conceptualized regarding factors natural in the condition that influence the sub framework. The Nigerian condition has been described by insecurity in political and monetary sub-divisions. The Nation experienced incessant administration changes that have brought about irregularities and absence of congruity in government approaches and projects. The country has never had an all-around arranged economy. The vulnerability in the earth is not favorable for financial advancement. World Bank delegate distinguished the moderate pace of monetary changes in the economy as the snag to remote venture.

The test for entrepreneurship in emerging economies is the means by which to give supportable work that both takes into account the utilized to fulfill their essential human needs through their pay and that which regards the natural supportability criteria, that is, occupations that do not decimate the earth. The different clear commitment that entrepreneurship can make to fulfill fundamental human needs is to convey in creative not so much harming but rather more viable new ways those essential administrations and products like vitality, sanitation, nourishment, lodging, medicinal services etcetera required by the poor social orders.

Many ventures, particularly little enterprises have shut shops because of absence of open force supply, transportation, coordination, nature of foundations and absence of modest credit office. Instability challenges have constrained numerous business people to remain in isolation or take shelter in different countries. Different difficulties remember irregularity for government approaches, arrangement of tax collection and absence of appeal in the economy when contrasted and different financial matters. Foundation encourages and requirements singular entrepreneurs and framework does not develop and change at the same time by the activities of one or even a couple of key entrepreneurs.

Or maybe, it rises through the gradual addition of various institutional assets and exclusive occasions that co-produce each other over an all-encompassing period. Helpful and serious connections between populaces of associations influence the conveyance of assets accessible to entrepreneurs in the earth. Sufficient to state that institutional factors, for example, government arrangements, political occasions, social standards among others shape the large scale content inside which these populace forms happen. To comprehend about the procedure and parts of a foundation for entrepreneurship requires recorded investigation of the transient succession of occasions and exercises that happen to make and change essential logical information into a monetarily suitable, arrangement of items conveyed to clients.

Various case narratives showed that new advancements are only occasionally if at any time developed by a solitary firm alone in the vacuum of an institutional domain. Numerous complimentary developments in specialized and hierarchical courses of action are generally required before a specific innovation is reasonable for business application. Business achievement or disappointment of a mechanical advancement is an extraordinary measure as impression of institutional developments that the social, monetary, and political foundation that any network needs to continue its individuals. It is imperative to be certain that entrepreneurs and administrators, not governments make business and work in private part, yet government can profoundly affect how all organizations work their opportunities to develop.

Government strategy and its impact on the 'institutional condition of a nation, region, or district has become a key focal point of enterprises to help improve the private segment. There are three primary measurements to the job of government in giving empowering and serious environment. Government and lawful principles decide how exchange rules work broadly and universally and the authoritative document of organizations, the degree of legitimate points of confinement on organization liabilities, prohibitive practices and against restraining infrastructure guidelines.

Government likewise influences guidelines on situations crushing away buyer insurance, food and welfare. Government charges duty expenses, raises obligations and spends. The manner by which this works has expansive impact on business money and hazard taking: Taxation and charge levels influence entrepreneurial impetuses and market passage; government obligation levels seriously influence the monetary climate. Spending impacts the serious condition acquisition rules, for government contracts impact markets.

The development of government administrations, for example, instruction, wellbeing, and transport administrations impact factor contributions for businesses. As a huge manager, government wage rates and work conditions sway on neighborhood and national compensation framework, the job of worker's guilds and business conditions. Government redistribution approaches and social building impact advertise motivations and the work market. Government money can be utilized to offer awards, sponsorships, credits, and other mediation activities or data or warning help to all classes of businesses and can try to improve the foundation of business factor sources of info, for example, training, and abilities innovative work showcasing and profitability activities International exchange insurance or barriers.

Government activity can be best where it improves the conventional condition for entrepreneurship and manageable monetary advancement. Two regularly government activities inconvenience financial advancement as a result of the diseconomies of scale that the division encounters in having the option to adapt to compliances with government systems, consequently, better guideline and improved government arrangements and administrations is typically the fundamental move that government can make to help the general business condition. The factors of the examination include force, correspondence, data, and transportation. The outcome indicated that organizations with utilitarian framework experience quicker deals development, quicker representative development, and higher advancement. Arrangement of foundations spikes firm development and firm development terribly relies upon the degree of framework improvement.

Contemporarily, globalization is viewed as one of the most far reaching powers that shape the progressive world. It prompted significant increments in overall exchange and trades in an inexorably open, incorporated, and borderless worldwide economy. The cooperation of developing countries in the globalization procedure made an opportunity for them to more readily use their relative favorable circumstances through entrepreneurs. Entrepreneurship is frequently connected with work formation, riches formation, advancement, and its related government assistance impacts. Along these lines, it is commonly credited with financial advancement instrument particularly for developing countries.

Globalization is the aftereffect of expanding mix of economies around the globe, especially through the development of merchandise, administrations, and capital across outskirts which likewise prompted the development of work and innovation across universal fringes. The term turned out to be increasingly normal during the 1980s, reflecting innovative advances that made it simpler and speedier to finish global exchanges both exchange and money related streams. Globalization alludes to an expansion past national outskirts of a similar market powers that have worked for a considerable length of time at all degrees of human monetary action, town markets, urban ventures, or money related focuses. Globalization is the inclination of venture assets and businesses to move past local and national markets to different markets the world over, permitting them to get interconnected with various markets. As needs be globalization furnishes associations an unrivalled serious situation with lower working expenses, to increase more noteworthy quantities of items, administrations, and customers. This way to deal with rivalry is picked up by means of expansion of assets, the formation, and advancement of new speculation opportunities by opening up extra markets, and getting to new crude materials and resources. Globalization has started to destroy the hindrances that generally isolated nearby business opportunities and neighborhood firms from their worldwide partners. Neighborhood markets are turning out to be indispensable pieces of more extensive, worldwide markets. Thusly, universally situated entrepreneurs would now be able to see a lot more extensive scope of opportunities and serious modes, unlimited by national limits. Right now condition, entrepreneurs, and emerging businesses face both new opportunities, and imposing new difficulties. Entrepreneurship is regularly viewed as a significant part in animating monetary development, advancement, seriousness, and mitigating destitution in developing countries. Right now globalization stage clearly affects level of entrepreneurship come into question.

The progression of science and innovations has enormously diminished the expense of transportation and correspondence, making monetary globalization conceivable. These days, sea shipping cost is just a portion of that in the year 1930, the ebb and flow airfreight one-6th, and media transmission cost 1%. The value level of PCs in 1990 was distinctly around 1% of that in 1960, and this value level in 1998 diminished again by around 80%. This sort of reality pressure impact of mechanical headway enormously diminished the expense of universal exchange and speculation, subsequently making it conceivable to compose and arrange worldwide formation. Obviously, globalization has something to do with expanded joining of the world society, with an accentuation on expanded monetary reconciliation. It additionally engaged with businesses changing their reference point thinking all around instead of locally and innovative change. Anyway in spite of the idea's by and large new none of these components have existed since, in any event the Second World War. The financial coordination of world economies has been continuous in the course of the most recent fifty years, as countries have worked through GATT and the WTO to lessen exchange limitations. During the 1960s and 1970s there was significant conversation of the development of the global enterprise as businesses changed their reference point from household to worldwide.

The job of entrepreneurship in financial advancement is the subject of a lot important to scholarly and arrangement circles the same. Entrepreneurship is regularly credited with numerous positive changes in developing countries. In any event, it is related with work formation, riches formation, advancement, and its related government assistance impacts. A solid independent venture part and entrepreneurship are commonly connected to a solid economy. Developing countries are starting to concentrate on their business surroundings and making a monetary space which is helpful for private enterprises, after bombed enterprises at advancement through import substitution and new-born child industry insurance programs and to some degree blended outcomes from export advancement procedures. To be sure, the advancement of entrepreneurship and the proclamation of little and medium estimated enterprises strategy has become a significant improvement remedy as of late. Entrepreneurship approach, at that point, joins a rundown which incorporates changes to countries' large scale monetary, conversion scale, exchange, and modern strategies and upgrades in administration. Advancement financial specialists recognize three significant phases of improvement in which entrepreneurship assume an essential job.

Cultivating entrepreneurship is broadly seen to be a basic strategy plan to extend work and gaining opportunities and to lessen neediness. Sound macroeconomic conditions and business condition including foundation, guideline, and legitimate condition have commonly been underscored to increment entrepreneurial exercises and make employments. While these stay applicable, in developing countries, expanding consideration is being paid to the job of work arrangements that intend to decrease imperatives and improve efficiency among the independently employed and little scope entrepreneurs. This is especially squeezing in developing countries where pay and compensation work is constrained and most of occupations are made and worked in independent work.

While giving greater improvement opportunities to developing countries, the globalization procedure is additionally presenting gigantic risks. Monetary globalization has developing countries' risks of being concussed by ominous outer components. Under open monetary conditions, the contention between the acknowledgment of outer financial harmony and that of inward monetary balance is an incredible limitation on the macroeconomic strategies of developing countries, debilitating their ability of macroeconomic control and guideline. Right now entrepreneurship is anything but an exact remedy for monetary advancement for developing countries, it can support financial improvement when polished advantageously. The entrepreneur is imagined as starting change and producing new opportunities. This outcome is affirmed for most developing countries in the 1970 and 1980s. The experimental proof unmistakably indicated that the firm-size dissemination in developed countries started to move away from bigger partnerships and toward entrepreneurial action. Some unmistakable properties of entrepreneurship in developing countries seem to improve the likelihood of achievement for development arranged firms, while others seem to keep down these organizations.

Emerging markets do not have a stable of develop markets and the consistency that such markets offer. Therefore, the opportunity for entrepreneurship in emerging markets is unavoidable. While entrepreneurial opportunities are more extensive and resultant procedures are normally self-supporting in developing countries, restricted individual and family reserve funds and a nonappearance of money related advancement seriously confines the development possibilities of promising new businesses in developing countries.

Technical, industry-explicit preparing is a significant part in the formation of universally serious firms. These organizations frequently structure into geologically engaged modern groups which prompted rise of comprehensively serious businesses in developing countries. Developing countries have investigated every possibility to accomplish financial improvement and development and globalization process have made an opportunity for them to use their similar points of interest, present trend setting innovations, outside capital and the executives experience. It is additionally good for killing monopolistic practices and fortifying business sector rivalry. With the ascent of globalization, entrepreneurial worldwide new businesses have risen in developing countries which are related with work formation, riches formation, advancement, and its related government assistance impacts. Surely, the advancement of entrepreneurship and the declaration of little and medium estimated enterprises approach has become a significant improvement solution as of late right now.

Somewhere in the range of 1945 and 1980 almost 100 provinces in Africa, Asia, and the Caribbean picked up their autonomy and started the way toward starting an improvement methodology for their residents. Tragically, a large number of those countries experienced neither huge per capita development nor monetary advancement. Without a doubt, moderate, and outrageous destitution stays a critical worry for some developing countries. While developing countries have utilized various approaches and procedures in their improvement interests, two types of mechanical strategy were especially noticeable. The first was import substitution a procedure of industrialization by delivering recently imported merchandise for the nation's household showcase. In any case, by the 1980's, even with financial emergency, many developing countries at that point went to a subsequent system export advancement.

Be that as it may, except for certain countries in East Asia, neither mechanical procedure has brought about significant financial improvement. Both improvement approaches depended on solid state intercession and industrious market bends to support their practicality hence regularly swarming out or obstructing through and through the conventional and significant job of the entrepreneur. Henceforth, after bombed enterprises at improvement through import substitution and new-born child industry assurance programs and to some degree blended outcomes from export advancement methodologies, developing countries are starting to concentrate on their business surroundings and making a financial space which is helpful for private undertaking both household (e.g., nearby entrepreneurs) and outside (e.g., outside direct speculation).

For sure, the advancement of entrepreneurship and the proclamation of small and medium sized enterprises (SME) arrangement has become a significant improvement remedy lately. Entrepreneurship approach, at that point, joins a rundown which incorporates changes to countries' full scale financial, swapping scale, exchange, and mechanical arrangements and enhancements in administration. Both national governments and the significant global associations, as a component of their destitution decrease, development, and financial improvement programs, are starting to concentrate on improving countries' business and venture situations for entrepreneurship.

The World Bank and United Countries Industrial Development Organization (UNIDO), for instance, have each settled units to advance private division improvement in developing countries and to give specialized help with the plan of SME and entrepreneurship approach. In 2003, the World Bank started an activity to quantify and rank countries' business divisions and speculation situations. Moreover, various developing countries have as of late drafted SME enactment and propelled projects to help private ventures and household entrepreneurs. While an attention on entrepreneurship for advancement may give off an impression of being a different way to deal with improvement, this examination offers that it is reliable with and even correlative to the more seasoned and progressively customary improvement methodologies.

As a matter of fact, there are wide and covers a scope of issues from culture and qualities; institutional obstructions, for example, budgetary division improvement, administration, and property rights; to the ampleness of instruction and specialized aptitudes. An expansive writing has likewise evolved on outside direct speculation and its positive and negative impacts on innovation move and entrepreneurship. As these economies moved from brought together economies to advertise economies, venture, and entrepreneurship got significant. However, different investigations analyze the impacts infrastructural improvement and the macro economy on entrepreneurship. With such a wide extent of issues, a system for blending the writing is required. This examination offers that the ID of the externalities which influence entrepreneurship gives a valuable structure to look at the writing on entrepreneurship in developing countries. These externalities have come about because of and have gotten inserted in countries' establishments and help to clarify the degree of entrepreneurship in an economy.

The quest for strategies to achieve both development and advancement

flexibility of interest for imported modern products is higher in the outskirts nation than in the propelled nation. The fringe economy has a decision of how to industrialize by either expanding its formation for trade or for residential utilization. Import substitution was believed to be the most effective path for developing countries to accomplish industrialization and salary development.

For sure, regardless of whether a developing nation decided to expand its fares and encountered an expansion in salary, as a result of its generally high pay versatility interest for imports, there would be a huge comparing increment in import request. Thusly, residential formation of the imported great (e.g., import substitution) would in any case be required. Among the approach proposals to keep up import substitution programs were high taxes, export assessments and formation sponsorships to local makers.

While countries could have decided to build fares to deliver the outside cash to import these modern products, industrializing developing countries would discover it at first simpler to create for a current and known local market than for an obscure worldwide market. Import substitution was a vital methodology for developing countries in light of the fact that these economies expected to give security to their new baby ventures. Much more as of late, it was likewise by and large idea that developing countries expected to deliver the merchandise that cutting-edge countries developed so as to keep away from the "destitution trap" of constantly creating low worth products with unstable costs. To accomplish industrialization through import substitution, countries utilized various market twisting apparatuses, for example, exaggerated trade rates and strategies which raised the expense of imports.

In advertise economies, these choices are left to a great extent to enterprises and entrepreneurs who are guided by costs and benefits. Be that as it may, for countries seeking after import substitution, there was solid government intercession. In the 1960's, for instance, when Zambia sought after its import substitution program, its recently made assembling part center formation around extravagance merchandise which had recently been imported for the countries' world class. In an ill-conceived joint enterprise between the Zambian Government and the automaker Fiat, the contracted number of autos to be developed yearly was nearly as incredible as the all-out number of vehicles in Zambia at that point. Formation under import substitution was additionally intensely slanted by the "request profile" of the well off.

The directing powers for formation were very unique. While contortions are a side-effect of blunders in advertise economies and give opportunities to remedy by entrepreneurs, import substitution required durable bends. Duties and different kinds of government mediations were utilized to guarantee that formation occurred in import contending enterprises while additionally ensuring those residential assembling firms. In any case, these strategies were frequently incapable, as the levy structure misshaped value signals and really gave motivators to firms to create the extravagant utilization products, as opposed to wanted capital merchandise

Countries which utilized import substitution additionally needed to keep up expanded trade rates to guarantee that household makes could manage the cost of the required capital sources of info. To be sure, as countries changed to the importation of capital merchandise, import request really turned out to be increasingly inelastic as the importation of capital products was never again a decision, however, a need. The import substitution arrangements additionally adversely influenced the nation's fares, "particularly when they include exaggerated trade rates and quantitative limitations on imports"—further decreasing remote trade profit. Given these extreme market bends which existed under import substitution systems, it would have been hard for the entrepreneur to find or follow up on socially ideal opportunities.

At long last, the colossal organization which must be built to help import substitution fit the propagation of changeless wasteful aspects in industry and defilement in government both significant obstructions to profitable entrepreneurship. Government strategies which effectively supported new passage frequently prompted markets with numerous little and wasteful firms. A large number of these organizations were working with abundance limit, high work costs comparative with efficiency and remote trade deficiencies which affected their capacity to acquire important data sources bringing about further leeway. The mind boggling import permitting frameworks likewise made devastating bungles between the time that capital ventures were really required and the occasions that import licenses were gotten-again bringing about underutilization.

On account of Ghana, organizations regularly picked providers dependent on the capacity of the remote organization to offer adaptable financing alternatives as opposed to the most proficient ones. Furthermore, as a result of the Ghanaian government's out and out or joint responsibility for of these organizations and the high joblessness rates in the countries, production lines kept on working in any event, when they were wasteful for political explanation.

The mind boggling administration additionally bolstered debasement. For instance, the import permitting process encouraged unscrupulous business dealings as permit designation choices came to be ruled more by defilement and individual kindness than by assessment of monetary feasibility. Indeed, the complex bureaucratic frameworks which had been made to help import substitution supported "expediters" whose salaries were gotten from encouraging the procedure of endorsements and desk work. Additionally, the provider credit endorsement process, opened new roads for debasement.

The import authorizing framework utilized during the nation's import substitution program, prompted agreement among provider and shipper, shipment of flawed product, payoffs, and overpricing. Given the wastefulness of the import substitution procedure and the intricacy of the organization made by import substitution, this audit offers that entrepreneurs would be bound to take part in rent seeking, sly, and ineffective entrepreneurial exercises as opposed to in socially gainful entrepreneurship. Import substitution was not effective. In reality, the normal efficiency and innovation upgrades and the indigenous learning forms expected to support high salaries did not develop.

The new born industry contention for assurance regularly comes up short in light of the fact that in any event, when a defensive obligation has been given, there is no assurance that singular entrepreneurs will attempt more prominent interest in getting mechanical information. As such, firms frequently worked with overabundance limit, offering an excessive amount of assortment. Without a doubt, an unintended result of import substitution programs was the presence and determination of wasteful ventures and market mutilations. Furthermore, the enormous administrations which must be made to help the import substitution programs regularly loaned themselves effectively to debasement.

Many developing countries' business sectors turned out to be seriously twisted by mechanical approaches. Economies were described by exaggerated trade rates, import, and remote trade controls, and huge wasteful imposing business models. Business guidelines related with the import substitution programs were frequently mind boggling and upheld the development of defilement. As economies performed more awful, more contortions were made, prompting upright and horrendous cycle. Given these government disappointments, it is anything but difficult to perceive any reason why import substitution neglected to accomplish significant development for the countries which utilized this procedure and made a situation which was inadequately fit to advancing beneficial entrepreneurship.

With the disappointment of import substitution and the achievement of the recently industrializing Asian countries, the standard way of thinking changed to the advancement of fares and an acknowledgment of universal exchange as a method for improvement. Global exchange is commonly seen to effectively affect monetary execution. Information on Asian produced sends out show a critical relationship among trades and monetary development. Exchange advancement is associated with more quick development than the last periods of IS [import substitution] which go before it. There is a critical and positive relationship among development and the level of exchange transparency.

Exchange advancement must be joined by a milieu of different approaches to guarantee that a nation is effective in incorporating all the more seriously with the world in a way that is positive for development and neediness decrease. Like import substitution, the revelation of the fare advancement methodology seemed to have happened coincidentally. The impacts of the "poor harvests" joined with the desires for downgrading and gossipy titbits about a U.S. disrupt which could have prompted nourishment and outside trade, deficiencies may have been the beginning of South Korea's fare advancement methodology in the mid 1960's.

By 1965, the fare advancement system was formalized inside South Korea's Ministry of Commerce and Industry's Export Promotion Subcommittee. South Korean fare advancement approaches incorporated the foundation of appropriations and access to modest credit for exporters which were attached to export focuses for firms in every area. The South Korean government additionally focused on keeping up the nature of fares and on showcasing enterprises to US companies Comparing the effective Asian economies with hailing Asian fare advertisers, in the fruitful East Asian economies, endowments were connected to "solid execution guidelines regarding yield, sends out, and in the long run, R&D."

Government support was all around given to firms as per their achievement in the commercial center, especially world markets. By one way or another East Asian, policymakers maintained a strategic distance from the impulse to guide most assets to sponsor misfortune making firms or to profit very much associated lease searchers. The experience has been that development execution has been progressively good under fare advancement techniques. Without a doubt, since open economies are presented to world costs got from worldwide profitability contrasts, household assets can be all the more effectively allotted contrasted with countries where twisted residential costs are the fundamental guide for a nation's formation blend.

There were, be that as it may, noteworthy hindrances to developing countries' made fares. These included elevated levels of security inside developed economies, the extra transportation costs related with delivering seaward and the impacts of political flimsiness on formation. Furthermore, innovation, preparing, and involvement with promoting their items to the last markets likewise established major interior hindrances to trade formation for some African countries. Consequently, it was regularly offered that "remote firms" would be more qualified to deliver export products in developing countries. Remote firms would wish to extend formation into abroad markets to get to "new opportunities."

Assets and experience of the parent concern, including administrative and specialized staff as well as that indefinable preferred position in its interior activities which a productive going concern common has over another one. There is additionally political economy contemplations related with moving formation to developing, low pay countries. Nonetheless, in spite of the potential for political fights inside developed countries because of the work disengagements, it was foreseen that this wonder the vertical incorporation of formation across countries would be an enduring marvel. Given the significance of the outward direction procedure, a significant inquiry is that how do trades influence development? To begin with, export direction is related with development through its effect on outside trade income. Fare direction additionally developed required remote trade to subsidize capital ventures in this manner dispensing with the requirement for unnecessary government mediation as required under import substitution.

Export development is related with "raising national salary" and more noteworthy remote trade profit. Dollar offers that as fare organizations work in outside money acquiring segments, they can all the more promptly and successfully use remote cash obligation contrasted with those organizations which produce for the household part. Without a doubt, the outward direction of the East Asian economies had spared them from the developing nation obligation emergency that assaulted Latin America. Export direction is likewise connected with auxiliary changes inside an economy which can greatly affect financial improvement. In reality, export advancement could turn into an impetus for these basic changes.

Moreover, emergent advancement systems take into account economies of scale in industry as formation is focused to a lot bigger market contrasted with formation for just the residential market. Outward arranged exchange approaches additionally took into consideration the age of scale economies, without the utilization of imposing business models. In any event, for little countries, the serious debilitation of diminutiveness cannot be nullified; however, it very well may be limited under an outward-looking methodology as a result of the economies of scale related with sending out to a bigger market.

Fares make it workable for developing countries to beat the restrictions of their local markets in abusing economies of scale and guaranteeing full limit use. Universal exchange can positively affect financial development, and accordingly on neediness, since exchange takes into consideration a progressively proficient utilization of assets and opens household makers to bigger, increasingly serious markets which empowers profitability upgrades. Export can likewise create significant profitability overflows.

There are significant similitude's between the items that wealthier countries export and those which less fortunate countries trade. In their investigation, they find that countries, which have moved to the formation of merchandise which are related with high efficiency, likewise have encountered significant levels of development. Despite the fact that, the capacity to change to increasingly profitable merchandise is constrained by human capital elements, anything that pushes the economy to represent considerable authority in goods with higher profitability levels-presents a dynamic (if transitory) procedure of financial development as emulators are attracted to deliver the newfound high-efficiency goods.

Countries should enterprises to address the market disappointments which lessen the motivating forces for entrepreneurs to enter new markets and produce new items which are related with higher efficiency. The expansion in item assortments across Latin America has commonly been valuable for decreasing the financial shakiness related with over the top fare specialization. Outward procedures were additionally bound to re-establish showcase efficiencies. Fare advancement was related with less distortionary and bureaucratic arrangements contrasted with import substitution which could positively affect development.

This is predictable with the finding that GDP development was altogether and adversely connected with genuine conversion scale twists a proportion of internal arranged approaches. At long last, formation is likewise bound to happen along a nation near bit of leeway under an outward-situated procedure. As exporters go up against a worldwide market, there is a motivator to improve profitability and innovation contrasted with makers who contend in ensured household markets. Asian fare arranged countries, for instance, experienced expanding levels of all out factor profitability with expanding levels of fares.

Efficiency development and government intercession were significant for clarifying the locale's 'supernatural occurrence' development. In any case, there is essentially no proof that sends out or outward direction was related with innovative externalities. There are relationships amongst fares and innovation overflows; he contends that causation cannot be resolved. Rather, another clarification might be that gainful firms essentially export more. To be sure, maybe the development in the East Asian supernatural occurrence countries was increasingly identified with an expansion in ventures and capital amassing which was encouraged by trade income.

Human capital is the significant factor in clarifying development differentials. It was perceived that human capital could be gained throughout creating products and taking part in exchange. However, it is not adequate to just build the volume of fares. Rather, the expansion in sends out must likewise be joined by an increment in the assortment and multifaceted nature of products developed through continuous advancement, or almost certain, progressing impersonation. Per capita pay development requires shifts from less beneficial to progressively gainful systems per specialist, the formation or selection of new wares, new materials, new markets, new authoritative structures, the making of new ability, and the aggregation of new information… the entrepreneur as hole filler and information completer is likely the main player of the limit formation part of these components in the development procedure.

Once more, monetary advancement includes change and the entrepreneur turns into the best specialist for this change. In fact, entrepreneurship matters for developing countries since business sectors matter. Hayek perceived that information was scattered all through society with every individual having a special supply of data. Nonetheless, the market, through its continuous changes because of the discrete activities of various individuals and the states of supply of different elements of formation, imparted new data through costs which empowered the effective assignment of assets. With the breakdown of midway-arranged economies, it has been seen that governments cannot dispense assets productively and that business sectors are, without a doubt, vital.

The exact proof is likewise solid on the side of a connection among entrepreneurship and financial development. Studies have discovered that local contrasts in financial development which is corresponded to levels of entrepreneurship. The acknowledgment of the significance of the entrepreneur and the need of the business sectors for the entrepreneur to work has driven numerous countries to start to chip away at culminating their business sectors by taking out boundaries to entrepreneurship and other market disappointments. In any case, approach creators should likewise make the extra move to guarantee that the positive externalities information, system, and showing and disappointment externalities can aid the development of entrepreneurship and monetary advancement. Entrepreneurship is necessary for advancement in light of the fact that in developing countries entrepreneurs fill in significant gaps left by fragmented and immature markets.

Without a doubt a key capacity of entrepreneurship in developing economies is decisively to prepare factors, for example, capital, and specific work which, being defectively showcased, may somehow or another not be provided or allotted to the exercises where their efficiency is most noteworthy. Be that as it may, in any event, when advertise defects are serious, entrepreneurs despite everything exist. To be sure, entrepreneurs react to these market flaws by utilizing different hole filling and, maybe, second best arrangements. In outrageous cases, where advertise and non-showcase disappointments are unavoidable, entrepreneurs are pushed out of the proper area into the casual part.

In less serious cases, enormous broadened indigenous business bunches have shaped in many developing countries in light of market disappointments. This is subsequently an intra-firm instrument for managing inadequacies in the business sectors for essential factors, hazard, and moderate items in the developing countries. Many of these gatherings were found to consolidate both banking and mechanical tasks and represent huge parts of business exercises in many developing countries. Huge gatherings were shaped in India to address the data and capital market insufficiencies. Significantly, these gatherings take part in entrepreneurial conduct while likewise providing the capital and the specialized and administrative assets.

All things considered, these congregations are not the ideal structure for entrepreneurship in developing countries as they bring about an extraordinary type of syndication private enterprise which can be troublesome to generally speaking long-term monetary advancement. It is in this manner, still important to keep on idealizing markets in developing countries instead of just depending on second-best choices. The entrepreneur had been disregarded in monetary theory. Financial analysts frequently disregarded the entrepreneur as a wellspring of monetary change and gave little consideration to the fundamental attributes of their monetary period the problematic, advancing vitality which came about because of the exercises of the entrepreneur.

The entrepreneur was a "tragically ignored" on-screen character in monetary advancement hypothesis notwithstanding his focal job in showcase forms. Neoclassical financial aspects' attention on immaculate data impeccable challenge and general harmony speculations neglected to clarify how showcases truly functioned and that entrepreneurial action had no spot at all in neoclassical microeconomics. Perceiving these lacks in neoclassical financial matters, Austrian financial aspects, specifically, offered elective perspectives on the working of the market and the job of the entrepreneur in monetary development.

How does the entrepreneur become alarm to and find benefit opportunities? Initially, Information was "scattered" all through society, while likewise understanding the significance of the uniqueness of every individual's load of data. Also, the market, through its continuous changes because of the independent activities of various individuals and the states of supply of different variables of formation, conveyed new data through costs. Mix-ups and misallocations do happen and give new opportunities to the entrepreneur. In this way, it is just the ready entrepreneur, drawing on his special information set, who can utilize this inventive manner. Hayek's hypothesis, in this way, underlined an information opportunity coordinating procedure of entrepreneurial disclosure. Information gathering, it could be said, extends the domain of 'shocks' that a ready entrepreneur can spot and follow up on. Information gathering is along these lines a significant restricting element for entrepreneurship.

It is imperative to explain what is implied by entrepreneurship in developing countries. Various terms are utilized reciprocally to depict entrepreneurial exercises. For instance, entrepreneurship, and SMEs have been utilized synonymously. Conversations of entrepreneurial exercises in developing countries have additionally incorporated the casual area and insignificant free enterprise. Numerous African assembling firms, for instance, had less than 150 workers and along these lines would fall into the SME part. Showcase intermediation in Africa is described by a plenty of little brokers, only here and there surpassing a bunch of representatives and family assistants. The World Bank, in its enterprises to target entrepreneurship, has concentrated on both the independent venture and the casual parts.

In 2003, the World Bank discharged another database on the SME division and the going with study found that when both the SME and the casual areas are considered, the joint commitment to GDP remains roughly consistent across pay bunches at around 65–70%. As salary increments in any case, there is a stamped move from the casual to the SME division. This finding demonstrated that the casual part in developing countries is a significant wellspring of monetary action. Another idea is trivial industrialists, or private ventures which utilize generally scarcely any representatives and depend vigorously on their proprietor's and the proprietor's family's work, incorporate a wide range of entrepreneurs from the various fare enterprises of Hong Kong, which produce pieces of clothing for trade, the furniture makers in Italy, to Taiwan's coordinated circuit makers. In developed economies, be that as it may, researchers have contended for a particular idea of entrepreneurship.

Despite the fact that there is significant cover between independent companyandentrepreneurship,theideasarenottheequivalent.Entrepreneurial firms may start at any size level, however, key on development without fail. The entrepreneur is portrayed by inclination for making action, showed by some imaginative blends of assets for benefit. Notwithstanding, while SMEs and entrepreneurship have various implications, both are significant in an economy. Without a doubt, the private company part may fill in as a vehicle both for entrepreneurs presenting new items and for individuals who just run and possess a business professionally.

Similar differentiations have been made between endurance or need entrepreneurs and opportunity entrepreneurs. Do these qualifications make a difference for developing countries? As the significant portion of firms in developing countries are little, as far as the quantity of workers and resources; and many working in the casual economy utilizing family work, this present audit's qualification of entrepreneurship cannot, accordingly, be founded on size. Any differentiations attracted this audit between entrepreneurship, the independent company division, insignificant private enterprise and the casual segment will be founded on the Schumpeterian idea of advancement new items, new markets, and new procedures. In any case, as Schumpeter brought up, that the "new thing" need not be awesome or of recorded significance. To see the wonder even in the humblest degrees of the business world is very fundamental, however, it might be hard to locate the unassuming entrepreneurs verifiably.

For approach purposes, improvement business analysts should concentrate when worried about explicit countries on examining the holes, obstacles, and hindrances in the market system of the economy being referred to and on the whole filling and information finishing limit and responsiveness to various persuasive conditions of the potential entrepreneurs in the populace. In numerous occurrences, doling out property rights or actualizing the obligation rule is not compelling on account of numerous positive externalities. Rather, she proposes the foundation of a regulatory office that would compensate the generators of positive externalities. This methodology should bring about the socially ideal arrangement being actualized. The contention displayed by Hupp would seem to work best where there is an open decent and hence would give a method for empowering the private arrangement of open products and different merchandise with positive overflows where client expenses cannot be evaluated. Such a methodology might be valuable in cultivating the positive overflows which empower entrepreneurial action.

The moderately modest number of instances of effective entrepreneurship renders exhibition and disappointment externalities critical in developing countries. Ruler and Robson depicted a comparable impact as learning by watching where new speculation extends in one segment of the economy have an exhibition impact on the proficiency of different segments. A significant part of their model is that the overflows are developed by the demonstration of venture itself and do not rely upon the genuine result of the task. Along these lines, each new venture yields efficiency overflows. In any case, the model accepts that the positive externalities to watching new activities (e.g., the increments in efficiency) continuously decrease after some time and that the profitability development rate (characterized as the innovative advancement boondocks) inevitably levels off.

Likewise, there are significant overflow impacts from having instances of business development and from entrepreneurs watching fruitful going concerns. Potential entrepreneurs watch the procedures and business activities of existing entrepreneurs and assemble data about potential markets, input providers, and formation strategies. Accordingly, advertise passage turns out to be progressively significant for creating these externalities. Moreover, potential, and existing entrepreneurs likewise gain from coming up short and bombed businesses. They realize what not to do or what to do any other way. Markets must, in this manner, be liberated from extreme mediations which do not permit firms to fall flat for these disappointment externalities to be compelling.

A nation's acknowledgment and resilience of pariahs and its degrees of comprehensiveness can affect entrepreneurial section. Here, the idea of social capital a started up set of casual qualities or standards shared among individuals from a gathering that licenses them to help out each other gets significant. The trust, caused by social capital empowers individuals from a general public to organize their exercises with lower exchanges costs. A general public's degree of comprehensiveness decides how enormous its range of trust expands. Elkan finds, for instance, that there is a doubt of pariahs which has restricted the development of firms in numerous African economies. All the for the most part, in developing countries entrepreneurs have regularly used their more distant families as these "connection relations" are the degree of the radii of trust in these social orders.

Be that as it may, this nearby control of business activities can adversely impact business achievement, as outside administrative and specialized ability is regularly barred. The significant level of ethnic discontinuity in many developing countries is likewise significant for clarifying entrepreneurship. For instance, that "untouchables," for example, ethnic minorities in developing economies regularly move into entrepreneurial exercises since they are avoided from different kinds of business. This prohibition, along these lines, brings down the opportunity costs of entrepreneurship. Ethnic Asian and Lebanese minorities in African countries were unmistakable undertaking proprietors and that their sentiments of uncertainty as minorities may have urged them to look for financial achievement as business proprietors.

While some social gatherings do have all the earmarks of being more entrepreneurial as migrants than others, the size of the foreigner gathering in the host nation and the relative phonetic disconnection of that gathering influence the probability of individuals from a specific worker bunch taking part in entrepreneurial exercises notwithstanding different factors, for example, training, and aptitudes. Comparable ends have been made in investigations of settlers to the United States. While both of these investigations identify with developed countries, the outcomes could be helpful for understanding the distinctions in entrepreneurship levels for some ethnic minorities in developing countries. Ethnic minorities which are generally separated from the indigenous populace would be bound to take part in high pace of entrepreneurial action.

Then again, be that as it may, while a few gatherings are regularly driven into entrepreneurship, limitations might be set on ethnic minority and non-indigenous neighborhood entrepreneurs in many developing countries when they are seen as being excessively entrepreneurial. An investigation of SMEs in the South Pacific found that there were authentic contrasts among indigenous and non-indigenous entrepreneurs in the South Pacific Islands. All the more critically, be that as it may, there was an observation among indigenous Pacific Islanders that non-indigenous entrepreneurs had a profundity of experience and asset to draw from which may have given them a bit of leeway in their entrepreneurial exercises.

Without a doubt, it was discovered that government arrangements were one-sided against non-indigenous entrepreneurs to make up for this advantage. The writing uncovers that there is a push-pull impact to entrepreneurship in developing countries with profound ethnic fracture. From one viewpoint, ethnic minorities might be driven into entrepreneurship; while then again hindrances may compel their exercises. Where there are serious ethnic strains, pariah gatherings might be avoided by and large to such an extent that the general public loses the advantages of their business showing externalities.

Monetary opportunity influences showing externalities by its consequences for both entrepreneurial passage and action. Mises finds that financial opportunity made ready for the significant improvement in expectations for everyday comforts in industrialist countries. For entrepreneurial action to happen, potential entrepreneurs must have the option to see an opportunity, yet to likewise have the option to lawfully follow up on it to turn into an "acting man." A general public's "social standards" ought to permit people to be allowed to pick their occupations. Without this monetary opportunity, then the market, relational trade, private responsibility for methods for formation, entrepreneurship, and private activity, essentially vanishes inside and out.

Giving the private division a more prominent job being developed has two features: initial, an adjustment in approach system that expels limitations on the private segment; second, the divestiture of exercises from the open segment privatization. In the first place, a few countries' governments disheartened entrepreneurship; while in others government movement is unavoidable to such an extent that it "swarms out" private entrepreneurship opportunities. Where government movement is unavoidable, an administrative sort of business culture is probably going to win instead of one which underpins imaginative entrepreneurship. In China, despite the fact that there has been some decentralization of monetary movement, government authorities meddled in the enterprises of big business supervisors. Portability of entrepreneurs looking for new opportunities is blocked. Entrepreneurs needing to hold the guidance and aptitude of remote specialists are hindered by the way that speculation choices are controlled outside the undertaking by higher specialists.

A second wonder which has prompted new opportunities for entrepreneurship in many developing and change countries is the influx of privatizations producing new exhibition and disappointment externalities. The formation of business sectors, through privatization, gives the space to entrepreneurs to work and to enhance, utilizing costs, and other data as a guide. The progress economies give an intriguing case to dissecting the significance of entrepreneurship. Like different locales, entrepreneurship is related with financial development. For instance, in spite of the fact that Russia has for the most part performed ineffectively regarding the arrangement condition for entrepreneurship, locales with higher entrepreneurial movement inside Russia likewise experienced more grounded monetary execution.

The view that entrepreneurial movement is a significant motor of development rises up out of the perception that post-communist economies that have encountered generally hearty examples of entrepreneurial improvement have would in general appreciate moderately high paces of monetary development. Without a doubt, following the breakdown of the communist framework there were high paces of new firm new businesses. While business arrangement continued at a quick pace, the conventional foundations which were expected to help expanding complex types of enterprises were non-existent and casual organizations developed to make up for the deficiencies of these new market economies.

The making of conditions which would aid the improvement of entrepreneurship was not the focal point of the transforming countries or the universal offices at first. Be that as it may, this absence of formal organizations made high hindrances to entrepreneurial exercises in the years following the change which has eased back the development of new businesses. McMillan and Woodruff call attention to that, Entrepreneurs require more from the state, in the medium and since a long time ago run, than the nonappearance of obstruction. On the off chance that organizations can develop to yield economies of scale, they need laws of agreement so they can take on unknown dealings and money related guideline so they can get bank advances and outside shareholding.

Indeed, a significant issue for progress economies is the absence of formal establishments identified with property rights, supervision of market exercises, question goals instruments, and improved monetary and bookkeeping frameworks. In this manner, the change to entrepreneurship in the once halfway arranged economies of Eastern Europe is not finished. While private ventures are currently the standard, accordingly extending the degree for entrepreneurial action, the business and administrative condition does not yet address the flaws in their new markets identified with high exchanges costs, data asymmetries and the missing markets for money related administrations in numerous countries.

Issues relating to a nation's macroeconomic dependability, the condition of its budgetary markets and its framework are inescapable in the writing on entrepreneurship in developing countries. Entrance to credit, poor transportation foundation and an absence of reliable utilities are a main requirement to firm development. The accessibility of advances is a significant factor in advancing the development of little beginning up firms. Financial decay came about because of various poor arrangements with the end goal that in spite of Nigeria's impressive oil pay, the government's reinvestment exercises did not quicken development. Be that as it may, the creators call attention to that post pioneer Nigerian government, in contrast to numerous other African countries, was not excessively antagonistic to the private division and had built up various projects to help the improvement of indigenous SMEs.

Entrepreneurs began businesses for various reasons during the period in audit. Be that as it may, extraneous prizes identified with making sure about pay were a higher priority than cleaner entrepreneurial inspirations (e.g., advancement). It would along these lines give the idea that in times of financial hardship need entrepreneurship as opposed to opportunity entrepreneurship turns out to be progressively significant. The deficiency, as far as both amount and quality, of framework in developing countries is another significant factor which limits fruitful business section and development and along these lines showing externalities.

Lack of foundation may restrain territories of future entrepreneurial development. Innovation is a moderately work escalated and capital-intensive industry. In like manner, administration enterprises ordinarily require minimal starting capital information. However, different regions that will require privatization later on may confront obstructions because of the absence of a proficient credit framework and absence of vital foundation. Notwithstanding physical foundation deficiencies, entrepreneurs in developing countries, for example, Cyprus additionally face the insufficiencies of strategy framework. The low infiltration of power in Africa constrains the capacity of countries to exchange. To be sure, the shortage of good foundation legitimately builds the expenses of working together and decreases the dependability of formation, in this way expanding costs by implication. Little firms cannot bear to make exorbitant ventures to meet their capacity needs. Given that SMEs are enormously influenced by temperamental force supply, the development of these organizations and the age of business are adversely affected. Similar ends can be drawn from the absence of foundation identified with transportation (e.g., streets and ports), correspondence (e.g., phones, web entrance) and land improvement frameworks (e.g., water system).

Information and data externalities influence entrepreneurship in developing countries in two significant ways: these externalities influence the capacity of entrepreneurs to find what to deliver and they sway the innovation and procedures utilized underway. Information and data externalities are affected by data asymmetries, exchange costs, training levels, innovative work opportunities, and remote direct speculation. To start with, data disappointments in regards to what to deliver portray showcases in developing countries.

In view of high revelation costs, entrepreneurs enter entrenched segments as opposed to looking for new formation and new market specialties. There are additionally significant expenses to finding what to deliver and that these expenses cannot be completely appropriated by an entrepreneur. In this way, in a market circumstance without government mediation there is probably not going to be the socially ideal measure of entrepreneurship and interest in business exercises. Furthermore, on the off chance that entrepreneurs who enter the market are permitted to exist as syndications, on the other hand the market flops as there will be over-formation of merchandise which do not epitomize the nation's similar bit of leeway. Data and search costs, thusly, may prompt lower levels of entrepreneurship.

Notwithstanding, the lack of accessible instructive assets is a significant restricting component for information overflows in developing countries. In an investigation of African entrepreneurs, it was discovered that African entrepreneurs' capacity to move into the formal modern part expanded with instruction. Furthermore, people with involvement with enormous ostracize or Asian-run businesses and individuals from the informed political first class were bound to become entrepreneurs. Training has a solid and beneficial outcome on entrepreneurship.

Most SME proprietor/directors are not sufficiently sorted out, qualified, or prepared. This truly hampers their presentation and their universal seriousness. Be that as it may, entrepreneurs for the most part had a bigger number of long stretches of formal instruction than representatives (e.g., 16% of entrepreneurs held college degrees contrasted with 2% of workers). The blend of instructive accomplishment additionally uncovered some significant contrasts between ethnic gatherings. Indigenous African entrepreneurs were bound to have an auxiliary or college instruction; Asian entrepreneurs for the most part achieved optional, college, and expert training; and entrepreneurs of European source in Zambia by and large had auxiliary school, college, and specialized preparing.

These distinctions may influence the sorts of entrepreneurial exercises that are enterprises by the various gatherings. Ringer and Pavitt offer that, it is generally perceived that instruction strategy impacts the viability with which innovations are absorbed and improved. Accordingly, proficiency is favorable in provider overwhelmed advances, and higher specialized and graduate designing abilities are essential in scale-concentrated and concentrated provider advances. The information channel the capacity to change information made by firms and in research centers into attractive items is probably going to be incredibly thick in developing countries.

There are numerous obstructions to information move. To start with, information, and development approach had been incoherent. For instance, national mechanical foundation will in general give little help to local firms that would profit by the transformative procedure of mechanical developing through discovering that is the sign of dynamic newbies. Innovation is additionally smothered in light of the fact that exploration associations need subsidizing and neglect to team up with one another.

FDI may help developing countries through: the arrangement of capital, the inflow of innovation, the inflow of administrative ability, and their effect on the making of productive markets. Ireland's supernatural occurrence development in the course of the most recent 70 years can be a significant model for developing countries. In fact, Ireland's change is credited to the nation's capacity to draw in FDI inflows through its recently shaped fare preparing zones starting in the 1950's. Be that as it may, the FDI was deliberately pulled in prompting bunches of high expertise exercises in the hardware, synthetics, and pharmaceuticals divisions.

The Irish instruction and preparing arrangement was additionally planned to guarantee that an inventory of gifted work fit to the division, so costs stayed serious. At long last, Ireland has been fruitful in shaping those significant in reverse linkages which transmit information overflows from FDI. In any case, it is perceived that "it sets aside effort for MNEs to get nearby providers, and dynamic strategy that can diminish the 'learning stage' about neighborhood supply may speed up at which linkages can happen."

There is a significant exercise to be gained from the instance of Ireland: utilizing FDI to accomplish information overflows requires going with approach, including training arrangement. In this manner, approaches to produce information overflows in developing countries require more than encouraging the progression of thoughts and data between firms by lessening the information channel, yet in addition encouraging the arrangement of fundamental and more significant levels of training, aptitudes while likewise promising information overflows from FDI through linkages with the household economy and residential entrepreneurs.

System externalities have risen as a significant subject in the writing on entrepreneurship in developing countries. There are various measurements. To begin with, there are arranges between entrepreneurs inside the nation (e.g., household affiliations) and afterward there are systems which broaden globally. A great part of the writing likewise centers around the absence of indigenous business organize in certain countries and the significance of ethnic minority arranges in others. A second, yet related, strand of the writing looks at the improvement of modern groups between firms in developing countries and their connections to universal bunches.

To be sure, arrange externalities of different kinds are significant in light of the fact that the little size of numerous ventures in developing countries regularly adversely influences exchanges costs, sizes of economies, and the consistency of formation quality. Business systems and modern bunches can help with conquering a portion of the drawbacks of diminutiveness through their formation of positive externalities. These systems may likewise assist with defeating a portion of the data disappointments related with business sectors in developing countries. Systems of entrepreneurs inside developing countries can greatly affect forming strategy helpful for entrepreneurship in developing countries.

The idea of "development alliances" or associations between business systems and the government to advance monetary development and improvement. They find that these gatherings are best where they comprise of a more extensive cross area of businesses as opposed to just a single explicit industry. This more prominent comprehensiveness reduces the conceivable outcomes for simply lease looking for exercises. Business systems ought to likewise be adequately sorted out and have the option to "profoundly connect with the state in professional style dialogues."

Business relationship in Nigeria and Tanzania has made some significant advances in affecting open strategy towards the private part and private undertaking. These gatherings have perceived that change is essential and alliances have framed across ethnic gatherings and huge and little business people to advocate for additional progression. In countries where the intensity of capital is not yet organized, the destiny of private enterprise may well rely upon the capacity of entrepreneur social developments to advance the arrangements, establishments, and changes important to long-term development. Therefore, systems are critical in developing countries in manners which go past the conventional system externalities of associating firms with data on providers, markets, and formation methods. Inside nation and outside systems of firms are regularly ethnic-based.

Ethnic business is the expert and social connections among entrepreneurs sharing a specific ethnic or social foundation. These systems fill significant holes in immature market frameworks identified with money, specialized information, and advertising data. Business systems were seen among non-indigenous entrepreneurs in the South Pacific where these systems offered a set up notoriety, most noteworthy access to capital and credit extensions. Initial, a thick system of business relations had been built up in Mauritius around the nation's fare preparing zones connecting neighborhood Chinese entrepreneurs with makers in China, Hong Kong, and Taiwan.

A significant number of these Sini-Mauritian systems depended on family relationship and other individual ties which induced a solid feeling of trust. In any case, a significant component of the Chinese systems was their job as an entryway for abroad Chinese entrepreneurs keen on putting both in Mauritius and somewhere else in Africa. Second, while indigenous Nigerian entrepreneurs in Nnewi, Nigeria, a town which fabricated extra vehicle parts likewise framed valuable business systems with abroad Chinese makers, these covering systems did not prompt expansions of credit, something that is basic in the inside activities of ethnic business systems. While not as thick as the Chinese-Mauritius arranges, the systems among Nigerian and Chinese entrepreneurs were helpful for building up access to data sources and innovation. It would, in this manner, create the impression that the quality of social capital affected the quality of these business systems.

Serious and effective groups center around constant advancement and redesigning. Composing on Brazil's shoe fabricating group, he finds that many developing nation bunches have been ineffectively structured and have concentrated solely on formation for the nearby economy and others many have been coordinated into the worldwide worth chain in disadvantageous ways. In an investigation of Latin America, noteworthy boundaries to bunch development are found to exist on account of shortage of entrepreneurial soul, hindrances to data sharing, absence of trust, and comparable delicate imperatives. In Latin America three sorts of bunches have been watched: need groups which frequently rise in the casual part; local enterprises groups (regularly of blended measured enterprises); and bunches of global firms leading complex exercises situated inside the nation.

Positive externalities of bunching lessen the hindrances to section for new firms, in this manner adding to make an overabundance supply of the group' primary item. In a low-aptitude condition this prompts ruinous challenge as opposed to offering ascend to contention driven updating as saw in inventive powerful groups. Both the socio-political and business systems of entrepreneurs and firms seem, by all accounts, to be significant in developing countries. The socio-political systems, which frequently appear as business affiliations, including offices of trade, are crucial instigators for change in numerous countries; if they can conquer the lease looking for propensities related with little, shut gatherings. Business systems of firms are likewise important to encourage information and exhibit overflows.

Empowering exhibit externalities is maybe the most significant issue for developing countries. This examination distinguished culture, qualities, and standards, a nation's perspectives on comprehensiveness; its level of financial opportunity and its essentials as affecting demonstrational externalities. The primary objective is guaranteeing market get to so capable potential entrepreneurs with smart thoughts can enter, set up businesses and flourish (or fall flat) without superfluous obstructions. While culture is significant right now entrepreneurship in developing countries, this overview additionally perceives that culture is not static and in this manner, the conversation of culture and entrepreneurship is not deterministic-with certain societies being perpetually ill-suited to entrepreneurship contrasted with others. Without a doubt, social examples helpful for monetary development may rise up out of endlessly various sources. A general public's way of life, qualities, and standards can affect showcase section in two primary manners: by impacting the engaging quality of entrepreneurship and second, as a boundary to entrepreneurial exercises. A third issue is the recognizable proof of regular characteristics among entrepreneurs.

To begin with, showing externalities and culture converge and impact a general public's recognitions about entrepreneurship. At times entrepreneurship might be seen as an ugly word related decision contrasted with different alternatives. In spite of the fact that socio-social factors are without a doubt significant, this survey places that the motivating force structures in the work markets of many developing countries are another clarification. This is particularly the situation where there are solid worker's organizations and feeble legitimacy based foundations. Approach producers in developing countries ought to look at the hazard rewards settlements to various parts. While entrepreneurship will consistently include more hazard that wage work, organizations, for example, liquidation rules bring down the normal opportunity costs. Such changes may improve the social acknowledgment of entrepreneurship.

Developing countries ought to likewise deliver social hindrances to entrepreneurship. Again, Botswana is an intriguing contextual analysis as the nation has adopted an immediate strategy to tending to a portion of its social boundaries. For instance, the Botswana government's enterprises to address the inclinations against female entrepreneurs and other social hindrances which keep certain citizenry from taking part in entrepreneurial movement. This will probably be a moderate procedure. Be that as it may, as the writing audit uncovered, societies change and adjust because of new data and opportunities. Developing countries and advancement organizations, at that point, ought not to stress a lot over social intangibles with the information that culture can change as motivations and conditions change.

Finally, the writing uncovers that there are some regular qualities across altogether different societies which are found in entrepreneurs. While some examination is centered around whether these characteristics are inborn (nature) or whether they can be instructed (sustain) regardless of whether we can instruct individuals to be progressively entrepreneurial this survey perceives that entrepreneurs cannot prosper without an agreeable institutional condition. The way of life must be one that, as a rule, underpins trade and entrepreneurship; however, the specific way wherein the soul of big business can be supported will be socially explicit. Therefore, approach creators should concentrate on making an empowering domain in which people who have entrepreneurial character qualities can thrive.

Strategy producers will likewise need to find a way to guarantee that their formal and casual guidelines do not victimize pariahs. The writing has indicated that ethnic minorities, returning émigrés and exiles can give significant entrepreneurial funding to developing economies. While building social capital is a moderate procedure, requiring rehashed associations, there are compensatory arrangement estimates which can be taken. For instance, to empower trust in business dealings, an economy's lawful framework can turn into a significant factor. An autonomous legal executive and enforceable agreement laws encourage unoriginal exchanges and reproduce the affirmations and trust picked up from long stretches of rehashed dealings or through familial and connection relations. Different foundations, for example, credit agencies encourage current financial frameworks and give the data expected to encourage a manageable distance exchanges. The point of arrangement creators ought to be to guarantee a playing field where every potential entrepreneur has an opportunity to produce and advantage from the showing externalities. Hence, establishments which diminish data disappointments and ensure property rights ought to be built and improved. Then again, developing countries face significant political economy contemplations as for indigenous entrepreneurship. By and large, indigenous gatherings have been the subject of past segregation.

While the program gave significant aptitudes and preparing and brought about higher salaries, the program was directed outside of the market and along these lines turned out to be to a greater extent a government assistance program than an entrepreneurial preparing program. In reality, the program's members seldom, if at any point, proceeded onward to become entrepreneurs in the private contracting part. This absence of progress to the private area demonstrates that while the program tended to significant social concerns, it did not address certifiable entrepreneurship. An issue which influenced show externalities was monetary opportunity. Monetary opportunity envelops a scope of issues.

Be that as it may, the central matter is that potential entrepreneurs ought to have the option to act. Absolutely, growing the degree for their activities through privatization of the economy is significant. Be that as it may, it is additionally critical to guarantee that government movement empowers instead of frustrates private undertaking. In many developing countries, government action is excessively inescapable. There is excessively unnecessary and complex guideline of business exercises expanding the potential for lease chasing, with respect to firms, and defilement with respect to government authorities. Even where markets have been made, through privatizations (for instance, in the change economies), the conventional organizations are as yet important to empower entrepreneurship.

At long last, as for show externalities, a nation's basics (e.g., its full scale economy, budgetary markets and foundation) matter. Countries in monetary disturbance experience issues supporting inventive entrepreneurs. While not inspected right now, impacts of physical clashes and wars ought to likewise have comparative impacts. Second, this survey has demonstrated that entrepreneurs need great framework and working budgetary markets. A significant inquiry emerges: Does entrepreneurship require financial development? Comparable inquiries have been posed in the improvement writing identified with neediness easing.

On account of the destitution writing, a developing economy implies that there is a "developing pie" or expanding assets with which to manage neediness. Financial development is to be sure an important precondition for tending to destitution. Destitution decrease procedures without development would be just redistributive. Also, advancing entrepreneurship without anyone else, without concentrating on the macro-economy might be redistributive-taking from certain pieces of the economy to help others. In this way, a nation's entrepreneurship arrangement must develop together with its professional development strategies.

Making an interpretation of research to advancement requires an arrangement of information foundation of certain quality. It gives the hierarchical motivating force to the long and regularly convoluted procedure of development. Information foundation is required at the most fundamental degree of instruction (preparing researchers and architects, just as at the degree of open logical innovative work). These information foundations should be made, at times, or changed as far as their objectives and ways to deal with coordinated effort in others to encourage information overflows in developing countries. A second, however, related idea was the significant expenses to finding what to deliver. These conditions limit information overflows and consequently add to the underproduction of entrepreneurship in developing countries.

Creative entrepreneurship requires a solid instructive establishment. Human capital is expected to make thoughts and in this way as human capital grows through training, so too will the domains of potential outcomes for advancement. Countries should pull together their instructive arrangements along the lines of their modern approaches at the better quality, while likewise improving fundamental training. Schramm effectively called attention to that instruction, both at the essential and the tertiary levels is significant for entrepreneurship in developing countries and gives the case of Institutes of Technology which have permitted high-power entrepreneurs to rise.

These changes are costly, yet vital enterprises. Given the imperative on the local economy, a nation's remote speculation and global exchange approaches are, in this manner, valuable devices for empowering information overflows. In reality, this present audit's examination centered around the fruitful change of Ireland utilizing the twin mainstays of vital and solid instruction strategy. Both of these methodologies aided the overflow of information between entrepreneurs inside Ireland and permitted Irish entrepreneurs to ingest overflows from outside of the nation. Be that as it may, Ireland, and the Asian marvel countries are exceptions as far as producing these positive information overflows. In any event, when FDI is available, linkages, and overflows are frequently feeble particularly when EPZ type gets together FDI is utilized. Forceful instruction redesigning must be joined with FDI strategy so as to profit by these information overflows.

System externalities in developing countries identified with the two relationships of entrepreneurs and groups of firms. Each had various purposes. This survey investigated the socio-political significance of gatherings in developing countries. Progressively, these gatherings are amazing lobbyists for financial advancement. Notwithstanding, it was recognized that these gatherings can be caught and take part in lease looking for conduct, particularly when there are commanded by one industry. The arrangement of multi-industry business affiliations ought to be empowered and encouraged. Bunch development, particularly where there is global formation ought to be supported.

Arrangement ought to be planned for accomplishing culmination inside the group. Then again, nonetheless, officially incorporated groups are by all account not the only arrangement. Taiwan's semi-conductor industry, for instance, was commanded by an enormous number of little firms that focus on certain market specialties and work together under various rooftops. Developing countries, along these lines, should consider their ventures to see which grouping methodologies are best. LDCs will likewise need to improve foundation, evacuate hindrances to imported sources of info and migration systems will likewise should be excused to permit access to pro outside work. Instruction will be critical to give the essential specialized and administrative abilities. Furthermore, FDI should be vital to guarantee that nearby entrepreneurs enter the worldwide chain at the correct spot. This requires a superior comprehension of fare markets.

Developing countries have attempted a horde way to deal with accomplish financial advancement and development. In the wake of increasing political freedom, much of the time, turned towards arranging and started to actualize import substitution projects to kick off their industrialization forms. To be sure, at the hour of freedom, a significant number of these approaches were upheld by the significant universal improvement organizations and driving monetary scholars. 35 years ago, the key components of a fruitful advancement technique were government arranging and import substitution. It was broadly underestimated that halfway arranged economies, whatever their different shortcomings, were truly adept at producing mechanical development. Practically all genuine individuals embraced the possibility of improvement through import-subbing industrialization, so obviously it must be correct. Nonetheless, the huge government contraption used to regulate the import substitution framework frequently made serious market bends, some of which exist even today. These twists included outside money controls, solid government mediation, and possession in the economy, high duties, and solid security of wasteful firms, and complex organizations which encouraged debasement. As import substitution methodologies fizzled, governments went to more noteworthy fare transparency many picked specific opening, through EPZs and other enclave measures to pull in FDI.

Notwithstanding, by, and large, these new procedures did not destroy the more extensive foundations set up for import substitution. The remnants of the import substitution system, it is contended, kept on adding to diligent market mutilations. A focal contention, at that point, is that given the present economic situations in many developing countries, it would be troublesome, however, not feasible, for nearby entrepreneurs to work. As in developed economies, entrepreneurship additionally can possibly be the motor of monetary development through its effect on innovation and advancement and the designation and preparation of the components of formation. Notwithstanding, seriously mutilated markets obstruct the correct working of the entrepreneur.

Entrepreneurship, along these lines, is being proposed as an approach objective where huge advantages to improvement additionally collect during the way toward moving to a progressively entrepreneurial economy. A portion of these arrangements, for instance, would be planned for building better business situations and reinforcing administration with the goal that entrepreneurs, both household and remote, can thrive. An entrepreneurship-based advancement system ought to likewise decidedly influence monetary development by making a domain in which more firms enter showcases, work, and fall flat, subsequently reassuring learning overflows and exhibition and disappointment externalities. By permitting the market to work with fewer encumbrances and through the activities of ready entrepreneurs, it is normal that assets (capital and work) in developing countries will be designated all the more productively prompting higher monetary development.

An advancement procedure which energizes entrepreneurship will likewise concentrate on training, abilities upgrades, and development. Such a center will have an enduring impact on financial development, yet additionally on monetary improvement and neediness. Entrepreneurship is additionally significant for new firm formation, work formation in the private segment and real riches formation. In many developing and change countries, the open division is a significant business and open segment work is frequently a channel on monetary development as rare government income must be allotted to pay rates instead of to different ventures, for example, instruction, and framework. Entrepreneurial strategy will, in this way, support private segment advancement and offer beneficial options in contrast to open part work.

Chapter 3

DIGITAL WORLD AND EMERGING ECONOMY

The test for entrepreneurship improvement in emerging economies is the manner by which to give the required empowering business condition, for example, security, foundation, keeping pace with mechanical progression, balancing out the economy and diminishing expense and methodology in new companies; that would draw in remote financial specialists into an economy to converge with the locally situated entrepreneurs for suffering monetary advancement. Government is both controller and monetary agent but government could undermine financial development through arrangement irregularities, erroneous financial insights, debasement, miss governance and disregard of the private division which is the sign of reasonable financial development.

The sorted out private segment should band together with the government in giving foundation offices, empowering condition, offer work tax-breaks, sponsor oil, lower power tax and reduce the pressure inborn in fire up strategies. Entrepreneurial development and foundation improvement ought to be energized through motivating forces, for example, charge occasion and through reconciliation, correspondence, PC administrations, and greetings tech firms as these factors are a portion of the world acclaimed monetary markers.

Advances in digitization and improvements in data and correspondence advances (ICTs) is changing the worldwide business scene, changing business rehearses and making opportunities for new sorts of entrepreneurial exercises. One such sort of entrepreneurial movement is computerized entrepreneurship, characterized as another business formation opportunity produced by ICTs web, portable innovation, social registering and advanced stages. Regardless of proof of increments in the quantity of little advanced ventures has simply skimmed the surface concerning how little web firms in emerging markets create and develop. Existing exploration on Africa has so far spotlight on independent companies that basically embrace and use ICTs to improve their business execution. Computerized entrepreneurs go past essentially adjusting and utilizing ICTs. To them ICT is both the trigger for their entrepreneurial exercises and the foundation that help partner collaborations.

While the appropriation and utilization of ICTs is a test, the quick development in the dissemination of ICTs recommends the need to comprehend the idea of advanced entrepreneurship. Advanced entrepreneurship is the act of seeking after new pursuit opportunities introduced by new media and web advances. It is like customary entrepreneurship as in computerized adventures target producing money related benefits and are legitimately engraved into the monetary domain, for example, formation of another organization or commercialization of a development. In computerized entrepreneurship a few or the entirety of the entrepreneurial enterprises happens carefully rather than in progressively conventional configurations.

Advanced enterprises are unique in relation to customary entrepreneurial enterprises since they have diverse business models and can seek after their items, advertising, and conveyance exercises utilizing computerized stages. Computerized entrepreneurship adventures go from enormous set up firms that create equipment, programming, and systems administration advances to little beginning up firms that utilization data and correspondence innovations (ICTs) to attempt their businesses exercises. Right now am especially keen on little beginning up computerized adventures.

This incorporate enterprises working in the ICT area (e.g., web based bookkeeping, Wi-Fi-hotspot, telephone reinforcement, man-made consciousness programming projects), social figuring sites (e.g., for music utilization) and little portable and web empowered businesses (e.g., grouping/indexing of specific data, travel/enlistment offices and purchase sell commercial center). It recommends the need to explain the limit between a computerized entrepreneurial enterprises and a customary entrepreneurial enterprise. Right now computerized venture is characterized as one that participates in utilizing ICTs to make value and to arrange value exercises with clients and accomplices.

This incorporates businesses whose center movement is to sell digitized items or administrations (e.g., multi-media formation businesses) notwithstanding the classifications of computerized enterprises referenced before. From this unique situation, inquire about on computerized entrepreneurship bars private ventures that just use ICT assets to lessen costs, improve inward tasks, or improve client administrations through for instance, the selection of sites. Rather, ICT should be considered as a trigger or supplier of entrepreneurship and development, in which ICTs or computerized segments grow or confine entrepreneurial opportunities.

This is reliable with the view that computerized entrepreneurship is still at a beginning period in emerging markets, which propose an examination need to concentrate on recently made advanced enterprises. This all around perceived benchmark gives a decent tantamount pointer of recently made businesses in emerging business sector. IT administration, business frameworks thinking, design arranging, and making innovation work. There are three web related firm-level ICT assets that decide achievement in web empowered markets: online notoriety (being noticeable on the web and being viewed as offering excellent support), online mechanical abilities (incorporating web applications alter online experience for specific markets and innovative advantage) and online brand networks (access to data about purchasers, providers, and accomplices.

On the grounds that most IT skill looks into has concentrated on enormous firms, applying the abilities to new SMEs must be treated with alert. In this way, as opposed to gauge the degree to which proprietor directors of new advanced ventures have what it takes and skills portrayed before, it is center around their encounters in exploiting ICT instruction and preparing in making computerized businesses. Regarding market direction, any new computerized adventure that has recognized and aced the innovation expected to attempt characterized business action must ponder advertise direction as another focal determinant of achievement in advanced entrepreneurship, with progress characterized as far as making another advanced enterprise.

Here market direction is characterized as the manners by which an advanced entrepreneur centers 'on client and other partner needs' in their objective market. There are three determinants of market direction in advanced entrepreneurship: innovative aptitudes to support the computerized adventure, instruments for dealing with a data rich business condition and information on the more extensive and increasingly various commercial centers accessible to advanced enterprises contrasted with non-advanced undertaking. When an entrepreneur has built up the privilege ICT skill and market direction, another test is to fabricate a business model that can produce incomes to guarantee endurance and benefit augmentation.

Because of liabilities of littleness and novelty, new little advanced firms attempt to enter the market by working together with set up accomplices (e.g., portable system administrators) to make authenticity and secure "the status of 'best-of-breed' item suppliers in the market." The degree to which ICT as operant asset shapes advanced entrepreneurship relies upon the entrepreneurs' ICT abilities/skills; showcase direction and liabilities of littleness and novelty as integral determinants of computerized entrepreneurship. These components clearly should be considered comparable to the neighborhood setting in which the advanced entrepreneur works. Right now impacts incorporate the decisions that entrepreneurs make in seeking after opportunities and managing related difficulties. Geographic setting incorporates the nation under examination while innovation setting remembers the ICT business for which the firm works. Notwithstanding nation and industry part, neighborhood setting likewise speaks to the spot and the local improvement of progressive entrepreneurial character.

Empowered entrepreneurs to participate in entrepreneurial exercises and advancement, while nation setting incorporate government strategies giving (e.g., to help private ventures), social, and monetary joining (introduction to worldwide business opportunities). In this manner, extensively neighborhood setting identifies with industry-explicit and nation explicit opportunities and difficulties that advanced entrepreneurs need to ponder while participating in computerized entrepreneurship. The relevant impacts incorporate the entrepreneur's decisions about the utilization of the ICT aptitudes to take part in advanced entrepreneurship as a lifelong decision and techniques they receive so as to work effectively.

Entrepreneurs who make advanced enterprises show specialized and relational abilities in computerized developments. ICT capabilities offer entrepreneurs the capacity to make innovation work such that empower them to give imaginative answers for the market opportunities they have recognized. The procurement of ICT aptitudes, through a college degree, proficient authentication, or self-investigation of PC sciences, data the board, and web/versatile improvement by the principle originator or possibly one fellow benefactor started the procedure for making of a computerized undertaking. Entrepreneurs who effectively made a computerized venture were effectively utilizing their insight into ICTs to recognize and offer creative answers for the issues confronting society.

All the entrepreneurs who had formal ICT training talked along a comparable line to Entrepreneur. In any event, for those contextual investigations with at least two fellow benefactors, the first business thought originated from the prime supporter with a foundation in ICT. The entrepreneurs clarified that they use understudy assistants on a specially appointed premise to assist with investigating new arrangements/advancements to keep pace with improvements in ICTs, particularly in an ICT imperative setting, for example, Cameroon.

For those without formal ICT instruction, however, who were energetic about new advancements, self-studying ICT furnished them with the aptitudes to build up their computerized enterprises. Such entrepreneurs exhibited that ICT as operand asset is emotional and relies upon an entrepreneur's discernment. Despite the fact that the entrepreneurs portray ICT as empowering influence, it is obvious from their business exercises that ICT is the trigger as in, without ICT, a considerable lot of the advanced developments that empower the entrepreneurs to seek after specific sorts of opportunities would be outlandish (e.g., the presence of an assortment of new computerized media).

Effectively propelling and working advanced enterprises additionally relies upon the entrepreneur's information on the innovation setting and abilities to manage the related relevant impacts. This is identified with the idea that innovation gives the engineering inside which key partners associate and react to any entrepreneurial/creative exercises attempted by the entrepreneur. Partners right now clients, providers, workers, and others related with the computerized enterprises. Those entrepreneurs whose computerized enterprises depend on negligible physical contact with key partners defended the viability of the business tasks as far as innovation being the center engineering. Computerized entrepreneurship in emerging economies is an incipient field needing hypothesis advancement by universal business researchers. Computerized enterprises can be nation explicit, yet their arrive at crosses worldwide limits. This calls for nation explicit universal business research to comprehend the job of ICT and neighborhood setting in empowering advanced entrepreneurship.

Innovation Entrepreneurship offers novel improvement opportunities for social orders to instruct and develop nearby ability, construct decent variety and long-term financial wellbeing. As a component of an underlying needs appraisal, Boston University and its systems administration accomplices are appropriating an overview to innovation entrepreneurs. Peruse progressively about the activity and review at the base of the page.

As emerging economies keep on developing far and wide, there is likewise a developing acknowledgment that entrepreneurship and market-driven arrangements in these countries are profoundly successful apparatuses for lifting individuals from neediness. Customary guide from rich countries to developing ones has been ineffectual after some time, however, even counterproductive. In a state of harmony with this point of view, numerous worldwide improvement associations, just as private speculation bunches and Invested Capital and numerous others are presently concentrating on entrepreneurship and socially dependable free enterprise as a motor for advancement.

Looking back, the main astonishing thing about this move in context is that it took such a long time. The knowledge of showing somebody deprived to angle as opposed to giving them a fish is, obviously, as old as history; given the opportunity and instruments, individuals wherever exhibit their ability for entrepreneurship and advancement. For the most part, the effect of entrepreneurship is talked about exclusively as far as riches formation and (ideally) enormous scope destitution decrease. Maybe, however, the genuine force and transformative influence of entrepreneurship is not just riches formation, yet the real strengthening and more extensive opportunities it gives individuals over their own lives. To be sure, contemplates have demonstrated this is commonly the essential intention in entrepreneurs beginning a business in any case.

Innovation, as well, is at last about strengthening, as it gives people the instruments to straightforwardly shape their condition in emotional manners (truly, for both great and awful). It is nearly expressing the conspicuous that, when broadly embraced, innovation's long-term sway on society has been more prominent tan some other social power. This reality, as well, is as old as history, however, has been brought strikingly into center by the present case of cell phones. The proceeding, riskous development of cell phones, received in practically every side of the world and by all degrees of the financial pyramid, is as of now laying the foundation for huge social changes in both developed and emerging economies.

Given the advances that both entrepreneurship and innovation are rolling out as positive improvement specialists in emerging markets, we accept there is presently a significant opportunity for developed countries specifically for their college based research networks to help explicitly innovation entrepreneurship in emerging markets. Innovative entrepreneurship is a motor for decent variety. Innovation entrepreneurship is more prominent than the total of its parts in that it empowers a nation's ability to make and fare new, imaginative items that at first exist no place else. To put it plainly, it is a motor for making decent variety.

As of late, a solid positive connection between's the decent variety of a nation's item offering and its general development has been appeared. Indeed, even asset poor countries that have concentrated on their innovative entrepreneurship economies have seen supportable long-term development and high caliber of life for their residents. On a more extensive social level, innovative entrepreneurship biological systems are fundamentally networks in which best in class training, worldwide, cooperative systems and worldwide points of view also resistance, receptiveness, and decent variety, essentially have a focal spot. To put it plainly, these are networks working not exclusively to address its present needs, yet are occupied with making what's to come.

Innovative entrepreneurship is the best method to reasonably spread innovation. Understanding and tending to neighborhood economic situations is without a doubt the best way to scatter the suitable innovation where it is required most. This adage holds wherever on the planet, yet economical scattering of progressive innovations in emerging countries has been a specific test for worldwide improvement gatherings, in light of the fact that the neighborhood economic situations are regularly not completely comprehended by groups working from developed countries. At last, it just makes great, clear monetary sense for developed economies to connect with innovation entrepreneurs in emerging markets. Emerging markets mean emerging opportunities for everybody, except these must be comprehended and acknowledged by collaborating with the nearby information base and workforce.

In the present period of globalization, emerging business sector firms (EMFs) have started to find those from developed economies as far as developing inventive abilities. Western organizations entered emerging markets figuring they could just gather the products of innovative work (R&D) and advancement abilities meticulously developed in their countries of origin. Be that as it may, while there are a few instances of effective innovation moves from Europe to Asia, there have been a few fruitless enterprises too. Western organizations are presently experiencing a turnaround impact of their interests in developing countries as a result of the exponential development of those business sectors. In the course of the most recent decade, these countries developed a normal development pace of about 4.5%, in spite of the worldwide budgetary emergency. While countries with a developed economy accomplished a development rate, lower than 2%. The quantity of center salary clients is relied upon to increment by three billion by 2030, indicating an ascent sought after of merchandise from US$21 trillion to US$56 trillion-with center around emerging countries.

Developed advertise firms (DMFs) favored forthcoming universal R&D areas are China (62%), the USA (41%), and India (29%) (UNCTAD, 2005). Be that as it may, developing items in and for asset requirement markets is far not quite the same as item advancement in Western countries. It implies for Western organizations to unlearn customary R&D approaches including the decrease of numerous complex and asset escalated steps. The capacity of coordination advancements and information developed in neighborhood establishments might be the empowering agent to serve client needs in mass markets. Some global organizations succeed as of now by getting advancements from developing countries the West. General Electric, as a notable model, has propelled a modest ultrasound gadget initially produced for the Chinese market. It has become the premise of a worldwide business with enthusiastic clients in both developed and developing countries. This pattern is evident in buyer merchandise too.

Subsequently, advancement, a regularly examined investigate subject among hierarchical hypothesis analysts, is progressively moving to emerging markets. The inclination of the developing significance of emerging markets and the mindfulness concerning advancement for monetary achievement are reflected in the sensational increment of articles in the press about advancement in blend with emerging markets. However, the new comes nearer from emerging markets can contribute strikingly to hypothesis, i.e., to the asset based view (RBV). Assets and essential abilities where assets are the 'load of accessible elements' and capacities are the ability to convey assets utilizing hierarchical procedures, to impact an ideal end. Organizations in emerging markets face solid limitations of assets and create abilities to make significant item arrangements by supplanting components of capital with nearby work at low costs. Such abilities are commendable for additional examination since expanding shortage of assets came into center in developed markets, as well. The creative ideas from emerging markets should be considered and comprehended.

Be that as it may, by perusing articles with respect to imaginative methodologies from emerging markets, it is obvious that there is no normal comprehension of utilized terms and the relations between the methodologies. The various terms are somewhat befuddling, and no depiction between the terms is made. That thwarts the ideal scholarly conversation increasing further bits of knowledge from alternate points of view. Along these lines, a typical comprehension of these terms is an essential for additional examination and an establishment for trading thoughts and building information. Consequently, the accompanying exploration question is asked: What are pertinent attributes to outline the terms from emerging markets? Therefore, the particular characteristics of the terms are recognized and combined. In this way, the combined qualities fill in as estimation where the terms can be adjusted to. Right now, linkages, and connections between the terms and their basic ideas are revealed. In the last advance, an applied system is acquainted with group the terms in a few measurements.

Economic development emerges from the procedure point of view when advancement is done in a thrifty manner. In any case, this is known as parsimonious designing or requirement based development. Right now, is considered the capacity to retain, adjust, and expand upon the advancements imported from abroad as opposed to create totally novel advances to diminish complete expense, quicken item improvement, and convey an incentive for cash. Parsimonious building or requirement put together advancement centers with respect to mindfulness and an intellectual methodology in developing new items, administrations, and businesses in constrictive conditions.

Since advancements address interesting necessities, the improvement of fitting items under constrictive conditions requires a reasonable customization of items, procedures, and administrations just as innovation and business models, as per the earth of neighborhood clients. It is to think about the perspicacious prerequisites for advancement in emerging markets, for example, moderateness, accessibility, availability, and usability, too making client mindfulness. To meet the prerequisites, synergistic work with the two clients and common society associations or governments. Moreover, to social improvement players, conveyance suppliers, and neighborhood entrepreneurs.

Parsimonious advancement goes past R&D by expanding the productivity of the entire store network: there is no utilization of current innovation, no fuel, and no capital venture yet an elevated level of administration and adjustment to conditions in the working condition. Additionally, the way to utilizing any item or administration as a stage for future development is to regard it as a heap of abilities as opposed to getting excessively obliged by its present highlights, marking, appropriation channels, or focused on clients. Tata Motors, for instance, is perceived for its modest vehicle, the Tata Nano. The Tata Nano costs about US$2,500 and is utilized by a large number of low-salary clients. Notwithstanding the low value, the vehicle has breezed through the European accident assessment security principles. The organization's capacities incorporate experiences into client needs in low-salary territories (e.g., India), restrictive advances, a provider arrange, and the disguised way of thinking of parsimonious building. Thus, if DMFs need to mimic such an item (or item improvement), they have to broaden their capacities behind the procedures, not simply duplicate the parsimonious methodology.

In rundown, the focal premise of parsimonious development is to believe emerging markets to be not kidding markets with potential for deals, as wellspring of assets, and potential purposes of starting point for merchandise and enterprises requested around the world. The items can move upmarket to fulfill clients' needs in developed countries too. We can develop for India we can likewise all the while enhance for the world. It can be assigned that the transcendent advantage of thrifty advancement as empowering a move of emerging economies from development driven by utilization into development driven by speculation, which is at present the noteworthy contrast among developed and developing economies. As observed over, a few EMFs are breaking this new ground yet.

Chapter 4

FINANCIAL MATTERS

The job of budgetary part in financial improvement has been long a fervently discussed issue. Nature of the linkage between monetary framework and monetary development might be in the interest following and supply-driving characters. Corresponding to the stock driving speculation, the endogenous development hypotheses reached out to incorporate money related advancement show that budgetary components might be one of the hotspot for expanding pace of return. Entrepreneurship is not just a static idea as a factor of formation yet in addition, a powerful idea and it, in this way, ought to be taken as a process. Entrepreneur is the person who creates and assesses new opportunities by defeating the troubles remaining against making new items.

The procedure of entrepreneurship can be subdivided into four unmistakable stages. These are recognizable proof and assessment of the opportunity, foundation of the business plan, assurance of the necessary assets, and the board of the subsequent enterprises. Everybody is an entrepreneur when he really does new blends. The declaration of "new mixes" proposes finding the new techniques to fulfill the present needs or making new items in the current innovation and formation designs. Development is the crucial piece of entrepreneurship, as the principle wellspring of financial advancement.

So, entrepreneurs look for and distinguish gainful opportunities as well as quick to face challenges in monetarily valuable exercises. Henceforth it would not be right to contend that distinguishing and picking the correct business opportunities among a few different choices is the specific difficulties right now. Bricolage and effectuation ways to deal with entrepreneurship might be particularly pertinent in the advancement of emerging economies, as assets are rare and markets immature. The rare assets of entrepreneurial firms in emerging economies lead to various types of systems administration among entrepreneurs and others, including providers and government authorities, to get required assets.

The manner by which entrepreneurs fabricate these systems likewise varies from that of develop economies, with people in emerging economies concentrating on distinctive key contemplations. In this way, money related limitations lead to contrasts in how firms in emerging economies accumulate assets. Nonetheless, one would expect that a rich arrangement of different micro process contrasts exists in emerging economies. Generally speaking, the assessments of how micro processes in emerging economies sway on procedure stay restricted to date. The large scale nature of the given condition too impacts the entrepreneurial activities of a firm. Assets are a key component that shapes entrepreneurship in emerging economies. Entrepreneurs must address at a large scale level not the area of assets, yet the determination of assets to use and, at last, the abilities to create so as to utilize those assets.

Assets are hard to get in emerging economies, yet which bundles of assets to use and how to construct those bundles of assets so as to build up an upper hand through some ability gets vital to the entrepreneurial firm achievement. Conventional emerging economies experience the ill effects of both the absence of institutional improvement and the absence of foundation and factor advertise advancement. In any case, much has changed as countries have modernized their foundations and establishments. Progressively, there is huge difference in foundation and institutional advancement of countries. Subsequently, a few countries are neither emerging economies nor developed economies. Such full scale level assorted variety can lead, thus, to significant contrasts in key entrepreneurship since large scale level factors set up limit conditions for the firm-level dynamic procedure.

The setting wherein a firm works, in blend with the smaller scale and full scale parts of the firm, prompts an assortment of potential entrepreneurial exercises. Extent of oddity, and kind of entrepreneurial exercises as key to understanding the assortment of coming about entrepreneurship in an emerging economy. Rate alludes to the quantity of adventures being made (or on the other hand added to existing businesses or developed through the side project or the board buyout of existing exercises) by entrepreneurs and entrepreneurial partnerships either separately or inside an area or economy. The pace of entrepreneurship can be very diverse in emerging economies. The distinction in rate may happen, to some degree, in light of the distinction in the idea of entrepreneurship. In emerging economies, entrepreneurship is frequently casual since entrepreneurs do not enlist with the government. For instance, the GDP gauges of casual economies obviously mean around 65% of work in Asia, 51% of work in Latin America, and 72% of work in North/ Sub-Saharan Africa.

In emerging economies, an exercise that may not exist in develop economies, for example, privatization of (or then again parts of) state-claimed substances, sway the pace of entrepreneurship. Such privatization can be the premise for the making of corporate entrepreneurial exercises as administrators become discharged from the imperatives of state organizations. While consideration regularly centers around privatization through first sale of stock (IPO) of focal government-possessed exercises, privatization may likewise happen at nearby government levels and may include littler exercises. The age of entrepreneurial enterprises including various degrees of government raises intriguing inquiries concerning the idea of proceeding with obstruction of government authorities in the running of the businesses, including the job of political systems and the division of increases from future execution.

In some emerging economies, family firms might be a significant wellspring of entrepreneurial movement. In others, strikingly previous Communist countries, family firms may turn into a critical component of the entrepreneurial scene as a market economy turns out to be increasingly settled. In a general setting of entrepreneurial deficiencies among the household populace, nationals who come back to their nation of origin after picking up involvement with developed business situations may create entrepreneurial exercises in emerging economies. Greatness of oddity alludes to the degree to which some entrepreneurial initiatives are new to the market in wording of new or existing information.

In emerging economies, the greatness of oddity may differ impressively. From one perspective, new pursuits may not be especially novel as far as information that exists in developed economies; however, they give ease opportunities and can be sold into these economies through transnational entrepreneurs. On the other hand, curiosity might be apparent in the advancement of new types of minimal effort items available to be purchased inside emerging economies, prominently to bring down salary collections.

A further component of curiosity, frequently disregarded in the emphasis on ease formation, is the improvement of innovative items as some emerging economies grow profoundly taught workforces.

These progressively novel types of entrepreneurial movement may turn out to be progressively significant as emerging economies create. Sort of entrepreneurial exercises alludes to the huge number of potential contrasts in information sources through which to recognize opportunities, the decent variety of authoritative structures in a market, and the number also, decent variety of restrictive procedures in a market. For instance, returning entrepreneurs (e.g., people who come back to their countries of origin after training as well as work in developed economies) may bring information and capacities from developed economies that both can fill holes in emerging economies and give overflow information benefits to local entrepreneurs. In this manner, the pace of entrepreneurial exercises in guaranteed country, the curiosity of the entrepreneurial opportunities that the firm can exploit, and the sort of entrepreneurship in the given area can affect the entrepreneurship in the firm in a rich scope of ways.

Despite the fact that we delineate these key ideas here, researchers ought to perceive that what we have displayed is not a thorough rundown of the exercises that sway the assortment of coming about entrepreneurship in emerging economies. Further, researchers should take note of that while we present the smaller scale or full scale level factors independently; these factors do not act in confinement. The small scale and full scale factors sway each other and at last produce the exhibition results that the firm encounters.

One of the key issues for researchers perceives that emerging economies do not stop. As we noted previously, the meaning of an emerging economy incorporates low-salary, high-development countries that depend chiefly on financial progression for their development. Be that as it may, numerous countries that were poor as financial advancement cleared the world during the 1990s are not poor today. For instance, in the 1990s, researchers could undoubtedly have grouped Poland as a new economy. Be that as it may, today, Poland is an individual from the European Union (EU) and has one of the most noteworthy development rates and wages in the EU.

Therefore, it would be a slip-up to arrange Poland, or previous Soviet Bloc countries, for example, the Czech Republic or Hungary, as new. Interestingly, a few countries that researchers would not have delegated new 20 years prior since they were not quick developing or they were excessively immature ought to never again be viewed as new. Nonetheless, a few economies that once showed up to be rising have stagnated, if not moved in reverse, as market and political changes have slowed down. In this manner, researchers need to perceive that a developing economy is an advancing idea and that researchers cannot consistently think about countries as emerging over time. Researchers and editors must be especially steady in their examination so they do not utilize obsolete characterizations of countries as emerging. Individuals must perceive the dynamic part of the term 'emerging economies' for the term to be important.

Perceiving the requirement for care in classifying countries as emerging economies opens up conceivable outcomes for an investigate plan that looks at the determinants of the condition of development of various emerging economies and the suggestions and difficulties for key entrepreneurship in these countries. From an approach viewpoint, such heterogeneity additionally suggests the requirement for the presentation of all the more fine-grained ways to deal with help for entrepreneurship that perceives logical mannerisms.

Worldly factors have suggestions for the existence cycle of every one of the four kinds (casual entrepreneurs, worldwide entrepreneurs, family entrepreneurs, and corporate entrepreneurs) of entrepreneurship in emerging economies. However, the particular ramifications for each type may contrast, maybe affected by the pace of development of the emerging economy and cooperation with institutional improvements. At present, we need experiences into these worldly procedures. We will examine this absence of bits of knowledge in more noteworthy detail later. Spatial components of setting incorporate both cross-national and provincial measurements inside an emerging economy. As for the cross-national measurement, researchers have perceived the job of returning entrepreneurs, yet researchers despite everything do not see well the entrepreneurs' area choices inside their countries of origin.

For instance, do they look to situate in the city where they grew up or do they settle on choices dependent on financial factors identifying with the area of clients and providers? Family entrepreneurs may likewise have significant cross-national measurements. Privately-owned companies in the emerging economy may have joins with family individuals that have emigrated to developed economies or they may give the neighborhood systems to bringing entrepreneurs back. In enormous, previous halfway arranged emerging economies, where enormous organizations might be topographically spread, the advancement of a market economy may have suggestions for the degree to which organizations keep on being so generally spread or conserve to all the more financially appealing territories.

A further spatial measurement concerns the ramifications of section by outside entrepreneurs or enterprises, such passage producing residential entrepreneurship inside a specific territory inside an emerging economy. From one perspective, such passage might undermine delicate early local entrepreneurs. Then again, rivalry from outside entrepreneurial firms brings new methods of conveyance that may invigorate increasingly imaginative entrepreneurial conduct. Other than the weight from such item advertises rivalry, there may likewise be learning overflows for residential entrepreneurs. As emerging economies advance, the making of a huge white collar class, with desires educated by presentation to 'Western' culture, underlines that request side conditions are switching that open up new opportunities for entrepreneurs in the event that they can adjust. These spatial changes may likewise call forward a requirement for conventional local entrepreneurs to change their transient outlook to turn out to be more receptive to an evolving condition. Fascinating exploration opportunities incorporate the possibility for investigations of neighborhood industry elements in such settings, which could incorporate thought of the exit of customary entrepreneurs close by the section of new ones.

Institutional guidelines likely impact both the authoritative document of entrepreneurship and the principles of the game by which each works. Further, as the institutional setting develops, various types of entrepreneurship may turn out to be pretty much reasonable. For model, casual entrepreneurship may win in the setting of frail institutional structures in the beginning periods of emerging economies. The communication between the ecological setting and entrepreneurial conduct may prompt execution results that do not really profit the general public in an emerging economy setting. Specifically, defilement furthermore, powerless lawful organizations may bring about an inefficient clouded side of entrepreneurship those groups out gainful entrepreneurship and blocks financial advancement. We need further examination of the degree, effect, and procedures associated with beneficial versus inefficient entrepreneurship in emerging economies.

The business systems firms work in emerging economies are molded by a particular star grouping of foundations and assets accessible to an officeholder firm. Be that as it may, these variables speak to an essential yet not adequate condition for a fruitful business technique. The association's key results are additionally formed by its entrepreneurial direction and asset coordination capacities. Vital entrepreneurship speaks to an enterprise to combine the resource-based view (RBV) from the methodology writing with opportunity acknowledgment from entrepreneurship. This approach stresses the need to choose and structure imperative assets and capacities while all the while aggregating, packaging, and utilizing these assets to create upper hand. The entrepreneur's asset choice and design process is impacted by the settings in which firms work.

What is not clear is the means by which firms build up the imperative entrepreneurial aptitudes for internationalization. Entrepreneurs with instructive and work involvement with developed economies can come back to their home economies (China) to make enterprises better set to internationalize than those new pursuits where this ability is missing. Social capital is essential to different kinds of entrepreneurship in all economies. While social capital might be particularly significant with regards to unsure markets and legitimate systems, we know close to nothing about the various jobs of social capital in emerging economies. Social capital may have drawbacks as well as upsides. Political social capital might be particularly significant in encouraging entrepreneurial movement in the beginning times of emerging economies, however, be prohibitive in later stages. We think minimal about the complementarily or substitutability of various types of social capital in emerging economies and how these collaborations change for various kinds of entrepreneurship as these economies develop.

Labor and capital are the fundamental info components of huge scope formation that overwhelmed the business world in current developed economies until the late 1980s. The expanding level of exchange costs acquired in huge scope formation directed expanding firm size after some time. This went together with the anticipated advancement of innovation, customer inclinations, and obtainment of assets. For sure, measurable proof focuses towards an expanding job of huge ventures in the economy right now. This advancement towards huge scope action was noticeable in most present day developed economies. Right now, the significance of independent work and private company appeared to be melting away. In spite of the fact that it was perceived that the independent venture segment required to be secured for both social and political reasons, there were not many that put forth this defense on the grounds of financial effectiveness.

The conventional formation variables of work and capital are most certainly not adequate in clarifying long-term development. Information turns into a crucial factor in endogenous development models. Innovative improvement is viewed as exogenous in the prior neoclassical development hypothesis. That is the reason the long-term development of work profitability stays unexplained. Endogenous development hypothesis gives models clarifying this long-term development utilizing information. Information has regularly been estimated as far as R&D, human capital, and protected innovations. The development of information as a significant determinant of development furthermore, intensity in worldwide markets would render independent work and little firms considerably increasingly worthless.

How might they produce the methods and bits of knowledge to misuse R&D exercises, to utilize profoundly prepared information laborers, and to carry their enterprises to the patent or even the business settings? Essentially, researchers infer that with the appearance of information as a formation factor the universe of business gets overwhelmed by sending out mammoth firms. This is the universe of worldwide markets, worldwide items, and worldwide players. Little firms were believed to be off guard versus bigger firms on the grounds that of the fixed expenses of finding out about outside conditions, imparting at long removes, and haggling with national governments. Solidification appears to have become a law of nature, while the quantity of worldwide players decreases consistently.

Notwithstanding these powers, little, and youthful firms have returned as the motor of financial furthermore, social advancement in profoundly developed economies. This arrival required an emotional monetary switch. It is the change from the overseen economy to the entrepreneurial economy. The model of the developed economy is the political, social, and monetary reaction to an economy directed by the powers of enormous scope formation, mirroring the transcendence of the formation components of capital what's more, (mostly untalented) work as the sources of upper hand.

On the other hand, the model of the entrepreneurial economy is the political, social, and monetary reaction to an economy progressively ruled by information as the formation factor, yet in addition, by an alternate, yet correlative, factor that had been ignored: entrepreneurship capital, or the ability to take part in and create entrepreneurial movement. Without new what's more, youthful firms it is not direct that information or R&D consistently overflows to a domain where it prompts substantial products. This differentiation between the models of the managed and entrepreneurial economy applies to both developed and emerging economies despite the fact that it has been set up to better comprehend the job of entrepreneurship, its drivers, its outcomes and its approach prerequisites in the structure of developed economies. For example, a confounding factor in many emerging economies is the high level of business familiarity. This wonder is regularly brought about by a duty framework which puts substantial managerial and money related weights on entrepreneurs and by stringent guidelines concerning work, items, and administrations. It is not just the state who loses through familiarity by method for missed income. Businesses pass up on the chance to partake in projects to invigorate advancement and worker preparing. They have no entrance to formal credit and appreciate no legitimate insurance. A significant advance forward is broadening government projects to animate advancement or preparing of workers to all small and medium-sized enterprises (SMEs) including those working casually under the condition that they begin partaking in the proper framework.

Until the late 1980s, the huge enterprises are the predominant type of business association. The lessening in the job of private venture in developed countries after the Second World War is all around reported. This is the period of large scale manufacturing where economies of scale become the conclusive factor in directing proficiency. There is no notice of 'independent ventures.' The corporatist association of social orders goes very well together with the developed economy. Strength, congruity, and homogeneity are the foundations of the developed economy. Enormous firms devastate this economy. Probably the best portrayal of the huge venture and its control of the developed economy is that they were progressive and bureaucratic associations that were in the business of making long runs of institutionalized items. They presented as good as ever assortments with unsurprising normality; they gave laborers with life-time work; and delighted in genuinely great relations with the monster worker's organizations.

Likewise, until late during the 1980s little firms are seen as an extravagance, as something western countries need to guarantee the foundation and wellbeing of downtowns, to ingest low maintenance furthermore, low gifted work, to help decentralization of decision-making, to protect the most established of all business models, the family firm, and so forth. One underestimated that they endure just at the expense of effectiveness. It is not astounding that numerous researchers from numerous scholastic orders have tried to make understanding into the issues encompassing this seen exchange off between financial productivity and political and monetary decentralization. The supposed achievement of the socialist, centrally led economies assumes an enormous job in the common perspective of that period. These economies blossomed with uniform, stable large scale manufacturing. It is direct that entrepreneurship is seen as conduct threatening to the socialist framework and proclaimed criminal. How unexpected that these economies separated in the late 1980s because of an aggregate absence of decentralized, test, free, unsafe, and little scope financial exercises.

While business schools flourish preparing youngsters for employments in huge scope tasks, these equivalent schools house scientists building up a restoration of little scope tasks. In the late 1980s and mid-1990s, interesting information material is distributed: the portion of diminutiveness differs in current economies, however, increments everywhere.4 In the United States the normal genuine GDP per firm expanded by almost 66% somewhere in the range of 1947 and 1989 from US$150,000 to US$245,000 mirroring a pattern towards bigger ventures and a diminishing significance of little firms. In any case, inside the consequent seven years it had fallen by around 14% to US$210,000, mirroring a sharp inversion of this pattern what's more, the reappearance of private company. Thus, little firms represented one-fifth of assembling deals in the United States in 1976, however, by 1986 the business portion of little firms had ascended to more than one-quarter.

The principal collection of qualities comprises of three significant fundamental powers; limitation versus globalization; change versus coherence; and employments and high wages versus employments or high wages. In the model of the developed economy, formation work and capital are the prevailing formation factors. The more portable capital moves to where the least expensive work (programming) is or such work moves towards capital once it is put resources into plants (equipment). Information is the prevailing component of formation in the model of the entrepreneurial economy.

It is something other than hard specialized and logical information. It additionally involves delicate viewpoints like imagination, the capacity to convey, passionate knowledge, and so on. The upper hand in the entrepreneurial economy is driven by imaginative action, while information overflows are a significant wellspring of this imaginative action. Subsequently, in the model of the entrepreneurial economy, nearby closeness is significant, with the district being the most significant locus of monetary movement, as information will in general be developed with regards to confined formation systems implanted in imaginative groups.

The model of the developed economy concentrates more on coherence, while the model of the entrepreneurial economy flourishes with change and even incites it. In spite of the fact that development is available under the states of change and progression, the nature and the locus of imaginative action, vary. The notable differentiation among steady and radical advancements is useful to explain this. Developments are viewed as gradual at the point when they are perfect with the center skill and innovative direction of the firm or the business. Conversely, an extreme development can be characterized as broadening past the limits of the center ability and the mechanical direction of the firm or the business. In the model of the developed economy, change is consumed inside a given mechanical worldview: the fruitful firm exceeds expectations at steady development. By differentiate; in the model of the entrepreneurial economy, the ability to break out of the mechanical lock-in forced by existing standards is upgraded by the capacity of financial specialists to begin new firms. Hence, gradual imaginative action alongside dispersion assumes an increasingly significant job in the model of the developed economy. While frequently requiring enormous interests in R&D, this sort of inventive movement creates gradual changes in items along the current innovative directions.

One of the most obvious approach choices in the model of the developed economy is that joblessness can be decreased uniquely at the expense of lower compensation. In the model of the entrepreneurial economy, high work can be joined with high wages and a low wage level does not really infer high work. A sign of the nonappearance of an exchange off between high wages and business is the enormous difference in joblessness rates across OECD (Organization for Economic Co-operation and Development) countries, albeit corporate cutting back has been omnipresent. Little firms when all is said in done, and new pursuits specifically, are the motor not just of business formation, 10 yet in addition of efficiency. This is not because of the pay differential among little and huge firms. On the opposite, the development of new firms may produce more noteworthy business, yet additionally higher wages.

New firm development guarantees that higher work does not include some significant downfalls of lower compensation, but instead the inverse higher wages. Under the model of the overseen economy, the activity formation by little firms is related with lower compensation. Consequently, while little firms create work at an expense of lower compensation in the model of the developed economy, in the entrepreneurial economy model little firms may make both more occupations and higher wages. The pertinence for emerging countries lies in the possibility that they need to make motivators for the information typified in their accomplished residents to remain in the nation of origin what's more, abuse their insight in business as opposed to moving to another country. A model of a nation which is by all accounts effective in doing so is India which houses various IT pros accomplishing work for customers over the globe, MBAs engaged with number crunching for large venture banks in London and New York, etc. The inverse is valid for a nation like Poland which has seen a monstrous mass migration of talented laborers which has really constrained neighborhood business to in-source work from countries like Ukraine.

The second collection of attributes differentiates the outside condition qualities in the models of the managed and the entrepreneurial economies. Choppiness, assorted variety, also, heterogeneity is vital to the model of the entrepreneurial economy. On the other hand, dependability, specialization, and homogeneity are the foundations of the model of the overseen economy. Note, be that as it may, that a piece of the entrepreneurial economy can likewise be 'sent out' to another economy. The idea of the new Argonauts is portrayed, by which it implies profoundly talented remote workers who come back to their nation of origin to fire up their own business misusing information and thoughts that they have acquired in their past business. These 'sends out' can impact this developed economy to turn out to be progressively modern or increasingly entrepreneurial or to make an entrepreneurial economy nearby the managed one.

Strength in the model of the developed economy results from a homogeneous item request, bringing about a low turnover pace of occupations, laborers, and firms. The model of the entrepreneurial economy is described by a high level of disturbance. Every year numerous new firms are begun and just a subset of these organizations endures. The job of decent variety and choice is at the core of producing change. This holds for both the managed and the entrepreneurial economy models. In any case, what contrasts in these models is the administration and association of the procedure by which assorted variety is made just as the determination component. In the model of the overseen economy explore exercises are sorted out and planned for offices committed to developing novel items and administrations.

The administration of progress fits into what allude to as the 'company's schedules.' The capacity of occupant businesses to deal with the procedure of progress pre-empts numerous opportunities for entrepreneurs to begin new firms, bringing about a low beginning up rate and a stable modern structure. In the model of the entrepreneurial economy, the procedure of producing new thoughts, both inside and outside of R&D research facilities, makes a tempestuous condition with numerous opportunities for entrepreneurs to begin new firm's dependent on extraordinary and changing sentiments about various and evolving thoughts. To put it plainly, the development process in the developed economy is shut while that in the entrepreneurial economy is open.

A few hypothetical contentions have recommended that the level of decent variety versus that of specialization represents contrasts in paces of development and innovative improvement. Specialization of industry exercises is related with lower exchange costs and, along these lines, more noteworthy (static) proficiency. Decent variety of exercises is said to encourage the trading of new thoughts and, along these lines, more noteworthy imaginative movement what's more, (dynamic) productivity. Since information overflows are a significant wellspring of inventive movement, decent variety is an essential in the model of the entrepreneurial economy where lower exchange costs are ideally relinquished for more noteworthy opportunities for information overflow. In the model of the developed economy, there are fewer gains from information overflows. The higher exchange costs related with decent variety yield no place for opportunities regarding expanded imaginative action, making specialization best in the model of the developed economy.

The exchange off among assorted variety and specialization centers around firms while that between homogeneity and heterogeneity centers around people. Present day correspondence and transport systems annihilated numerous obstructions. In a heterogeneous populace of the entrepreneurial economy, correspondence across people will in general be increasingly troublesome furthermore, exorbitant than in a homogenous populace: exchange costs are higher and proficiency is lower. Simultaneously, new thoughts are bound to rise up out of correspondence in a heterogeneous than in a homogeneous world. Despite the fact that the probability of correspondence is lower in a heterogeneous populace, correspondence right now condition is increasingly inclined to deliver curiosity and advancement.

The lower exchange costs coming about because of a homogeneous populace in the model of the developed economy are not related with high opportunity costs, since information overflows are generally insignificant in creating imaginative movement. In any case, information overflows are a main thrust in the model of the entrepreneurial economy, counterbalancing the higher exchange costs related with a heterogeneous populace. The third gathering of attributes differentiates firm conduct in the models of the developed also, the entrepreneurial economy: control versus inspiration; firm exchange versus advertise trade; rivalry and collaboration as substitutes versus supplements; and scale versus adaptability.

Under the model of the developed economy, work is considered as unclear from the other information factors. It is viewed as homogeneous and effectively replaceable. Firms compose their work as per the standards of direction and control. Under the model of the entrepreneurial economy, the direction and control way to deal with work is less compelling, as the upper hand of the progressed industrialized countries will in general be founded on making and approving new information. This is practiced by inspiring specialists to encourage the disclosure procedure and execution of new thoughts.

The board styles underscore the supporting of relational connections, encouraging instead of regulating representatives. In the entrepreneurial economy model, the focal point of exercises is on investigating new capacities, instead of abusing existing ones. Exchange costs financial matters recognize trade by means of the market and intra-firm exchanges. Vulnerability also, blemished data increment the expense of intra-firm exchanges. Low vulnerability, joined with straightforwardness and consistency of data, makes intra-firm exchanges productive comparative with advertise trade. In the developed economy model, where there is a high level of assurance and consistency of data, exchanges inside firms will in general be more proficient than showcase trade.

On the other hand, in the entrepreneurial economy, model market exchanges are more productive on account of the high vulnerability. Since the mid-1970s, the monetary field has become progressively unsure and flighty, managed by a decline in both mean firm size and the degree of vertical incorporation and combination. Models of rivalry for the most part accept that organizations carry on independently, while models of collaboration accept unavoidable linkages among firms. These linkages take different structures, including joint enterprises, key unions, and (in)formal systems, et cetera. In the model of the developed economy, rivalry, and participation are seen as being substitutes. Firms are vertically coordinated and essentially contend in item markets. Participation between firms in the item showcase decreases the quantity of contenders and lessens the level of rivalry. In the model of the entrepreneurial economy, firms will in general be vertically free and represented considerable authority in the item showcase.

The higher level of vertical crumbling under the model of the entrepreneurial economy suggests a substitution of interior exchanges inside a huge vertically coordinated enterprise with collaboration among autonomous firms. Simultaneously, there are more firms, bringing about an expansion in both the serious and helpful interfaces. The probability of a firm contending or helping out different firms is higher in the entrepreneurial economy model. Costs-per-unit are decreased through misusing economies of scale. In product offerings and businesses where an enormous size of formation converts into a significant decrease in normal costs, huge firms will have a monetary bit of leeway, prompting a concentrated modern structure.

Stable and unsurprising items, shopper tastes, and lines of asset arrangement added to the accomplishment of the abuse of economies of scale. The significance of scale economies has surely added to the rise and predominance of huge enterprises in substantial assembling businesses, for example, steel, cars, and aluminum. The elective wellspring of decreased normal expenses is adaptability, portraying the entrepreneurial economy model. Enterprises where interest for specific items is moving continually require an adaptable arrangement of formation that can satisfy such a capricious need. The last gathering of differentiating attributes of the models of the entrepreneurial economy and the developed economy alludes to government approach, including the objectives of approach (empowering versus obliging), the objective of approach (inputs versus outputs), the locus of strategy (local versus national), and financing approach.

Under the model of the developed economy, open approach towards the firm is basically compelling in nature. There are three general kinds of open approach towards business: antitrust approach (rivalry strategy), guideline, and open proprietorship. Every one of the three of these arrangement approaches confines the organizations' opportunity to contract. Under the model of the overseen economy, the applicable arrangement question is: How can the government retain firms from manhandling their market power? The entrepreneurial economy model is portrayed by an alternate arrangement question: How would governments be able to make a condition cultivating the achievement and suitability of firms?

Though the significant issues in the model of the developed economy are worries about overabundance benefits and maltreatment of advertise predominance, in the model of the entrepreneurial economy the issues of worldwide seriousness, development, and business are significant. In the developed economy model, the accentuation is on compelling business sector power through guideline; though the concentration in the entrepreneurial economy model is on invigorating firm or rather mechanical advancement and execution through empowering strategies.

Striking instances of how not to manage this theme are plentiful in pretty much every emerging nation. The clearest one is Venezuela which constrained remote speculators to acknowledge altogether less beneficial conditions for existing concessions in the oil division. Also, it has renationalized oil, concrete, and steel organizations. Bolivia too nationalized its oil and gas industry. Other telling models are guideline in Mexico relating to media transmission, power, and oil. Argentina has been attempting to endorse to organizations what costs they ought to request their items as saw when the previous president Kirchner asked Argentineans not to go to the Shell service stations at the point when the organization was attempting to pass on higher oil costs.

Government mediation and enterprises to limit remote impact do not just imply that the nation foregoes opportunities for information overflows, yet they will likewise negatively affect choices with respect to potential new outside interests in the nation which will antagonistically sway decent variety and heterogeneity. Brazil made autonomous controllers in numerous divisions during the privatization blast of the 1990s. Since the present president got down to business in 2003, an alternate, more interventionist, approach has won. A significant model is the presentation of HD-TV in Brazil where the service played a functioning job in the choice which standard the nation ought to receive. The government settled on the Japanese ISDB standard as a by-product of Japanese ventures in the Brazilian semiconductor industry, financing, and innovation moves.

Governmental strategy can include focusing on chosen yields in the formation procedure as opposed to focusing on chosen inputs. As a result of the relative assurance with respect to business sectors and items in the model of the developed economy, the proper arrangement reaction is to target yields. Explicit businesses and firms can be advanced through government programs. Though in the model of the developed economy formation depends on the conventional contributions of land, work, and capital, in the entrepreneurial economy model it is fundamentally dependent on information input.

There is vulnerability about what items ought to be delivered, how, and by whom. This high level of vulnerability makes it hard to choose fitting results and improves the probability of focusing on an inappropriate firms and ventures. Henceforth, the fitting strategy in the model of the entrepreneurial economy is to target inputs and specifically those information sources identified with the formation and commercialization of information. Government turns into the facilitator making joins what's more, systems, making types of social advancement, proposing motivations to firms and information establishments, animating unique and practical adaptability of work, and so forth.

The vulnerability related with the results of a procedure where information is viewed as a significant info implies that policymaking is increasingly troublesome right now circumstance. Many emerging countries are deficient with regards to the important information and experience for appropriate policymaking. Genuine instances of a characteristic method to defeat this issue can be found in Israel, Taiwan, and India where exceptionally gifted residents have come back from abroad to set up new imaginative businesses or put investment in other new companies.

These people regularly assume the job of consultants to the government along these lines spreading the information for input arranged approaches. The locus of approach is a third trademark where the models of the developed and entrepreneurial economy vary. Under the model of the developed economy, the proper locus of policymaking is the national or government level. The most significant policymaking organizations will in general be situated at the national level, in spite of the fact that the focused on beneficiaries of approach might be limited in one or a couple of districts. Under the model of the entrepreneurial economy, government arrangement towards business will in general be decentralized what's more, territorial or nearby in nature. This differentiation in the locus of arrangement results from two factors. To start with, on the grounds that the serious wellspring of monetary movement in the model of the entrepreneurial economy is information, which will in general be limited in provincial bunches; open approach requires a comprehension of territorial explicit qualities and characteristics.

Second, the inspiration hidden government strategy in the entrepreneurial economy is development and the making of occupations, to be accomplished chiefly through new pursuit formation. New firms are normally little and represent no oligopolistic risk in national or global markets. In the model of the entrepreneurial economy, no outside expenses—as more significant expenses are forced on customers in the national economy similar to the case in the model of the developed economy. Cultivating neighborhood economies forces no expense on shoppers in the national economy.

The inquiry is whether neighborhood governments are really prepared to structure and execute neighborhood approach which invigorates businesses to profit by nearby points of interest furthermore, moderate nearby disservices. Also, it is critical to evaluate whether a fitting arrangement of balanced governance is set up to guarantee that nearby policymakers act in the most proficient way. Various illustrative models can be found. Mexico is a nation where decentralization has expanded quickly in the most recent decade despite the fact that the important system was deficient. Therefore, the impacts of decentralization have not emerged true to form. The countries now influence to contemplate how participation between such differing countries could prompt the advancement of a profoundly entrepreneurial locale.

Associating financial on-screen characters through systems administration and data sharing makes it conceivable to improve business and outside direct venture opportunities, subsequently making a difference the more unfortunate countries to get up to speed all the more rapidly and the more extravagant to infiltrate an enormous market all the more effectively. Be that as it may, the emerging countries in the district, for example, Russia, Poland, and the Baltic states, are as yet deficient with regards to the administration structures to harvest the full advantages from this provincial activity notwithstanding broad help from their neighbors which are further developed as far as administration.

An intriguing case of restriction is the marvel of the special economic zones (SEZs) in China. These are geographic elements permitted to pioneer the procedure of opening up to remote speculation since the 1980s. They coordinate science with industry what's more, exchange. An alternate administration framework and uncommon guidelines were set up to guarantee that neighborhood governments to adjust policymaking towards accomplishing the vital objectives that the focal government set for these specific territories. At long last, financing arrangements for business shift between the two models. Under the model of the developed economy, the frameworks of fund furnish the current organizations with only liquidity for speculation. Liquidity is viewed as a homogeneous info factor.

The model of the entrepreneurial economy requires an arrangement of fund that is not quite the same as that in the model of the developed economy.12 in the model of the developed economy, there is sureness in yields just as sources of info. There is a solid association between banks and firms in their joint enterprises to cultivate development. In the entrepreneurial economy model, sureness has offered approach to vulnerability requiring diverse money related foundations. Specifically, the enterprises and casual capital markets, giving fund to high-chance what's more, inventive new firms, assume a significant job in the model of the entrepreneurial economy. Right now loses its homogeneous picture and is frequently coupled with types of exhortation, information, and changing degrees of inclusion (business heavenly attendants, hatcheries, and so on).

Remote budgetary foundations have obtained or set up businesses in many emerging countries. Much of the time, this has implied that nearby banks have lost the vast majority of their huge corporate business to these remote gatherings. Emerging countries could improve the entrepreneurial piece of their economy by invigorating nearby budgetary organizations to receive current methods for financing imaginative new nearby business. The model of the developed economy overwhelmed most developed economies until the late 1980s. It depends on relative assurance in information sources and yields. Huge plants and the quick interaction among man and machine are the foundations of this economy.

Economies of scale expanded significantly. The model of the developed economy brought extraordinary development. The joint impact of the technology and media communications insurgencies and globalization has decreased the capacity of the overseen economies of Western Europe and North America to develop and make employments. On the one hand, there is the coming of new challenge from ease, yet moderately high instructed and expertise serious, countries in Central and Eastern Europe just as in Asia. Then again, the broadcast communications and technology upheavals have definitely diminished the expense of moving, capital, yet in addition data out of the significant expense areas of Europe and into lower-cost areas.

Taken together, this joint impact suggests that monetary action in significant expense areas is no longer perfect with reutilized enterprises. Or maybe, the upper hand of significant expense areas moved to information based exercises, and specifically savvy search exercises. These exercises cannot be costless moved the world over. Information as a contribution to financial movement is inalienably unique in relation to land, work, and capital. It is described by high vulnerability, high asymmetries across individuals, and high exchange costs. An economy where information is the fundamental wellspring of serious advantage is increasingly reliable with the model of the entrepreneurial economy. The substance of the model of the entrepreneurial economy is not simply making information, yet likewise misusing it.

There are huge portions of the progressive developed and emerging economies where reutilized formation is fundamental or where shut types of advancement are effective. There are enormous parts where misuse of what exists is significant and where investigation of what does not exist is immaterial. The progressive economy is an economy of which the group of stars varies definitely from that of twenty years back. There is a lot to depict and to find about the major changes of the most recent twenty years. Moreover, there is an extraordinary arrangement to find about what great strategy rehearses are under the model of the entrepreneurial developed economy.

It appears evident what the ideal use is of a machine, a running belt, or a whole manufacturing plant in the overseen economy. In any case, it is misty what the worth is of information with its some delicate furthermore, idle viewpoints, for example, inventiveness, correspondence, and feelings. The over fourteen qualities with their accentuation on the job of entrepreneurship capital might be useful understanding the progressive economy. Emerging economies are in an intrinsically progressively muddled circumstance as anyone might imagine outlined in the accompanying focuses. In the first place, we ought to recognize that while developed economies change from the figured out how to the entrepreneurial economy, emerging economies face a significantly additionally testing task.

Much the same as emerging economies are a blend of a developed and a developing one; they are likewise a blend of a developed and an entrepreneurial one. For example, Indonesia has numerous attributes of developed economy taking into account that it has a background marked by advancing certain ventures while compelling numerous others and policymaking is regularly centralistic. Be that as it may, a genuine case of entrepreneurial arrangement is Indonesia's demeanor towards encouraging the improvement of SMEs. Commonly SMEs in Indonesia, and especially Java, will in general group.

Various such firms have become effective exporters of rattan furniture, wood furniture, and pieces of clothing utilizing the quality of subcontracting associations with outside financial specialists and purchasers as well as agglomeration economies accomplished by bunching in chosen areas. Indonesian SMEs taking an interest in bunches are more prone to trade and to embrace item and procedure developments when contrasted with additional scattered and detached firms. This is an immediate aftereffect of the BIPIK (Program Pembinaan dan Pengembangan Industri Kecil) program which was begun in the late 1970s to invigorate geographic convergence of private ventures. Such a focus encourages generally modest preparing in essential entrepreneurial aptitudes for some SMEs simultaneously. Emerging economies normally have not completely wrapped up the union phase of the developed economy.

Models are wasteful and profoundly divided retail and inn and cooking divisions. All things considered, they need to attempt and create or import portions of a yet more up to date economy. The developed piece of an emerging economy goes well together with a concentrated force framework where similarity and homogeneity assume critical jobs. This force framework, joined with typically more vulnerable vote based weights in emerging economies, may disappoint the halfway change to an entrepreneurial economy where innovation and decent variety play significant jobs.

A high level of business casualness implies that while the state is gone up against with missed incomes and data about the outcomes of its administrative activities, businesses fail to meet expectations with regards to access to formal credit sources and to lawful assurance. Fifth, a channel of the brainy, the innovative and the entrepreneurial ones is no simple beginning stage for cultivating a fresher entrepreneurial economy. 6th and barely examined above, there are differing manners by which entrepreneurship can be inconvenient to monetary advancement, as through its unreasonable designation towards exercises which are by and by beneficial, however, socially unfortunate or through low quality entrepreneurship producing negative externalities.

This impact can be noticeable in emerging economies of numerous shapes like the Russian what's more, the African models appear. Clearly, a considerable lot of these impediments are counterbalanced by points of interest of emerging economies like the opportunities of gaining from the mix-ups of the developed economies (making up for lost time systems, returning exceptionally talented specialists) and the casualness of the way of life (microcredits). The assortment among the emerging economies requires a more exact examination than given above about what ought to be finished advancing components of the new entrepreneurial economy.

Access to fund is especially basic, with advancement, monetary development and budgetary improvement saw as inseparably interweaved. Except if new businesses have adequate substantial advantages for promise as security, bank advances are commonly not accessible to them. Regardless of whether they have such resources, banks in emerging economies are frequently hesitant to loan without adequate credit data and poorly characterized lawful rights relating to make sure about exchanges. As anyone might expect, thusly, credit to GDP proportions in emerging economies by and large miss the mark concerning those in progressive economies, recommending that a critical number of organizations are underserved or even unserved by banks and should depend on their authors' assets or those of loved ones.

While new companies in progressive economies face a similar test, they are bound to have the option to take advantage of elective subsidizing pools, for example, heavenly attendant contributing, investment, and emerging types of financing. Likewise, with their financial frameworks and sorted out monetary markets, most emerging economies' elective subsidizing pools presently cannot seem to accomplish comparative entrance levels to progressive economies. Microcredit has had a restricted effect in easing credit requirements and filling entrepreneurship, development, and development in emerging economies. Be that as it may, computerized money and new improvements in FinTech can help prod entrepreneurial movement and advancement not just by making existing types of intermediation increasingly proficient and less expensive, in this way upgrading the loaning limit of banks and microfinance organizations, yet in addition by developing new types of intermediation.

While China and India are uncommon venture capital (VC) magnets, financial speculators are taking a developing enthusiasm for other emerging economies too; economies as various as Brazil, Egypt, Kenya, Nigeria, and Russia are pulling in expanded consideration from investors. Free VCs (IVCs) are by all account not the only financial speculators who may back entrepreneurial firms. Numerous organizations likewise have corporate enterprises programs, normally executed as a vital decision to supplement inner R&D programs.

Albeit corporate VC (CVC) is fundamentally littler than VC as far as its venture volume, for a significant number of new businesses it is a significant wellspring of entrepreneurial money. CVC ventures are not really roused by indistinguishable goals from VC speculations; while the last are commonly determined by monetary return desires, CVC ventures are regularly key and connected to the business interests of the organization. Government-supported and private VC is reciprocal. Open financing ought not occur in segregation; except if governments try to improve the business condition in which entrepreneurship can flourish, their job as investors is probably going to be insufficient

Emerging markets are additionally observing the ascent of non-institutional types of entrepreneurial money, explicitly blessed messenger contributing, hatcheries, and group contributing. Like VC, blessed messenger contributing is progressively a worldwide wonder, with a developing number of heavenly attendant gatherings framing in emerging economies. While business quickening agents and hatcheries may give just a limited quantity of subsidizing to new companies, the tutoring these projects give can be basic to entrepreneurs. While emerging on the web stages may be able to accomplish a prevalent match among entrepreneurs and financial specialists, we note that various significant difficulties stay before swarm contributing can accomplish a similar scale as heavenly attendant and VC contributing.

These difficulties lie particularly in educational asymmetries, insufficient due perseverance, potential grouping conduct, the absence of bespoke legally binding courses of action, and the nonattendance of obviously characterized exits for speculations. While these non-institutional sources of financing are as yet early stage, volumes are developing quickly. In China, for example, business swarm loaning totaled under $1.5 billion out of 2013. After two years, the volume previously surpassed $40 billion. To distil and outline exercises from emerging advancement pioneers like China and India, we likewise examined Chinese and Indian computerized economy pioneers Tencent and Flipkart.

As these organizations structure Google like advancement environments, they (and others like them) start to cross outskirts and become worldwide change-producers, quickening advancement, work formation, and financial improvement at home and abroad. Both Tencent and Flipkart were at first supported by funding. Further, Tencent has today become a significant supplier of investment itself, backing countless entrepreneurial firms that have developed as unicorns' new companies valued at $1 at least billion. There is proceeded with ascend in the emphasis on advancement and entrepreneurship in emerging markets. This will require an expansion in both the expansiveness of and profundity of the channels of financing accessible for entrepreneurship and development. Exercises can be taken from developed markets, yet emerging markets should make financing situations that are likewise custom-made to their one of a kind setting.

Development is one of the most looked into issues in the monetary field. Profitability factors, information, and innovation are the most well-known sources of monetary development, by the by in the most recent decade contemplates have come back to consider to be movement as a wellspring of development. Creators have tended to this issue in numerous perspectives: overflows, Schumpeterian, inspiration, and risk, capital (Urbano and Aparicio, 2016), and development, to name a few. Right now, has been a developing collection of exact writing identified with the job of entrepreneurship on financial development. This issue has been profoundly breaking down with the development of the worldwide institutionalized measurements of entrepreneurship developed by GEM. In the majority of the cases, the examination was led relating development and entrepreneurship estimated by the complete total early-stage entrepreneurial activity (TEA) or independent work gauges.

Different specialists have moved in the impact of the various sorts of TEA which incorporate reasons why people choose to engage in entrepreneurial exercises, for example opportunities, need. Therefore, likewise investigating the dynamic piece of entrepreneurial exercises which compare to the exclusive standard development entrepreneurs. Regardless of the enterprises of social researchers to comprehend the systems under entrepreneurship prompts better conditions for the countries, an extraordinary piece of their exploration have taken uniquely regard for the relationship in essence in any event, when theoretical writing propose that distinctions between phases of advancement exist. In the enterprises to give a light, right now, the impact of entrepreneurship for developed and developing countries independently. They found that new firms' formation does not have a certain impact over monetary development for the two phases of improvement. This outcome can be attached to a nearby connection between the diligence of new businesses and the entrance to a proper market; recommending that this sort of entrepreneurial action does not ensure quicker paces of development.

While the facts confirm that they have referenced that not all entrepreneurship is prompting advancement, they additionally exhibited that there is a sort of entrepreneurship that legitimately influences monetary development, the "gazelle" entrepreneurship. This conviction is especially valid in progressive economies; in any case, they did not discover proof of this impact for the emerging economies. This proposes that, for developing countries it is expected to arrive at an edge level of advancement previously encountering this impact completely.

In worldwide terms, late exact proof recommends that new business formation estimated by TEA has a beneficial outcome over development rates (Coulibaly, Erbao, and Mekongcho, 2018; Dhahri and Anis, 2018). In such conditions, it is less certain whether entrepreneurship action has a bit, or even critical effect on development rates for emerging countries. It was to a great extent hard to formalize it until the most recent decade because of the nonattendance of a "formal" metric for entrepreneurship. With the development of information assortment by GEM and other sources, the theoretical plans of this hypothesis have propelled numerous researchers to experimentally test the impact of entrepreneurship over development rates.

The channels through entrepreneurship prompts financial development are a few, speaks to the breakpoint to the connection among entrepreneurship and development. On the other hand, to the neo-old style development hypothesis that have focused on the commitment of efficiency factors capital and work to the procedure of monetary advancement. A few creators begin to think in entrepreneurship as a wellspring of development under the Adam Smith's vision of development where entrepreneurial exercises are seen as benefit opportunities. Along these lines, the procedure matter more than contributions to the formation consequently monetary development entrepreneurship could be tied with development through these benefit opportunities. Afterward, the new monetary hypothesis of development handled these thoughts and permits us to fit the entrepreneurship into development models.

Thusly, endogenous development hypothesis has concentrated on the moderate factors: capital (human) arrangement and advancement. Endogenous development likewise attempts to clarify development through the overflows of information. Entrepreneurship is one system that changes over information into development. There is a significant discussion thusly the genuine impact of entrepreneurship over the worldwide economy. For the one hand, there is writing that bolsters the way that adventures help to build development rates in developed countries, for the other one, less is thought about its impact in developing countries.

The impact of entrepreneurship is not established for this sort of economies and entrepreneurial action is a long way from advancement and development for developing/emerging countries. In doing as such, it is conceivable to notice that the connection among development and entrepreneurship in developing countries in not clear by any stretch of the imagination, in addition, there is not convincing proof that relate these components (Prieger, Bampoky, Blanco, and Liu, 2016).

It is notable that not all independent work is entrepreneurial; in addition, the system in which entrepreneurship improves financial advancement is mind boggling. Emerging economies have higher paces of independent work, all things considered; they accomplish low degrees of salary. Understanding what is falling behind the impact of entrepreneurship in emerging markets is conceivably one of the most significant points right now. Therefore, the principle goal of this paper is to address this issue for emerging economies by characterizing entrepreneurship in a fitting way. All the more plainly, we try to respond to the topic of whether the dynamic piece of entrepreneurship would increment monetary development rates in the emerging economies.

Numerous governments (exceptionally in developing countries) have developed uncommon projects to empower entrepreneurship, trusting it will add to development, business, and financial government assistance. There is an open discussion on the real impact of entrepreneurship on financial factors, particularly in developing countries where entrepreneurship has a solid part dependent on need. Moreover, it is hard to recognize the type of entrepreneurship that opens approach should encourage. This work plans to mostly responding to this inquiry by breaking down information for 100 countries over a multiyear time span test. Entrepreneurship can be a wellspring of development both for developed and developing countries.

In any case, not all entrepreneurship has this impact. Dynamic (or high-development) entrepreneurship has a critical impact in monetary development both in progressive economies as in emerging markets. It is especially fascinating the outcome for emerging markets, where commonly entrepreneurship has been related with little, low-development adventures. This outcome ought to energize open strategies that advance the improvement furthermore, financing of dynamic entrepreneurs through an increasingly developed entrepreneurial biological system. Despite the fact that entrepreneurs act in quest for their own benefits, they may create advantages to the more extensive society all the while, for example regarding making new openings, escalating rivalry, presenting advancement, and expanding efficiency. Likewise, among policymakers around the world, developing indigenous enterprises has increased expanding prevalence as a motor for reasonable neighborhood financial development (Thurik, 2013).

In spite of the fact that cultivating entrepreneurship is not new, it speaks to a move away from the macroeconomic mediations that commanded among (neighborhood) policymakers in earlier decades, at the point when it was generally basic to attempt to draw in enormous firms by giving generous motivations (Chatterji et al., 2013). Lamentably, a large number of these top-down strategy intercessions have not had the option to address quick and transient nearby monetary issues. Entrepreneurship is currently advanced as a base up, 'minimal effort high effect' approach, which can address singular level needs identified with pay and business, and can work with negligible foundation and assets.

One of the best commitments of entrepreneurship to the economy is the acknowledgment and usage of opportunities so that it gives 'new blends' (e.g., items, markets, association), which comprise better approaches to fulfill existing need. Be that as it may, not all opportunity abuse will fundamentally add to the benefit of society. Contingent upon the 'rules of the game' in the economy, which may change starting with one time and spot then onto the next, entrepreneurship can once in a while be useless, and even damaging. Ineffective firms are frequently replicative, rather than imaginative, and take a portion of the other's pie as opposed to expanding the size of the pie itself.

The multi-nation overviews led under the global entrepreneurship monitor (GEM) inquire about program have contributed emphatically to seeing how various sorts of entrepreneurship influence financial development across countries and areas (Xavier et al., 2013). A significant qualification inside entrepreneurship investigate that was presented by the GEM consortium, and which is especially important in emerging markets since it is identified with the level of financial improvement, is between opportunity-driven and need driven entrepreneurship. Another regular differentiation while looking into entrepreneurship in emerging markets, identified with the institutional setting, is between formal what's more, casual entrepreneurship. As a rule, the two qualifications are related.

The qualification between opportunity-driven and need driven entrepreneurs starts from the way that most emerging markets have significant levels of entrepreneurship, however, these organizations just have a restricted commitment to financial development. While the opportunity driven entrepreneur, settles on a functioning decision to begin a business to exploit an unexploited or underexploited business opportunity, the need driven entrepreneur has no better alternatives at finding a (good) work. This evident oddity affirms that not all entrepreneurship is fundamentally gainful. Since opportunity-driven entrepreneurs are maneuverer into entrepreneurial exercises, they are for the most part better propelled, and frequently likewise increasingly gifted at maintaining a business.

Accordingly, they can work increasingly effective and be progressively gainful. Along these lines, they are additionally more prone to gain admittance to outside account, and, therefore, their organizations will in general become quicker and bigger. For need driven entrepreneurs, the basic inspiration for beginning a business is very unique. Since these entrepreneurs are for the most part 'drove' into independent work for subsistence reasons, they generally work taking things down a notch, including straightforward business exercises. Their entrepreneurial aptitudes may not make any difference a lot to the working of their businesses. They just have constrained individual or family investment funds, and need access to outside account, which seriously hampers the development possibilities of their organizations.

Other than giving a pay to a family, need driven entrepreneurship for the most part has next to zero impact on financial development, while opportunity-driven entrepreneurship can for sure have huge beneficial outcomes (e.g., work, rivalry, development). Be that as it may, a generally high portion of the entrepreneurship rates in emerging markets is essentially determined by need intentions. All things considered, significant levels of entrepreneurship might be a pointer of low levels of advancement as opposed to a potential motor for financial development. This relates with the thought that the connection between entrepreneurial action and monetary advancement is U-shaped. Independent work decreases as economies become progressively proficient, and elective blue collar openings for work are made, possibly to increment again when economies arrive at the significantly further developed advancement driven stage. The significant distinction, be that as it may, is that these entrepreneurs are transcendently portrayed as goal-oriented, creative, opportunity-driven entrepreneurs.

It is notable that a considerable extent of financial action in emerging markets takes place in the casual segment. The clearest qualification with a proper entrepreneur is that casual entrepreneur works a business without enrolment. In any case, firms may appear various degrees of familiarity. Indeed, even enrolled firms may every so often resort to casual tasks, for example by charging without receipt, or offering easy-going types of assistance to companions what's more, family members. Aside from totally 'covered up' firms, the casual part likewise incorporates (somewhat) 'covered up' yield. Since casual firms work (to a great extent) outside the legitimate structure of an economy, one of the most concerning issues when concentrating casual entrepreneurship is the absence of solid information.

Around the world, gauges estimating casualness (or independent work) run from 30% in Eastern European economies, up to practically 60% in Sub-Saharan countries (WBES, 2013). It is broadly expected that having a huge casual division is bothersome and conceivably hurtful to the economy. Casual firms may create unreasonable challenge to formal firms, and deny governments of potential income through pay and work charge. Others restrict this 'parasite see' by contending that abundance guideline and significant expenses of working a conventional business is driving potential entrepreneurs into familiarity. Casual businesses may lift people or families out of neediness and may consequently likewise add to monetary development.

At long last, the alleged 'double view' focuses on the concurrence among formal and casual firms. Casual firms speak to little risk to formal firms since they for the most part work on various markets, with various clients, yet additionally contribute little to financial development since they are regularly profoundly wasteful. Proof without a doubt recommends that casual entrepreneurs by and large will in general begin, and remain littler than formal firms, utilize fewer specialists, and have less access to business financing than their proper division partners. Most by far of casual entrepreneurs are in reality need driven entrepreneurs, beginning their businesses as a result of absence of elective business opportunities (Autio and Fu, 2013). From more than one point of view, it appears to be alluring to animate businesses to enroll as formal firms, since it could lead to significant effectiveness gains. Nonetheless, there is practically nothing proof that proper firms have recently worked casually.

The decision, beyond what many would consider possible, between formal or casual entrepreneurship is regularly founded on a computation of relative expenses and advantages inside a particular institutional condition. Most firms in emerging markets are gone up against with numerous exorbitant and tedious administrative what's more, managerial boundaries while enrolling. Add to this the numerous circuitous costs, for example, rewards, and administration expenses for handling business grants immediately (Autio and Fu, 2013). Therefore, in countries with troublesome section guidelines, a powerless principle of law, and powerless security of property, numerous entrepreneurs will most likely like to remain casual.

Entrepreneurship is practically synonymous to development. In a procedure of 'innovative devastation,' entrepreneurs challenge existing firms by presenting new mixes that make current advancements and items out of date. A fairly more extensive methodology alludes to advancement not just as the improvement of new items or then again, (mechanical) forms, yet in addition as the misuse of new markets and the improvement of better approaches to compose business. Likewise, applicable right now the differentiation between advancements that are 'new to the world,' developments that are 'new to the local market,' or developments that are 'new to the firm' (Aulet and Murray, 2013). Economic situations, approaches, and the institutional condition can advance or thwart creative conduct.

In emerging markets, the motivator for entrepreneurs to develop is regularly restricted, on the grounds that the risks presented by financial, political, and administrative vulnerability are regularly high. Markets are frequently flawed, and improper property rights and powerless agreement requirement make returns on advancements risks, while inadequate foundation, low per capita wages, and institutional obstructions make it hard for developments to spread. Most advancement, will in this way, best case scenario, occur at the firm level, since just few entrepreneurs can effectively contend at national levels, not to mention worldwide levels.

All things considered, in managing both market and government inadequacies, entrepreneurs in emerging economies regularly resort to a wide assortment of flighty strategies and systems, for instance to get account. Indeed, even mechanical backwardness is not really a disservice as long as the absorptive limit and imagination of entrepreneurs as for new advances is adequately evolved. This absorptive limit goes past simple impersonation, and may bring about new, and even problematic, advancements without bearing all the expenses and risks of putting resources into developing new information. The procedure of financial improvement is not straight, conveniently following certain phases of improvement, however, may likewise include 'jumping.' Entrepreneurs may even profit by showcase and government inadequacies in light of the fact that the requirements, and in this manner new business opportunities, are across the board. Since serious risks are likewise progressively restricted, opportunities for entrepreneurs in emerging markets are likewise more extensive in scope, permitting firms to seek after a portfolio approach.

This technique can likewise effectively deal with the more significant levels of business and market risk. Entrepreneurship as a motor for neighborhood monetary development, specifically in emerging markets. Despite the fact that it is regularly considered as a 'minimal effort high effect' approach, its commitment to financial development has, in no way, shape or form, accomplished its latent capacity yet. Due to the regularly testing entrepreneurial condition as to levels of advancement and institutional setting, the quantity of little scope, casual, independently employed, and regularly ineffective entrepreneurs exceed the quantity of profitable, creative, opportunity-driven entrepreneurs.

So as to make a situation that empowers gainful and imaginative entrepreneurship so that it can contribute all the more adequately to nearby monetary development, an expansive and coordinated methodology is basic, since it is impacted by numerous determinants (e.g., instruction levels, business atmosphere, legitimate, and political conditions). Enterprises to advance entrepreneurship as a motor for monetary development ought to along these lines incorporate the three most significant partners included: the open part, the private area, and information organizations. All partners ought to accordingly share an unmistakable and elite spotlight on encouraging driven, imaginative, and high development situated firms.

With respect to the job of the government, in most emerging markets there still is a great deal of ground to be picked up to improve the business atmosphere, and make it simpler and less expensive to begin and run a business. What's more, tending to other market inadequacies (e.g., access to account, foundation, work markets) additionally falls inside the obligation of the open space. The commitment of the (neighborhood) private division in encouraging creative and profitable entrepreneurship might be multi-facetted. The negligible degree of commitment might be in sharing best works on, offering apprenticeships, and instructing fire up firms, yet it might likewise incorporate putting resources into promising firms and building up (increasingly) formal associations.

Maybe the most significant obligation lies with information organizations. Training and the advancement of entrepreneurial abilities assume a significant job in improving the probability of endurance of new firms, and in improving their financial presentation. Since information foundations generally assume a significant job in new worth formation, they are the most fitting partner in stepping up to the plate in advancing inventive business arrangements, furthermore, change the outlook concerning entrepreneurial perspectives (e.g., opportunity discernment), capacities (e.g., fire up abilities), and yearnings (e.g., development, high-growth) (Acs et al., 2013).

In the event that effective, creative firms can possibly develop exponentially and yet these organizations for the most part additionally, need greater interest in capital, time, and exertion before they will bring returns (Aulet and Murray, 2013). Since numerous organizations are destined to early disappointment when they are generally powerless, instructive enterprises ought to be joined with different activities, such as setting up business hatcheries that offer beginning up help to promising entrepreneurial thoughts. By connecting innovation, capital, and ability inside an ensured and empowering condition, the procedure of business formation can be speeded up, while the likelihood of disappointment can be diminished.

From the perspective of neighborhood monetary development, one of the long-term destinations might be the arrangement of a bunch of imaginative firms, with a pool of all around prepared, and similarly invested entrepreneurs, and a culture that supports advancement and new businesses (Chatterji et al., 2013). The way toward executing such a coordinated methodology, with a reasonable and solid center and including every single applicable partner, will be long and without a doubt covered with various misfortunes and traps, yet it will inevitably likewise profit those gatherings of society that still depend on need driven entrepreneurial exercises.

The little commitments made by numerous entrepreneurs drive the development in the economy; scaling entrepreneurs push the limits of their condition, and through these enterprises, the advancement they produce may add to destitution mitigation. With more space to develop, the developing economies have an extraordinary potential for advancement: this is the place the entrepreneurs come in. The entrepreneurs that scale profit by the capability of development, enhancing the advancement and working as an all-encompassing arm of the government to drive industry explicit advancement. This yields a solid positive connection among entrepreneurship and development in such emerging economies.

Because of the little beginning sizes of the new businesses, radical imaginative changes are progressively reasonable, attainable, and engaging; the entrepreneurs need seek after opportunities with high risk advancement to win serious lottery: the high development opportunities. In this manner the new companies with imaginative mechanical items consistently, with certain exemptions, lead the best group of new companies in a nation. With it's all in or all out nature, mechanical new companies, once on the correct side of development, immediately become a High-impact organization: making new businesses; expanding productivity in the ventures utilizing their innovation; adding force to the economy because of their high development nature.

In emerging economies, the social impression of entrepreneurs holds a significant job too: in Turkey for instance, study finds that most of the open considers entrepreneurs as corner-turners, attempting to enter a higher financial class. Worldwide improvement is entering a stage where entrepreneurship will progressively assume an increasingly significant job. There are at any rate three purposes behind this, every specific to particular kinds of countries. Right off, the bat, in the West, the developed economy of the 1970s–2000s, described by dependence on enormous business and large scale manufacturing, has offered path to a supposed entrepreneurial economy. Here information driven merchandise and enterprises are currently more deftly gave by littler firms, and the rise of an inventive class requires a less meddling, however, additionally encouraging state.

Besides, in the emerging countries, most eminently the BRICs (Brazil, Russia, India, and China) great development has been driven by a genuine entrepreneurial insurgency. The need in these economies to support development through reasonable access to assets, information, markets, and low-carbon industrialization puts a premium on creative entrepreneurship. At long last, at all developed countries, where help reliance is high, contributors have been moving the accentuation being developed collaboration towards private area advancement. In a significant number of these countries, including asset poor North African countries, populaces comprise of numerous youngsters who see little possibilities of picking up work with not too bad wages. Advancing youth entrepreneurship here has gotten an imperative strategy target of numerous advancement associations and contributors. It is normal that entrepreneurship will, considering the abovementioned, add to development and work formation in progressive, emerging, and least developed economies the same.

There are two significant admonitions be that as it may. The first is that for entrepreneurs to assume a suitable job, the job of the state stays significant, if not more so than previously. Solid states, as controllers and watchmen, assume an especially indispensable job. Without suitable 'rules of the game,' entrepreneurship may bring about unfortunate social results, including defilement, wrongdoing, theory, and money related emergencies, and may decline the vulnerabilities of individuals during cataclysmic events. The second is that while entrepreneurship may raise monetary development and material government assistance, it may not generally bring about upgrades in non-material government assistance.

The expansion in worldwide venture and cross-fringe entrepreneurship during the century mirrors the developing opportunity of national economies. The entrepreneurial movement has assumed a focal job during the time spent monetary change by making new businesses and administrations in the worldwide networks. In this manner, globalization has essentially affected entrepreneurial opportunity and execution. Since entrepreneurship is worried about the disclosure and misuse of gainful opportunities, it has followed certain waves in its own improvement over the world, much like other financial procedures. The times of the 70's and 80's speak to one of these rushes of entrepreneurial exercises during this time, the entrepreneurial idea and impacts mirrored the business attitude and it made huge commitments to the economy and society.

These entrepreneurial impacts lead to an expansion of efficiency in labor and capital, which improve monetary development and to the advancement of new administration ideal models implanted in business techniques and practices. The twenty-first century faces new difficulties in the monetary and the executives' framework as the worldwide entrepreneurial age creates. Emerging multinationals' internationalization procedure regularly gives entrepreneurs access to new clients, advancement, and innovative center points just as a few potential outcomes to encounter new things that were not accessible or attainable in their neighborhood markets.

Accordingly, scientists have as of late moved consideration away from approaches that attention on distinguishing those individuals in the public arena who like to become entrepreneurs towards understanding the nexus of ambitious advancement and important opportunities in the emerging nation setting. This new center has expected researchers to clarify the job of opportunities during the time spent entrepreneurship. Mistreating these opportunities in the new setting expects firms to assemble an entrepreneurial ability that permits them to at the same time influence their inborn capacities while extending to manufacture new ones in the emerging markets.

For as far back as decades, the prevailing speculations in entrepreneurship have looked to clarify entrepreneurship as an element of the sorts of individuals occupied with entrepreneurial movement and, therefore, have to a great extent ignored the opportunity for entrepreneurship. An opportunity concentrate accordingly requires thought of the procedure of entrepreneurship with advantage, risk, and cost for the breeze vitality business in the worldwide emerging condition. Entrepreneurial opportunity includes not just specialized abilities like monetary investigation and statistical surveying, yet in addition less substantial types of innovativeness, group building, critical thinking, and administration. Entrepreneurial opportunity is characterized as a circumstance where new merchandise, administrations, crude materials, advertises, and arranging techniques can be presented through the development of new methods, closures, or means-cuts off associations. This definition proposes that recognizing and choosing right opportunities for new businesses are among the most significant capacities of a fruitful entrepreneur.

Entrepreneurial opportunity acknowledgment is the capacity to distinguish institutional hypothesis and practice where new products, administrations, crude materials, showcases, and sorting out strategies can be presented through the arrangement of new methods, finishes, or means-cuts off associations. It is our idea that entrepreneurial opportunity acknowledgment is likewise major to institutional theory. Foundations are characterized as regulative, standardizing, and subjective structures and exercises that give dependability and significance to social conduct. Organizations administer cultural exchanges in the territories of governmental issues (e.g., defilement, straightforwardness), law (e.g., financial advancement, administrative system), and society (e.g., moral standards, mentalities toward entrepreneurship). Consequently, incorporating the thought of opportunity-acknowledgment into inquire about on entrepreneurship would add a significant measurement to the institutional hypothesis and give a valuable and intriguing method for clarifying the enterprises advancement in the worldwide business condition.

Three distinct phases of monetary improvement impact the apparent entrepreneurial opportunities and abilities in the various countries. The primary stage is factor-driven economy. Right now, contend dependent on their factor enrichments: essentially untalented work and characteristic assets. Keeping up intensity at this monetary improvement arrange pivots fundamentally on well-working open and private establishments, all around developed framework, a stable macroeconomic condition, and a sound workforce that has gotten in any event essential instruction. In the second phase of proficiency driven economy, entrepreneurs with high desires admission better in countries with a stable financial and social atmosphere, notwithstanding other all around developed organizations.

Now, entrepreneurial opportunities are progressively determined by advanced education and preparing, effective merchandise markets, well-working work markets, developed money related markets, the capacity to tackle the advantages of existing innovations, and a huge household or outside market. In the third phase of advancement driven economies, information is common, however, work is costly. Entrepreneurship-explicit opportunities become the switches that drive dynamic, development arranged conduct, while the establishment of fundamental necessities and productivity enhancers should be kept up.

Entrepreneurial opportunity is an advantage improvement action that includes the revelation, assessment, and misuse of opportunities to present new merchandise and enterprises, methods for arranging, markets, procedures, and crude materials through sorting out enterprises that recently had not existed. Drawing on the above commitments to the exercises of advantage increment in the emerging economies, entrepreneurial opportunity is distinguished as the show capacity and readiness of countries to see new monetary opportunities and to present their methods for taking advantage of these lucky breaks into the worldwide market even with vulnerability.

Entrepreneurs are perceived as the absolute most significant player in a progressive economy in light of the fact that they from numerous points of view represent showcase powers, and it is normal that entrepreneurs will be the focal figures in financial aspects. Opportunities, in the feeling of entrepreneurship and the board benefits, are treated as a build that is showed in entrepreneurial activity venture, making new associations, putting up items for sale to the public, and create approaches for national development.

Consequently, we accept a perspective that open doors can exist autonomously of the diverse advantage advancement levels. In any situation, qualities of size of economy, government motivating forces, or wind asset capacity may make various advantages for wind-vitality entrepreneurship in the emerging markets. Entrepreneurial opportunities are progressively perceived as the primary driver of financial development and flourishing at nearby, national, and territorial levels, and deserving of significant help and cost interest in framework, innovation improvement, and human asset quality. These exercises are altogether impacted by entrepreneurial expenses. If the nation when all is said in done has uplifting perspectives toward entrepreneurship, this will produce monetary help, money related assets and costs, organizing benefits and different types of help to present and potential entrepreneurs.

In this way, the expenses toward entrepreneurship are influenced by natural backings and character attributes and the venture improvement can profit by individuals who can perceive significant business costs, and who see they have the necessary abilities to lessen the expenses in the worldwide activity. The idea of risk taking and its linkages with develop of entrepreneurial opportunity have been sensible to catch. Subsequently, it has been reasonable for clarify why entrepreneurs surge in to make the most of opportunities that others neglect to see or follow up on. Entrepreneurs may not consider themselves being any bound to face challenges than non-entrepreneurs, yet they are in any case inclined to subjectively order business circumstances all the more emphatically. Right now, for drawing in another business incorporate the debasement risk, opportunity, and rule of law chance, and legitimate frameworks and insurance chance. These risks challenge entrepreneurs to distinguish and abuse business opportunities, in any event, when they are occupied by the apparent high risk of these enterprises.

Brazil is on the front line of elective vitality ventures with a deliberate pledge to decrease its ozone depleting substance outflows by 2020; with the national utilization of ethanol in autos outperforming gas utilization in 2008; and with 45% of vitality needs provided from inexhaustible sources. Advancement of wind power is one positive overflow impact of the elective vitality extends; and has been helped by political will communicated through state motivators, the improvement of streamlined efficiencies, and the enhancement of wind turbine speeds. Government bolster structures incorporate the Alternative Sources Incentive Program which tries to advance the enhancement of the Brazilian vitality framework through joint enterprises in wind, biomass, and little hydroelectric frameworks.

Be that as it may, much enthusiasm for wind power has been gathered in the North-eastern locale in accordance with the way that this district has the biggest breeze power potential. Moreover, there has been an expansion in the advancement of differing entrepreneurial substances right now, giving a prepared application to vitality age. There exists an interest hole that remote financial specialists can misuse right now. The elevated levels of tax assessment are right now being tended to, and participants need to have a long-term point of view on their contribution.

China turned into the biggest breeze vitality supplier around the world. The improvement of wind vitality in China, regarding scale and cadence, is totally unmatched on the planet. The huge land mass and long coastline gives excellent breeze assets to China, which can be outfit to fuel development in the economy. The potential for misusing wind vitality in China is huge, with an absolute exploitable limit with respect to both land-based and seaward wind vitality of around 700–1,200 GW. The requirement for elective vitality sources in China is extraordinary, given that it has now become the world's biggest vitality purchaser depending on coal to supply around 70% of its vitality needs. By the by, the bigger Chinese breeze turbine producers have additionally entered the universal challenge for huge scope wind power gear-developing 5 MW or bigger turbines and venturing into abroad markets with the help of a few part makers.

China is a unitary express that has encountered a drive to build up a working legitimate framework, and proclaimed more than 300 laws and guidelines from the late 1970s to the mid-1990s. Because of a pending exchange war with United States over infringement of protected innovation right of U.S. enterprises in the mid-1990s, China's trademark law has been changed, and now offers critical insurances to remote trademark proprietors. Despite the fact that China has kept up its solidarity and household strength, and has accomplished fast monetary development and a better quality of living for the mind dominant part of its kin, there are difficulties for its current political circumstance. Other than the test of Taiwan's accepted freedom, developing urban joblessness, rising wrongdoing, social issue, and debasement challenge the government's capacity to look after steadiness.

Businesses planning to put resources into China may charge ineffectively except if they get sound guidance. It is an idea basic to one's viable working in the Chinese society in light of the fact that the Chinese regularly feel committed to work with their companions first. Existing estimating approaches, in any case, influence the degree of dynamic venture by designers. In the event that a remote organization has the budgetary muscle to counter the passage obstructions, remembering some innovative points of interest for turbine plan, for instance, at that point a long-term way to deal with entering the Chinese market will be attractive.

South Africa is the predominant financial player inside the Southern African Development Community. It is likewise seen as a portal to numerous other African countries. South Africa is the best African nation wherein to work together, next just to Mauritius by positioning. The International Monetary Fund (IMF) estimates that financial development rates in Africa could outperform that of Asia in the following five years, six of the world's ten quickest developing economies were in Africa. The solid development of Foreign Direct Investment (FDI) in Africa, particularly from China, can be viewed as flagging the preparation of Africa to work with the world. Right now, higher occurrence of modern ventures will put a considerably more noteworthy strain on the current restricted vitality assets, and fortify the case for supply-side intercessions on the mainland. Moreover, Africa's populace surpassed 1 billion out of 2009, is developing at a normal pace of

2.4%, and is relied upon to twofold constantly 2050.

Inside this bigger setting, South Africa has a developing economy, a minimum amount of businesses and a related requirement for solid sources of power. It's expanding industrialization and the powerful development of enterprises like mining, vehicle get together, metalworking, hardware, and materials has put exceptional requests on its vitality assets. A serious power emergency intruded on monetary advancement in 2007, requiring the import of a few billion KW of capacity to satisfy need. The dedication of the government to vitality security was communicated in the 2011 State of the Nation address and followed the 2010 arrival of the nation's integrated resource plan (IRP). The IRP looks to produce 10,000 GW of power from elective sources by 2013, and incorporates private sustainable power source providers. There are additionally administrative and commonplace government impetuses, other than a set up clear Power Purchase Agreement, to empower interest in the breeze vitality area. A deliberate passage through concurrences with Provincial Governments, while holding the limit and adaptability to rapidly increase formation in the wake of accessing high volume ventures might be a valuable methodology in South Africa.

While developing countries have utilized various strategies and procedures in their improvement interests, two types of mechanical approach were especially conspicuous. The first was import substitution a procedure of industrialization by creating recently imported merchandise for the nation's household advertises. Nonetheless, by the 1980s, in the face of monetary emergency, many developing countries at that point went to second system export advancement. Be that as it may, except for a few countries in East Asia, neither modern procedure has brought about significant monetary improvement. Both improvement approaches depended on solid state mediation and tireless market mutilations to support their reasonability along these lines regularly swarming out or ruining through and through the conventional and significant job of the entrepreneur.

Consequently, after blown-up enterprises at improvement through import substitution and new-born child industry insurance programs and to some degree blended results from trade advancement systems, developing countries are starting to concentrate on their business surroundings and making a monetary space which is helpful for private venture both residential (i.e., neighborhood entrepreneurs) and outside (i.e., remote direct speculation). To be sure, the advancement of entrepreneurship and the proclamation of SMEs arrangement have gotten a significant improvement solution as of late. Entrepreneurship strategy, at that point, joins a rundown which incorporates changes to countries' macroeconomic, conversion scale, exchange, and modern arrangements, and upgrades in administration.

Both national governments and the significant global associations, as a major aspect of their destitution decrease, development, and monetary improvement programs, are starting to concentrate on improving countries' business what's more, venture situations for entrepreneurship. The World Bank furthermore, United Countries Industrial Development Organization (UNIDO), for instance, have each settled units to advance private area improvement in developing countries and to give specialized help in the detailing of SME and entrepreneurship approach. The World Bank started an activity to quantify and rank countries' business areas and venture situations. Also, various developing countries have as of late drafted SME enactment and propelled projects to help independent companies and residential entrepreneurs.

While an attention on entrepreneurship for advancement may appear to be a different way to deal with advancement, this investigation offers that it is reliable with and even integral to the more seasoned and progressively conventional advancement techniques. We overview the writing on entrepreneurship in developing countries which, as a matter of fact, is wide and covers a scope of issues from culture and qualities; institutional obstructions, for example, money related division improvement, administration, and property rights; to the sufficiency of training and specialized aptitudes. A wide writing has additionally evolved on outside direct speculation and its positive and negative consequences for innovation move and entrepreneurship. After the breakdown of the Soviet Association, various investigations analyzed the advancement of little and medium-sized ventures experiencing significant change economies. As these economies moved from brought together economies to advertise economies, enterprises also, entrepreneurship got significant.

However, different investigations look at the impacts of infrastructural improvement what's more, the macro-economy on entrepreneurship. With such a wide degree of issues, a system for integrating the writing is required. This study offers that the distinguishing proof of the externalities which influence entrepreneurship gives a valuable system to look at the writing on entrepreneurship in developing countries. These externalities have come about because of and have gotten installed in countries' foundations and help to clarify the degree of entrepreneurship in an economy.

Likewise, with any change-orientated movement, social business and social entrepreneurship have not developed in a vacuum, but instead inside a complex system of institutional, political, monetary, and social changes happening at the worldwide and neighborhood levels. The institutional condition (the financial and political milieu in which an entrepreneur works) impacts individuals' readiness to take part in socially gainful action. The nature and nature of foundations in a nation decide if people will seek after entrepreneurial movement. In South Africa, social entrepreneurship has unequivocal application where conventional government activities cannot fulfill the whole social shortfall, where an exertion on the decrease in reliance on social government assistance/awards is at present being founded, and where the endurance of numerous non-governmental organizations (NGOs) is in question.

Such difficulties are exacerbated by a social setting described by enormous imbalances in training, lodging, the helps pandemic, and high joblessness and neediness rates. Under these conditions, social entrepreneurs assume the job of progress specialists by receiving a crucial make and continue social incentive by perceiving what's more, perseveringly seeking after new opportunities to serve that crucial. The entrepreneurial procedure is frequently conceptualized as the aftereffect of a mix of different inspirational and conviction parts where natural conditions additionally assume a job. Being inspired is not just viewed as an essential part of the entrepreneurial procedure yet should be enhanced with the imperative abilities and skills. Except if people see themselves as fit and ready to be entrepreneurial, their enterprises will stay uncompetitive and failing to meet expectations. The exploration finds those with higher entrepreneurial self-adequacy as seeing their condition as craftier as opposed to loaded with risks, and they will in general put stock in their capacity to impact the accomplishment of objectives.

Nonetheless, in spite of the fact that inspiration is suggested, or accepted, in papers on convictions, goals, and perceptions in connection to entrepreneurial practices, it remains generally under the inquired about regardless of its basic significance to anticipating and clarifying various sorts of entrepreneurial practices. The language of social entrepreneurship might be new, yet the wonder is not. Increasingly, specialists are looking past entrepreneurship as just having a monetary segment or Schumpeterian reason where entrepreneurs prod development and accelerate auxiliary changes in an economy, yet additionally perceive a social part which recognizes that individuals seek after their requirement for autonomy or have no elective choices for work and thus take part in independent work.

Establishments can be depicted as moderately broadly diffused practices, advances, or decides of social connection that have gotten settled in the feeling that it is exorbitant to pick elective practices, advances, or rules. The institutional system of a general public involves the central political, social, and lawful standard procedures that build up the reason for formation and dispersion, and associations must adjust to it in the event that they are to get backing and authenticity. Consequently, foundations are seen as helpful for good strategies, which thusly will encourage gathering of capital and work.

Administrative foundations allude to the officially classified, instituted, and authorized structure of laws in a network, society, or country. Less formal do proficient what's more, exchange affiliations, and business bunches set up the standardizing foundations, which regularly show in models and business shows, for example, those. Intellectual foundations advise the proverbial convictions about the normal gauges of conduct that are explicit to a culture, which are ordinarily learned through social connections by living or experiencing childhood in a network or society. Reliable with the idea that the institutional condition does in reality influence entrepreneurship, the following area further grills how an individual's readiness to seek after a certain course of conduct (right now entrepreneurship) is resolved without anyone else viability convictions while taking perception of the institutional condition.

Proof is amassing which proposes that improving the administrative condition may have positive advantages on the development and endurance of new pursuits in South Africa. The normal new firm commonness rate for all productivity driven countries was more than twofold South Africa's rate. The pervasiveness rates for set up business movement were much all the more upsetting, with the normal for all productivity driven countries being very nearly multiple times higher than South Africa's rate. The monetary ramifications of these discoveries illustrate the South African division's present potential to contribute genuinely to work formation and monetary development.

Not exclusively does the macroeconomic condition together with the prompter business condition influence the degrees of entrepreneurial movement in a nation, yet additionally more explicitly suffering national attributes have been anticipated to affect entrepreneurship. Calls have been made for countries to reorient their qualities and practices towards entrepreneurship. In the event that entrepreneurship is not valued in the way of life of a specific nation, at that point not exclusively will it be related with guiltiness and defilement yet in addition different types of monetary support will demonstrate insufficient. Ongoing work recommends that social entrepreneurs who are individuals of a hindered network appear to have exceptional knowledge into that network's needs. Be that as it may, they may not generally have the option to secure the assets required to dispatch a social enterprises proposed to address the needs, and are not in every case solid and steady to oversee and lead such a social adventure.

The focal reason of the subjective point of view is that entrepreneurial conduct develops because of the entrepreneurs' basic comprehensions. Basically, the entrepreneurial comprehensions point of view permits specialists to see how entrepreneurs think and why they do a portion of the things they do. Intellectual establishments are the aphoristic convictions about the normal principles of conduct that are explicit to a culture, which are ordinarily learned through social connections by living or experiencing childhood in a network or society. Research proposes that while such a psychological undertaking is hard to accomplish, it is decidedly related to choice execution in settings that can be portrayed as mind boggling, dynamic, and characteristically unsure. The entrepreneurial setting, especially the nation's institutional condition, epitomizes such a choice situation. In South Africa, most entrepreneurs are confined by their shortage of abilities, business information, and assets in their capacity to develop and make work.

While political activities and global coordinated effort are fundamental to bring issues to light about entrepreneurship as a rule and all the more as of late, social business rehearses; at last, change can just occur through changes in singular convictions, mentalities, and practice. Expanding on this thought of self in a social setting, this paper tended to the degree to which the institutional condition is connected to a person's self-conviction to participate in social entrepreneurial movement in an emerging showcase setting. Moderately great impression of the administrative and regularizing measurements and positive relationship. This implies these two institutional profiles are altogether associated with social entrepreneurship regarding social effect, imaginativeness, expandability, and maintainability. This is significant thinking about that social new pursuits offer the guarantee of enabling underestimated portions of the populace in emerging economies. Social enterprises are significant to the development and improvement of the South African economy, what's more, inseparably connected to monetary strengthening, work formation, and work inside burdened networks.

Arrangements to make employments, advance entrepreneurship, and development are key needs for some emerging economies. Structuring and executing changes is especially testing as approach creators 'enterprises to find some kind of harmony across areas, firm size, and motivations that can support development in a quickly changing worldwide economy. High-development firms representing around 3–20% of the assembling and administration businesses are specifically noteworthy as a development model considering their commitment to in excess of 50% of new openings and deals in these divisions. A regularly shared perspective on a run of the mill high-development firm is a little beginning up in a progressive segment that becomes quickly over a continued period through some ideal quality characteristic to the firm another trend setting innovation, a splendid showcasing advancement, or an amazingly able staff. Utilizing this focal point, it is not exceptional for some arrangement creators to look for specific focusing of firms apparent as having the potential for high development and giving them access to money related and specialized assets to understand this potential.

High growth firms are youthful yet not really little. Firms will in general be more youthful than the normal firm. Despite the fact that for some, the high-development scene starts after the beginning up stage. New businesses represent around 40% in Brazil, Cote d'Ivoire, Ethiopia, and Hungary, and around 30% in Indonesia. Likewise, high-development firms in developing countries are not really little. Many are bigger than the normal firm toward the start of a high-development scene, for example, in Indonesia, where almost 50% of High growth firms utilized in excess of 50 laborers. It is additionally not astounding that High growth firms end up bigger toward the finish of the high-development scene. Except for Hungary, High growth firms in all countries remembered for the examination wind up being at any rate 4% bigger than a normal firm after the high development scene.

High growth firms are found in a wide range of parts and areas. It is a typical misguided judgment that High growth firms are found in just progressive enterprises. Actually, these organizations exist in a wide range of segments and work over a scope of areas. The experience over the various areas bears no reasonable cross-country design characteristic of target parts with a more prominent possibility of watching High growth firms. Parts with a more information or innovation escalated profile frequently show higher than normal High growth firms, however, so do different areas that are significantly less progressive. For instance, in Hungary, High growth firms are progressively pervasive in information serious administrations. Be that as it may, in Mexico the quantity of High growth firms is especially high in PCs, gadgets, electric machines, and interchanges, estimation, and transportation gear, yet in addition in materials.

High firm development is fleeting and roundabout. It is hard for firms to continue high development. Actually, the probability of a rehashed scene, either promptly or later in the association's life cycle, is low. A few firms change from high development to low development or the other way around, while numerous others leave the market inside and out after a high-development scene. Proof in the report emphatically approves this knowledge. For instance, in Tunisia, more than 33% of firms that was in business between 1996–2009 accomplished HGF status at any rate once. Be that as it may, simply 0.01% of firms experienced high-development consistently all through a similar period.

Development, arrange economies, administrative capacities and specialist aptitudes and worldwide linkages contribute essentially to the likelihood of a high-development scene. Development can fortify firm development. In India, administration firms that present new items and fare are altogether bound to encounter a high-development scene. Likewise, high-development occasions in assembling and administrations are driven by diligent as opposed to infrequent R&D, and by firms that lead R&D to arrive at outer instead of only local markets.

Agglomeration and system economies offer learning and specialization opportunities because of more prominent firm thickness. This is a significant factor in deciding the probability of being a HGF. For instance, Ethiopian plants situated in or near enormous urban focuses have a more noteworthy opportunity of achieving high-development status versus the ones found more remote away. In Thailand, firms that are increasingly associated with others by means of proprietorship systems are likewise bound to encounter high development.

Outside market linkages as estimated by an association's sending out status, portion of exporters or FDI beneficiaries in a given area or part, or imports of innovation have added to high-development designs for firms in India, Hungary, Mexico, and Tunisia. Firms that pay higher wages have a more noteworthy probability of along these lines accomplishing high development mirroring the key job that human capital plays in firm execution. The commitment of establishing chiefs and workers is seen as basic in deciding future firm development in Brazil. There is solid proof that little and developing businesses are significant motors of thriving, representing a lopsided measure of work development. Projects intended to help start and scale these businesses which we characterize as economically practical, with 5 to 250 workers, and potential and aspiration for development have gotten well known among benefactors. Many significant establishments, including the International Labor Organization, World Bank, and USAID, are supporting activities to assist entrepreneurs with extending their businesses through aptitudes advancement, financing, mentorship, and market linkages.

However, even huge scope, business-bolster programs oftentimes neglect to experience thorough effect appraisals and battle to fuse best practices from existing examination into program structure. Projects frequently choose various models for instance, a light-contact study hall model that arrives at a huge gathering of entrepreneurs versus a higher-contact, counseling model that arrives at just a couple in view of hunches instead of proof. In any case, what does the proof scholarly proof, in light of trial examines really inform us regarding whether these projects help businesses develop? What's more, what can the associations that run these projects gain from it to structure increasingly compelling intercessions?

Among little firms, awards, value, and other risk tolerant capital structures drive more development than customary credits. Capital is regularly a significant requirement to business development in emerging markets, which need vigorous banking and credit frameworks. The risk development of the microcredit business over the most recent quite a few years has somewhat filled this hole with credit items for smaller scale and independent ventures. In any case, ongoing proof proposes that the exacting installment structures of these advances keep businesses from utilizing them for the higher-risk and longer-term ventures that are fundamental for development.

An enormous collection of research shows constrained long-term impacts of conventional microcredit advances on business execution, while one examination found that just presenting a two-month effortlessness period into the credit reimbursement plan prompted businesses utilizing the advances for more risks yet better yield ventures. Conversely, businesses are bound to utilize awards and value, or semi value items, for ventures that relate to more prominent generally development. Randomized analyses on awards to microenterprises have demonstrated continued normal month to month returns of 5–30%. What's more, a later appraisal of $50,000 awards to new businesses found that the awards prompted a 37 rate point improve in the probability of business endurance three years after the fact, and a 23 rate point improve in the probability of a business utilizing at least 10 laborers.

The regular presumption that specialists consistently know best, which underlies most business-bolster program structures, is not in every case genuine. Studies propose that it is amazingly difficult for givers to choose high-potential firms, and even specialists perusing full business plans battle to anticipate business execution any superior to forecasts that utilization essential information on firm socioeconomics and execution. Interestingly, at any rate one examination of microenterprises in India found that peer entrepreneurs are essentially better at anticipating future firm accomplishment than expectations dependent on review information alone.

Past choosing businesses, business systems, and different stages that include routinely trading data among entrepreneurs, for example, month to month gatherings among supervisors from various ventures are likewise successful at dispersing best practices and at last driving development; one thorough investigation discovered deals increments of 8–10% from taking part in a friend information sharing system. Yet, the structure of this commitment matters a ton: similarly, that it is ideal to rehearse tennis with somebody who is somewhat superior to anything you in the event that you need to improve your game, considers show that entrepreneurs get the most incentive out of friends whose businesses have comparative qualities yet higher generally speaking execution than their own (while not being immediate contenders).

Standard study hall preparing may cost not exactly individualized help, however, is commonly less powerful. The requirement for minimal effort, versatile arrangements has made institutionalized homeroom preparing models an especially mainstream approach to give business preparing. Nonetheless, a wide collection of research shows that a large number of the most across the board programs utilizing this model do not really prompt businesses changing their practices to spike development. Conversely, individualized counseling administrations, while costly, have demonstrated significantly more strong impacts. Bigger firms expanded profitability by 11% following administration counseling, recovering the moderately significant expense of counseling administrations in under a year. When contemplating cost-viability, it is enticing to concentrate on the cost side, however, it merits remembering that modest mediations that do not deliver results are at last less savvy than progressively costly ones that show genuine effect.

Mentorship can be useful, yet extraordinary mentorship structures accomplish various results. Accessible proof proposes that mentorship can assist entrepreneurs with changing their practices and quicken business development. In any case, not all mentorship programs are similar, and various sorts of tutors can influence entrepreneurs in an unexpected way. An examination in Uganda found that a program with worldwide guides made entrepreneurs bound to fundamentally "rotate" their general business procedure, while an investigation in Kenya indicated that nearby tutors helped drive a 20% expansion in firm benefits during the mentorship time frame (in spite of the fact that businesses did not support this development past the mentorship time frame).

It's significant not to overlook the interest side. Most business bolster programs normally center around the stockpile side of the market, since business limit is legitimately under the organizations' control and can be impacted by one-time mediations. Facilitating imperatives on the interest side can be an amazing pathway to development. This can incorporate direct market linkage assistance with global purchasers, government agreements, or associations with worldwide corporate stock chains, which have all demonstrated specific guarantee as roads for quickening the development of private companies. For instance, one program interfacing Egyptian floor covering creators to European purchasers prompted an expansion in item quality and income every hour, even with no critical capital speculation or extra conventional preparing.

We need more proof, specifically around various business portions. While the current scholastic proof on supporting little and developing businesses gives us a solid beginning stage for structuring progressively successful projects, significant research holes remain. The vast majority of the present proof depends on programs that emphasis on microenterprises or enormous firms, and does not take into account more-nuanced focusing of various help structures for various business sections, specifically around the alleged missing center those unreasonably huge for microenterprise-cantered programming yet not yet huge enough to get to a scope of market bolster benefits all alone. An ongoing report from the Collaborative for Frontier Finance gives an increasingly careful division approach, and future research can be substantially more pertinent to specialists by expressly consolidating this kind of division.

Projects intended to help little and developing businesses without a doubt mean well, yet thorough tests show that not all projects really lead to business development. While there are still holes in our insight into what works, ebb, and flow investigate gives us a fantastic beginning stage for structuring proof based projects to assist entrepreneurs with satisfying their latent capacity, make occupations, and eventually prod financial development. Around the world, policymakers need to know how they can best utilize their assets to spike a flourishing economy an economy that can contend and develop, create employments, increment livelihoods, and give improved items and administrations to the populace. They perceive that for economies to flourish, rivalry, stir, or dynamism is required; where new pursuits rise and develop and different firms exit. Right now, consideration has as of late cantered around a little subset of alleged high-development firms. These organizations enter, improve, and scale inside a relatively short time allotment, making unbalanced an incentive as business, salary, and improved items or administrations.

Improving our insight and comprehension of developed firms in developing countries is basic to improving viability of intercessions to spike work formation and increment profitability. Notwithstanding, the greater part of what we comprehend about development entrepreneurship today depends on information from Europe, North America, furthermore, the more extensive gathering of upper-pay OECD-part countries, just in light of the fact that this is the place most dependable information is accessible. We hence know far less about development entrepreneurship in a developing nation setting. Getting entrepreneurship, the procedures by which firms enter and leave the market, and specifically, the idea of growing firms, is essential to our comprehension of the procedure of auxiliary change, and eventually, expanded profitability.

Auxiliary change is the way toward reallocating society's elements of formation across areas. This happens through the withdrawal and exit of certain organizations, which at that point opens up assets that can be reallocated to extending firms. Right now, we can comprehend the significance of entrepreneurship as a principle driver of inventive decimation diverted by means of firm section, development, compression, and exit. A structure interfacing entrepreneurial movement to monetary development ought to recognize the smaller scale monetary establishments of development, accentuate the job of information externalities in the development process, and distinguish middle of the road linkages from entrepreneurial movement to financial advancement. Information overflows encourage development, which thus drives development. Entrepreneurship adds to development by filling in as a component to encourage information overflowing from existing exercises of occupant firms or colleges to new and creative ones. Since it encourages the overflow and commercialization of information that may in any case have stayed torpid and commercialized inside the occupant firm, entrepreneurship has a positive sway on development and in this way on development.

There are general two sorts of entrepreneurs: those that need to misuse an apparent business (opportunity entrepreneurs), and those that are driven into entrepreneurship since all different opportunities for work are either missing or inadmissible (need entrepreneurs). Along comparable lines. Individuals taking part in various sorts of entrepreneurship are distinctive in nature and react in an unexpected way to arrangement changes and financial cycles. Truth be told, many bombed entrepreneurial strategies are defective in that they neglect to recognize heterogeneous sets of entrepreneurial entertainers. Specifically, just an unimportant portion of subsistence entrepreneurs will progress to transformational entrepreneurs.

The progression of jobless to independently employed small scale entrepreneurs is multiple times higher than the progression of jobless to entrepreneurial business (proprietors of firms that employ others). Further, section into independent work is frequently portrayed by a low degree of human capital. It is spurred predominantly by a longing to help families. In the meantime, turning into a business proprietor that procures others (transformational entrepreneur) is by and large described by more significant levels of human capital, and higher readiness to take risks. The differentiation between the two ordered kinds of entrepreneurship can take a wide range of names, contingent upon the creator. High-impact entrepreneurship is essentially particular from just the production of new firms, in essence. High-impact entrepreneurship is advancement driven and makes riches and development through extension, and bringing new formations to business sectors.

In general, more elevated levels of transformational/opportunity entrepreneurship are regularly connected with higher levels of total financial development. To this end, contemplates that take a gander at the absolute entrepreneurial movement (without recognizing transformational versus subsistence) may not disclose to us much. Significant levels of all out entrepreneurial movement regularly connote elevated levels of need entrepreneurs, which is regularly not demonstrative of an effective economy. A key pointer might be whether the kind of entrepreneurial movement being considered envelops advancement exercises.

Global entrepreneurship monitor (GEM) describes (information on entrepreneurship from both developing also, developed countries), that significant levels of aggregate entrepreneurship are related with higher financial development just in higher-salary countries where advancement is progressively normal. In developing countries, the relationship between absolute entrepreneurial movement (of which the tremendous sum depends on need) and monetary development is negative. Lone potential high-development entrepreneurs are emphatically connected with financial development, while different types of entrepreneurial action are most certainly not.

While need entrepreneurs despite everything give significant sources of work and salary for some destitute individuals in developing countries, they do not appear to have the same differential effect on total financial development as transformational firms. Further, there is a unique arrangement of high-development firms that normally seek after advancement as a way to development among transformational/opportunity entrepreneurs. Hence, entrepreneurship writing shows a recharged center around high-development firms. It is likewise critical to take note of that people are most certainly not simply separated into classifications of "subsistence" and "transformational" entrepreneurs by minor mishap. Or maybe, the settled in decides of the game that determine the family member settlements to various entrepreneurial exercises play a key job in deciding the assignment of entrepreneurship.

More to the fact of the matter, society's standards and organizations help decide if entrepreneurial exercises will be put toward gainful or ineffective bearings that can altogether influence an economy's beneficial growth. This proposes a significant job for approach to change the "rules of the game," to assume a functioning job in the assignment of entrepreneurial movement, and in this way to possibly decide the breakdown of entrepreneurial movement toward either need driven or transformational purposes.

Firm-level exact research underpins the idea that high-development firms contribute extraordinarily to item and process advancement, in this way driving efficiency gains and including an incentive for their economies. While huge firms may put more in all out dollar value in advancements, entrepreneurial firms are increasingly innovation intensive comparative with size and produce developments all the more proficiently. The nature of developments turning out of entrepreneurial firms might be higher and levels and nature of commercialization of advancements are higher furthermore, more radical for entrepreneurial firms than for other kinds of firms. Entrepreneurial firms are more R&D escalated than the normal perpetual firm. Moreover, entrepreneurial firms give a moderately huge portion of a state's worth included development y decidedly influencing efficiency development. Emerging firms are significant in light of the fact that they produce business for different organizations in the neighborhood economy. Their audit attests that emerging firms regularly begin little and nearby, in this way, an enormous piece of the expense of their products sold and capital uses goes to other residential businesses. This demonstrates an amazing monetary multiplier impact of the achievement of only a hardly any development situated firms. Furthermore, they state, emerging firms help fill in as market aggregators by buying contributions from miniaturized scale and little firms, in this manner filling in as a basic connection between littler providers and clients further up the worth chain.

Advancements by entrepreneurial firms may have positive ramifications by upgrading rivalry also, expanding markets, in this manner eventually upgrading purchaser decision. The accompanying structure: in the more drawn out term, fruitful quickly developing new firms elevate expanded effectiveness because of strengthened rivalry and procedure advancement and upgrade showcase request because of item advancement. This prompts a more noteworthy assortment of items and better correspondence to the assorted variety of buyer inclinations, which has significant suggestions for purchasers in developing countries where propelled products and ventures may not arrive at remote territories.

High pace of firm section in the U.S. is related with work development; higher start up rates are related with positive business development for agglomerated/high efficiency regions; higher start up rates lead to since quite a while ago run business formation in 30 Portuguese locales; higher start up rates lead to business formation in 40 Dutch areas; higher start up rates are related with national business development over the long-term for all OECD countries. Be that as it may, we come back to a qualification between the arrangement of all firms entering the market at some random point and the unique set of high-performing firms that will in the end develop.

Solitary a little arrangement of entering firms will endure and in this way develop. Most discoveries on endurance rates recommend that up to 33% of every single new firm do not make due past two years. Therefore, when we talk about youthful, little firms, we are discussing a unique arrangement of firms that constantly enter and leave the market, at the same time making and obliterating employments. More current research from the U.S. proposes this dynamic of new and youthful organizations being made and kicking the bucket in a condition of extreme challenge is answerable for the additions in net occupation formation. The net business impacts of the fast procedure of passage what's more, leave (beat) among little; youthful firms are thought to be certain by and large, at any rate for developed countries.

As opposed to customarily held convictions that private ventures make most private part employments, more up to date look into that utilizes statistics information from the U.S. also, controls for age, finds that it is youthful firms and new businesses that are the most significant sources of net employment formation. Early look into by Birch41 built up the view that SMEs are the significant motors of work formation in the U.S. Many years of SME strategy in the U.S. what's more, different countries depend on this view.

In any case, employments the U.S. Registration Bureau Business Dynamics Statistics and Longitudinal Business Database, finds that, when controlling for age, there is no orderly connection between firm sizes what's more, firm development. They recommend that on the grounds that new firms tend to be little, the finding of a precise backwards relationship between firm size and net development rates in earlier investigations is completely inferable from the way that newest firms are characterized in the littlest size classes. The suggestion for these discoveries is that strategies that target businesses of a certain size, while overlooking the job old enough, will probably have constrained achievement in improving employment formation.

They utilize this as the reason for suggestions to target strategy mediations to address difficulties that youthful firms and, especially, new businesses face (administrative difficulties and market disappointments). The constructive outcome of firm passage on business development is inferable just to a small amount of the alleged high performing firms. Any given associate of firms will never have higher business levels than when they are first made. Once more, this is identified with the way that a tremendous number of those organizations made would not get by in the long-term. He recommends that of those enduring firms, about 90% would not develop by any stretch of the imagination, and will be left with the equivalent number of representatives as when they began. Just around 5 to 10% of enduring firms will have a bigger number of representatives any time after they were made.

Across various countries and topographies, little quantities of firms add to unbalanced measures of new openings. Be that as it may, this end cannot be unhesitatingly drawn without information from additionally developing countries. Youthful and little firms are the primary drivers of net occupation formation apply similarly to developing countries, utilizing dependable evaluation information. Moreover, there is proof that the accomplishment of development situated firms has more extensive monetary benefits past commitments to work development.

These more extensive advantages incorporate cultivating advancement and profitability gains, reallocating the elements of formation what's more, driving auxiliary change, upgrading rivalry, and expanding markets, the entirety of which at last improve customer decision. Be that as it may, quite a bit of this examination will in general originate from developed countries. There is a deficiency of direct investigation of High growth firms in developing countries, both as far as their commitments to work, and their economy-wide advantages.

Furthermore, a few creators note that there are not many hypothetical systems that connect entrepreneurship to monetary development. Progressively exact research should be possible on the microeconomic establishments and moderate information sources that interface the two, especially for developing countries. Writing that centers around the individual level characteristics the accomplishment of entrepreneurial firms excessively to the qualities of individuals, for the most part the establishing entrepreneur or establishing group. Basic attributes regularly referred to incorporate instruction levels, work understanding, what's more, gender, and furthermore mental characteristics of people.

Inside the investment business, for example, as much spotlight is put on the limit of the administration group of the firm as on the business itself. In fact, in one review, financial speculators credited 65% of disappointments inside their portfolio organizations to issues inside the new businesses' administration teams. Higher degrees of instruction of the firm originators will in general anticipate firm development. There is an edge impact of instruction on firm development designs. SMEs with exceptionally taught proprietors will in general develop all the more rapidly, yet a nation explicit limit must be gone after a firm to encounter this development impact.

Entrepreneurs with more long periods of work experience will in general have more quickly developing firms. Work experience will in general assistance entrepreneurs both straightforwardly, through improving direct information and firm abilities, also, by implication, through systems and contacts. Entrepreneurs with a specific limit of work involvement with endlessly beat the individuals who had less experience. Work experience is especially significant on the off chance that it happened inside a similar division. In developing countries, development entrepreneurs will in general originate from having been recently utilized as administrators in the equivalent or on the other hand comparable division, frequently by an outside firm. High growth firms are normally possessed by guys, yet women can be viable proprietors if certain authoritative requirements are lightened. Women owned firms face altogether more obstructions than male-possessed firms regarding uneven rights, commitments, and lawful securities. They subsequently develop at more slow rates than male-possessed firms on average.

This could likewise be on the grounds that women watch out for possess firms that are packed in more slow developing parts, frequently due to obstructions to section confronting females in emerging firms. Regardless of this, women are exceptionally successful firm proprietors, with more elevated levels of work efficiency on normal than normal and practically identical conclusion rates to firms owned by men. While the traditional conviction is that entrepreneurship is for the most part the region of the extremely youthful, which is apparently liberated and ready to face challenges what's more, challenge set up methods for getting things done, the information proposes something else.

Development entrepreneurship will in general be concentrated among mid-profession people, somewhere in the range of 35 and 45 years of age. The mean and middle age of all entrepreneurs in the study was 45, and the age dissemination of first-time authors was most elevated in the late 30s and mid-40s. Notwithstanding, the likelihood of beginning a business decreases after 50. The greater part of this examination is centered around the U.S. furthermore, other developed countries. Locus of control, risk hunger, inspiration, and a craving to learn and organize by the entrepreneur all appear to be identified with entrepreneurial victory. Much has been expounded on the potential normal mental attributes of effective entrepreneurs.

Advances in credit chance approaches and prescient conduct exploit forefront look into in this field by utilizing realized mental attributes to anticipate entrepreneurial achievement or disappointment. While the adequacy of prescient conduct techniques is as yet questionable, a few investigations have enterprises to utilize thorough strategies to recognize potential entrepreneurs. Extraversion, chance taking, what's more, receptiveness to encounter is fundamentally identified with entrepreneurial goals among business graduates. Neither interior nor outside locus of control was found to significantly affect entrepreneurial expectations in spite of different investigations finding so. In any case, in an investigation of entrepreneurial pioneers, Ernst, and Youthful found that effective entrepreneurs join an inside locus of control with an eagerness to face challenges what's more, hold onto opportunities, alongside enthusiasm, perseverance, also, an eye for specialties and market gaps. An inner locus of control is characterized as a confidence in the capacity of an individual to control one's condition and results.

High-performing competitors; while everybody can learn a game and become capable, just some have the possibility to get serious at a national or universal level. Additionally, among those that do have potential, the individuals who approach know-how and systems outflank contrasted with those that do not. Funding financial specialists in developed economies have since quite a while ago utilized an individual focal point to evaluate opportunity and risk. They reliably property a high extent of disappointments to issues inside the supervisory crew. In any case, it is not clear if financial specialists in developing countries would see a similar reason for disappointment in their portfolios, or on the other hand if firm-level elements or parts of the business enabling condition assume a progressively conspicuous job.

These most normally identify with age of the firm, size of the firm, and the division inside which the firm is working. Activity formation comes for the most part from youthful firms furthermore, new businesses. Almost all net occupation formation since 1980 has happened in firms not exactly five years of age, and that, without new businesses, net employment formation for the American economy would have been negative in everything except a bunch of those years. As a rule, the net expansion of employments from year to year originates from three sources: new businesses, youthful firms (ages one to five), and the biggest and most established organizations. This produces to some degree a free weight impact, with work formation happening at the most youthful and most seasoned parts of the bargains age range, and low occupation formation happening in between.

The affirmation that high-development firms are regularly youthful firms in the U.S. is validated by information from a few developing countries. Concentrates in both Latin American and Africa show that youthful, little firms are bound to appear high paces of development, as contrasted and more established firms of comparative size and sector. Organizations will in general experience their significant extension periods in their third year of activity (on average). The normal development pace of firms diminishes with age. An explanation behind this is firms will in general either develop rapidly from the start, or on the other hand leave the market, and afterward level off their development ways once they arrive at the ideal size for their area and geology. A little number of youthful and little firms are the most unique as far as including employments, on net. In taking a gander at geographic breakdowns of employment formation in districts of India, position development is anticipated by higher groupings of new and youthful foundations. In any case, regardless of whether high-development firms are constantly youthful. Firms are in reality generally old, with a normal age of 25 and right around 95% of them being more seasoned than five years. Actually, there is no relationship between a development firm and either age, size, or part.

Some exact investigations covering the developing world locate that littler firms become quicker than bigger firms. However, there are a few researches writing on whether this holds useful for all countries. Huge firms assume a significant job for work makers among high-development firms. In their enterprises to expose certain legends in regards to the profile of High growth firms, most of High growth firms are in actuality bigger than recently accepted. This is a significant discussion around the job of firm size and development rates, and one that merits consideration through future research, particularly in developing countries.

Emerging firms can be found across numerous different divisions in the economy. In spite of the fervor in numerous approach hovers over the progressive segments, there should be an alert against such a concentration as an indicator of development. High growth firms are not really synonymous with innovative firms and that there is, truth is told, an expansive sectoral heterogeneity to emerging firms all in all. Just around 15% of emerging firms work in innovation sectors. Policymakers ought to be wary toward strategies furthermore, sectoral advancement plots that anticipate quick development coming about solely from IP or new innovation advancements.

We can look to specific high-development divisions over the past decade to distinguish potential high-development firms. In the U.S., the data innovation division, alongside retail, social insurance, convenience, nourishment administrations, proficient, logical, and specialized administrations have demonstrated solid occupation formation, and we can look to these divisions to discover emerging entrepreneurs. Emerging firms will in general exist in all ventures, yet that they are generally progressively visit in information serious administration businesses and in instruction and healthcare.

Additional firm attributes that are thought to add to firm development are outside ownership, commitment in trade activities, what's more, extending to laborers formal employment opportunity training. There are various nation explicit investigations that investigate these highlights of firms as being connected with periods of high-development. Fruitful entrepreneurs, who lead High growth firms, flourish in situations with different variables cooperating to structure an entrepreneurial environment. The entrepreneurship environment important for developing entrepreneurs contains helpful strategy, markets, capital, human aptitudes, culture, and bolster components meeting up to give an empowering environment.

Studies that assess the coupling limitations to development for potential High growth firms tend to locate numerous interconnected components, which consolidate to either make or farthest point an effective entrepreneurial biological system. Acquiring long-term risk capital, access to protection, aptitude deficiencies in potential. Representatives, excessively oppressive work guidelines that limit their capacity to employ laborers under adaptable conditions, absence of administrative abilities, and the accessibility and cost of premises.

The OECD's demonstrative structure characterizes an entrepreneurial environment as a lot of interconnected entrepreneurial entertainers, entrepreneurial associations, organizations, and procedures that officially and casually blend to interface, intervene, and administer the presentation inside the nearby entrepreneurial environment. Similarly, they all take a multidimensional way to deal with estimation, considering the different spaces that can influence entrepreneurship in a district and how they interface with each other. Which components of an entrepreneurial biological system matter most for entrepreneurial results is an issue of some discussion. The following is a concise conversation of the different components that are thought to create an entrepreneurial biological system. There is proceeded with banter on which of these data sources ought to be organized by policymakers also, which matter most to an effective environment.

Governmental guideline is a significant part of any dynamic private division, yet excessively difficult administrative systems regularly fill in as restricting limitations to firm development. There is solid proof that an overwhelming administrative weight adversely impacts the pace of new firm entry. While little and casual firms are regularly ready to work by bypassing government guidelines and tax collection, they risk getting increasingly unmistakable as they develop; consequently, high-development firms will in general be formal enterprises. Agreements with governments and huge universal purchasers are frequently forbidden for casual firms, due to lawful documentation necessities. Along these lines, casual little firms will in general develop more gradually than formal firms. Finding formal status has a positive impact on firm development, significantly in the wake of controlling for firm size, age, and proficiency. This postures critical boundaries to development for some organizations in developing countries, as by far most of these organizations will in general be casual.

A flourishing and energetic SME part (portrayed by a high pace of section of new and creative entrepreneurial firms and exit of less fruitful ones) is related without hardly lifting a finger of passage and exit because of a low authoritative weight, have sound contract implementation systems, successful property rights enlistment systems, solid lenders' privileges insurances, low taxation rate on new and little firms, and progressively adaptable work markets.

A well-working entrepreneurial biological system has plentiful accessibility of human capital in the type of talented representatives and supervisors. A developing proof base focuses to the differential effects of administrative limit and the board rehearses on firm development. For instance, in Mexico, a randomized investigation discovered that counseling administrations to SMEs produced an 80% expansion in deals and a 120% increment in profits. Rather, entrepreneurs in the two countries featured the significance of human capital increments (counting the executives and specialized preparing) as a huge need.

New companies may, truth be told, be increasingly reliant on human capital than officeholder firms. New companies may require explicit aptitude and exceptionally talented laborers more than officeholder firms, since they frequently need different assets, for example, capital, assets, and access to back. Right now, human capital contained inside the authors and laborers of a start-up is frequently its most noteworthy resource. A study of 338 Italian new technology-based firms from 1995 to 2008 estimated the long-term impacts of the authors' underlying human capital at the hour of firm beginning up. It found a positive and critical nearness of an "entrepreneurial engraving impact" applied by authors' degrees of human capital on adventure development.

Access to back is a key element of an entrepreneurial biological system and one that is frequently deficient for little and new firms in developing countries. A wide assortment of writing recommends that little firms have more trouble getting to back than bigger firms. Access to fund might be fundamental for little firm development, however, insufficient without anyone else. Ease of credit imperatives can prompt improved firm execution and work growth. Entrance to outer fund builds the development of both work and deals among little firms.

There is a solid positive connection between firm financing and the pace of work development and that there is a 70% more noteworthy impact for SMEs than for enormous firms. Regardless of whether earlier access to bank fund is an indicator of firm achievement is something that is discussed. Access to back for advancement is regularly a result of the general business condition. Bigger firms or firms with higher development potential were influenced all the more legitimately by the general business condition, as their development is tied intimately with venture, which is in turn is dictated by and large financial instability. In additional unpredictable economies, reserve funds and venture are reduced.

For sure, some case that one of the greatest market disappointments for potential high growth firms in developing countries is identified with the challenges in financing development, as these organizations frequently depend on development concentrated development. Development infers dubious rewards. Development risks will in general be exacerbated in the setting of developing countries, where the way proportional is progressively unpredictable, and capital is increasingly hesitant to get involved. Of specific note is the pretended by enlightening asymmetries in limiting access to fund for little and youthful firms. Money related segment framework changes are intended to diminish such enlightening erosions.

Changes help increment SME access to fund and lower intrigue rates, alleviate negative impacts of low bank rivalry inside countries, diminish insurance required to make sure about advances, increment loaning collateralized by moveable resources, and lift firm execution in zones, for example, deals, and employment. A key component of a fruitful entrepreneurial biological system is the capacity of an entrepreneur to get to business sectors, both worldwide what's more, residential. Having a broad interpersonal organization is an advantage that can encourage an entrepreneur's entrance to markets.106 Many investigations across countries and ventures affirm the thought that development entrepreneurs tend to originate from affectionate networks, agglomerated systems, and particular ethnic networks that control methods of formation for certain sectors. Bunches (geographic and sectoral agglomerations of ventures) may likewise encourage little firm development by upgrading level, just as vertical, linkages.

Of specific note are the impacts of alleged agglomeration economies, or businesses that bunch together in explicit geographic zones, normally urban communities. The beneficial outcomes on firm advancement and development because of agglomeration are because of a superior accessibility of foundation, more opportunities for learning, impersonation through work turnover and connection with providers, what's more, bigger markets for gifted work, crude materials, and output. The provincial component of high-development firms ought not to be downplayed truth be told, this is apparently the main quality of high-development firms where there seems, by all accounts, to be across the board understanding. These systems of firms include a high level of specialization and tend to profit by overflows because of geological vicinity furthermore, are found across countries and enterprises.

There are, indeed, few districts in most industrialized countries that stick out with a lot higher portion of quickly developing firms than their numbers in the general number of firms would suggest. Culture, characterized as the fundamental framework of qualities specific to a particular gathering or society, is thought to shape the improvement of character attributes and may inspire people in a general public to draw in, or not connect with, in specific practices. In this manner, a culture that supports entrepreneurial action through its determination of qualities is an element of the entrepreneurial biological system.

Entrepreneurial direction (an inner locus of control joined with an inclination toward advancement) is bound to show up in individualistic, low-vulnerability evasion societies than in collectivistic, high-vulnerability evasion societies. The drivers of financial development are identified with inclination arrangement and the transmission procedure of families. Additionally, the current conveyance of inclinations in the populace decides the potential for financial development, mainly through the probability of people's quest for entrepreneurship. They show that quickly developing countries have bigger portions of the populace showing inclinations helpful for imaginative exercises. The impact of venture capital (VC) on entrepreneurial section was more fragile in progressively various leveled and preservationist societies.

The basis for open mediation in private markets is frequently supported by method for clarifying restricting limitations on firms, and how open mediation can ease those imperatives. The coupling imperatives to firm development contrast extensively among transformational and subsistence entrepreneurs.

Though subsistence entrepreneurs might be restricted by access to transient credit or difficult business start-up systems, transformational entrepreneurs with desires for development doubtlessly face imperatives in the guideline of work and item advertises access to longer-term hazard capital, and generally macroeconomic stability. Constraints that influence high-development firms and advancement exercises, in specific, will in general identify with showcase disappointments that confine the free progression of information and new thoughts, the arrangement of and support of systems and social capital, and the progression of hazard capital that can be utilized for innovation.

The main wellspring of market disappointments alluded to in the writing includes organize externalities, which happen at the point when an association's worth is restrictive on the geographic vicinity of integral firms, foundations, and people. Along these lines local or geographic stages, which enterprises to cultivate entrepreneurial systems that advance information overflows are regularly sought after as approach. This identifies with the "entrepreneurial environment" approach. The second wellspring of market disappointment centers around information externalities. Information is regularly taken to be an open great.

Since neighborhood conditions may decide an association's or a person's capacity to get to information, it is imagined that open arrangement can assume an immediate job in advancing speculations in information, which can give the premise to prodding entrepreneurial firms into turning out to be high-development firms. The third wellspring of market disappointments includes the exhibition impact radiating from knowledgebase entrepreneurial action. Early entrepreneurs that have the opportunity to watch other fruitful firms and demonstrate the reasonability of specific advancements commonly have a bit of leeway over different firms in districts or on the other hand, countries that do not have this exhibit impact.

The exhibition impact ought to instigate consequent information based entrepreneurship, and along these lines, regions that need self-evident examples of overcoming adversity may stay troublesome conditions for yearning HGFs. There is banter on whether firms ought to be legitimately directed, or whether arrangement should concentrate on improving system conditions. The writing is agitated on which approach is better: focusing on explicit firms or concentrating on full scale approaches that upgrade rivalry what's more, ease requirements developed by advertise disappointments? Arrangements that invigorate development entrepreneurship and development ought to recognize the qualification between transformational and subsistence entrepreneurship also, focus on their methodologies as needs be. The essential qualification between subsistence/need furthermore, opportunity entrepreneurs.

However, numerous specialists note that by far most of entrepreneurship strategies in developing countries has neglected to make this differentiation, and in this manner has neglected to target appropriately the privilege gathering of firms. Rather, quite a bit of entrepreneurship approach is planned for supporting wide based entrepreneurship and firm start-up, which has little ramifications for business development, advancement, and auxiliary transformation. Only promising making of new businesses would not change stagnated economies.

Despite the fact that the significance of high-development entrepreneurs has been generally settled, in a mind-boggling number of cases government approaches despite everything will in general spotlight on broad-based entrepreneurship, without focusing on development exercises or development situated firms. Truth be told, in numerous developing countries, the money related foundation and going with arrangement condition is better prepared to give miniaturized scale financing to little, useless subsistence firms, which makes bottlenecks for transformational entrepreneurs, and produces the unintended outcomes of advancing inefficient entrepreneurship.

Thus, governments ought to recognize strategies that bolster all entrepreneurship from one viewpoint, and strategies that help the formation and support of high-development, creative firms on the other. As talked about in the past sub-area, many market disappointments that compel the advancement exercises of potential HGFs identify with issues in the business condition. Maybe the greatest one is an absence of access to extension capital, which, for potential HGFs specifically, requires the extension of establishments that encourage the development of investment and private value.

Much research has set up that vehicles that expand entrepreneurial fund to little yet developing firms are effective at both apportioning credit (and choosing fruitful firms), and at helping firms to develop. What's more, utilize a relapse brokenness way to deal with assess the effect of holy messenger financing on firm development, finding that the expansion of entrepreneurial capital is related with a 20 to 25% higher probability of firm endurance after four a long time and a 16 to 19% improve in the probability of inevitably extending to at any rate 75 workers. Along these lines, there is a contention that governmental approach ought to be engaged on opening up private funding to arrive at potential HGFs. Approach that bolsters high-development potential, transformational firms ought to incorporate components of entrepreneurship arrangement, SME bolster systems, furthermore, development approach.

Inventive Entrepreneurship Perspective is outfitted explicitly to supporting the development of HGFs and varies from wide based SME approach in various regards. While SME approach is essentially about firm endurance, IEP should concentrate on the development of a couple select firms; while SME approach will in general take a gander at the firm as the standard unit of investigation, IEP will take a gander at the firm, and the individual transformational entrepreneur; while SME arrangement is fundamentally worried about leveling the playing field for little firms opposite huge firms, diminishing formality, and improving efficiency, IEP is concerned with defeating particular market disappointments at early focuses in the company's lifecycle, developing missing pieces of the environment (primarily identified with access to capital), and spots an exceptional accentuation on advancement over profitability.

This will frequently involve governments assuming a functioning job in framing solid connections among colleges and the private segment, giving appropriations to R&D ventures for directed firms, where proper, developing specific speculator abilities (for instance, governmental help to heavenly attendant and VC financial specialist networks), and work market and training strategies that explicitly plan to increment the stock and nature of entrepreneurs. A few instances of cement governmental arrangements that are effective at executing IEP are national acknowledgment grants for inventive entrepreneurs (Singapore), government arrangements to advance development and R&D at colleges, co-investment plans (Taiwan, Singapore), and diminishing prohibitive migration approaches (Chile, Singapore). Government strategy can assume a functioning job in setting up a fruitful entrepreneurial environment.

Anyway, it must take an all-encompassing perspective on the biological system. As a promoter for the "entrepreneurship biological system" way to deal with supporting HGFs, numerous governmental enterprises turn out badly in that they address just a couple of components of the biological system. Notwithstanding, the entrepreneurship biological system comprises of a lot of numerous components that associate in complex manners, and subsequently expansive based government backing ought to mirror this. They incorporate, among others, molding the biological system around neighborhood conditions and culture, abstaining from coordinating assets to just high-innovation segments, however, recognizing that most of HGFs are definitely not essentially tech-driven, handling social change when important, maintaining a strategic distance from over-designing bunches, however, helping them to develop naturally, distributing cash to new pursuits cautiously, and perceiving that numerous hatcheries do not developed triumphs, and transforming legitimate, bureaucratic, and administrative structures, without over-accentuating changes, and without accepting that these are sufficient to set up a fruitful entrepreneurial biological system.

The changes that have the best sway on adventure formation are decriminalizing insolvency, protecting investors from loan bosses, and permitting bombed entrepreneurs to rapidly begin once again. Governments have a significant job in building up the appropriate organizations to help spike the development of potential HGFs. Governments should center on alleged "system conditions" that have sway on firms at beginning times of the lifecycle. These incorporate strategies for example, decides, and guidelines that impact the expense of contracting the primary worker, the security of scholarly property rights for youthful and creative firms, lessening managerial obstructions to firm start-up, and monetary motivators, for example, lessening the negative results of leaving and firm disappointment.

Other structure conditions that are critical to cultivate firm development incorporate getting rid of backhanded expense systems preferring little enterprises (that can make unreasonable motivations for firms to stay little), center around redesigning also, making accessible quality framework, for example, force, streets, and transportation, update information foundation by boosting the private part to increment R&D uses, and advance approaches that help channel beginning period chance money to inventive movement. The most governments can (and ought to do) is dispense with approaches that impediment potential HGFs, for example, unified wage setting foundations, business insurance enactment, and foundations that decrease the motivating forces for VC speculation (for example, high capital additions charges). Positive things that governments can do incorporate executing solid social security and social protection frameworks, which can give pay security during times of vulnerability for both entrepreneurs and new representatives in entrepreneurial firms.

Therefore, enterprises to advance development money are likewise normal, either through direct arrangement of capital, or by improving system conditions and advancing jamming in of private capital. Models of this incorporate co-speculation vehicles, development of heavenly attendant financial specialist systems, and the improvement of VC reserves planned explicitly for firms that seek after advancement exercises in developing countries. Given the heterogeneous idea of HGFs, there is banter in the writing around whether potential HGFs can be distinguished ex-bet. As HGFs are heterogeneous in their qualities also, need steadiness in their development levels, there are genuine challenges in foreseeing which firms will develop, making them probably not going to be vehicles for focused open approach.

Consequently, goes this line of reasoning, approaches ought not to target explicit firms, yet rather ought to target institutional changes designed for the more extensive business condition to cultivate high-development firms. On the opposite side of the discussion is the contention that, while there is no arrangement of widespread attributes that permit us to foresee adequately which firms will develop, we can in any case make some fundamental expectations with respect to firm achievement and results. Especially, for firms or people that have effectively exhibited some moderate accomplishment in ahead of schedule organizes, or dependent on what we know from genuine HGFs.

In many cross-country contemplates, firm development has all the earmarks of being irregular or if nothing else roundabout in nature, and accordingly not unsurprising. Therefore, the accessible proof is not urging for policymakers to target HGFs to advance future firm development. Rather, additionally reassuring outcomes originate from examine that underpins a connection between business dynamism also, institutional components of the business condition for example, budgetary advancement, banking rivalry, and establishments that encourage better agreement authorization. Regardless of the proof that HGFs are without a doubt heterogeneous furthermore, in this manner hard to foresee ex-risk, there are some new testable models to foresee firm development.

Private companies can expand their odds of achievement and ensuing development in the event that they have sufficient capital, keep up great records and money related control, have the board understanding, have explicit plans, make use of expert exhortation, and have great financial planning. HGFs in the United Kingdom are heterogeneous and do not fit any pre-decided shape regarding part, age, or size. Be that as it may, they do not desert having the option to foresee the high development capability of these organizations. While they question that a solid prescient limit exists that can correctly spot firms that will experience a time of high development, they contend that a few firms may show "early signs," and subsequently focusing on them can be advocated.

Advancing new start-up formation by means of institutional changes, "potential" HGFs can and ought to be sourced from existing SMEs that show early indications of accomplishment. Such early signs incorporate a momentary period (over the course of one year, for instance) of better than expected development (between 10 to 30% incomes). While momentary development does not qualify as "high-development" by definition, it could be an indicator of future achievement. Also, certain subjective measures could be utilized, for example, evaluating organizations for late association changes, embracing another business model, looking for access to development capital instead of working capital, looking for help for internationalization (not simply sending out), and late expanding of staff numbers.

A promising new center region to recognize potential HGFs is through the perspective of the individual entrepreneur. When applied over a broadly delegate test, just 2% of show elevated levels of entrepreneurial ability, and as it shows low outstanding ability. Its appraisal claims that those distinguished as having excellent ability are 24 times bound to discover entrepreneurial achievement, and there is a 1 of every 20 possibilities of distinguishing an effective entrepreneur through its framework, versus a 1 of every 100 possibility through the all-inclusive community. Gallup's program is being guided with high schoolers in Costa Rica to test their prescient model of entrepreneurial talent, 134 and should it be fruitful, could enormously add to our comprehension of prescient models.

These strategies show a ton of guarantee in having the option to adequately anticipate development. A business plan rivalry was effective at distinguishing entrepreneurs with the potential to utilize a lot of capital. Using capital, they had the option to produce enterprises that enlist representatives and show quick development. The synthesis of the master boards, and their capacity to meet entrepreneurs eye to eye is a significant segment of the accomplishment of a challenge's prescient capacity.

Meeting potential entrepreneurs in person is a major part of the challenge's prescient limit, as there are numerous things that are as it were learned by means of vis-à-vis contact, for example, the individual's inspiration, readiness to learn, capacity to arrange, receptiveness, and comprehension of the general business in which the person in question works.

Another key part of the program is that the boards are made out of a mix of arrangement specialists, and specialists from the budgetary business, for example, funding or private value speculators. Numerous projects endure on the grounds that they do exclude the decisions of expert speculators. These financial specialists have key abilities that help to foresee the suitability of a business thought and the entrepreneurial characteristics of an association's head.

The menu of policy choices is a first enterprise at grouping the scope of instruments as of now accessible. To the degree conceivable given the points of confinement of time and assets, the Flagship study will look to survey the adequacy of the full cluster of strategies generally conjectured to have first-request impacts on the rise and consequent practicality of high-development firms. These incorporate not just government activities planned for improving entrepreneurs' access to capital, markets, information, and workforce ability, yet in addition rivalry approach, administrative arrangement, what's more, acquirement strategy. These strategies, alongside others, for example, advancement strategy and expertise improvement, are by and large "flat" or economy-wide. Likewise, there can be spatial methodologies (extraordinary monetary zones and so forth.), which give a solid entrepreneurial biological system/culture. There can likewise be firm-level intercessions given that, for instance, the executives redesigning is not programmed and requires development.

Social ventures are subject to getting an enormous part of their pay through the immediate offer of items and administrations to end customers. Incomes through deals to the open segment or to third division associations are a lot littler. This is likewise in accordance with the way that over portion of the social enterprises demonstrated that they got no help from open organizations and now and again were even impeded in accomplishing their objectives. Considering this, social enterprises are restricted in serving the most reduced salary classes and to work in parts that identify with meeting the essential needs of individuals (e.g., water and sanitation) as these offer less potential for benefit.

In the most recent decade, a move has occurred with respect to the job of private part ways to deal with taking care of social issues in developing and emerging countries and market direction have gotten far reaching being developed participation. Partners from people in general, private and common society segments are progressively giving assets to gainful organizations as opposed to open or non-benefit associations. While the portion of non-benefit associations in the arrangement of social speculators has sunk, a solid increment can be seen in revenue driven social enterprises just as associations that consolidate non-benefit and for-benefit lawful structures (known as cross breed structures). Social entrepreneurs who got financing from social speculators will in general be individuals from the instructive world class in the countries analyzed. By far most has a higher instructive degree, which does not amaze given the mind boggling difficulties in the administration of social enterprises. In any case, concentrating on the instructive first class leaves aside significant opportunities to pick up information from low-pay entrepreneurs whose instructive foundation might be increasingly constrained, yet who can add to building endogenous answers for their networks. Elective sources of pay, for example, long-term supply contracts with social enterprises are important to offer associations the chance to likewise support individuals living in the most minimal pay levels of the base of the pyramid.

More grounded collaboration between supporters of people in general, private, and third segments are expected to ideally use the qualities of every part and reclassify obsolete subsidizing structures being developed participation. To ensure non-benefit social ventures, an activity is required with respect to social speculators specifically to give progressively imaginative financing instruments that meet the financing needs of non-benefit social entrepreneurs. Numerous social issues do not at first loan themselves to a productive arrangement or require quite a while of planning to set up business sectors. Non-benefit social ventures assume a key job here and along these lines should be reinforced.

At last, comprehensive business models (e.g., social diversifying) are a promising method to include low-pay entrepreneurs. Social financial specialists ought to likewise re-evaluate their choice criteria so as to turn out to be increasingly available to a more extensive scope of entrepreneurs. What's more, umbrella associations, just as policymakers, are significant entertainers in advancing preparing and tutoring programs that get ready entrepreneurs from every instructive foundation to get to financing.

Chapter 5

ENVIRONMENT

In the event that we are to by and large handle environmental change, lift a huge number of individuals out of destitution, and comprehend our vitality, populace, and other asset requirements over the coming decades, the private division progressively holds the appropriate responses. Entrepreneurs, especially in quickly developing markets, are now giving answers for natural and social issues by building and developing businesses that preserve assets and improve employments. By finding better approaches to neatly give vitality or water, for instance, entrepreneurs are making gainful organizations that advantage the two individuals and the assets they rely on. Furthermore, entrepreneurs who lead little and medium estimated enterprises are frequently the best prepared to comprehend the bunch asset and social issues they experience in their networks, and discover answers for explain them.

Albeit ecological entrepreneurship keeps on holding incredible guarantee for economic improvement, it additionally faces extraordinary difficulties from a general market point of view: a requirement for a consistent stock of productive and versatile organizations, interest for these organizations from financial specialists prepared to convey capital, and strong value-based framework to associate this market interest. These difficulties have been clear in the part since financial specialists started to genuinely take a gander at ecological organizations in emerging markets as potential speculations longer than 10 years back.

To discover a few responses to these difficulties, we met various pioneers in ecological entrepreneurship improvement (a few of whom were instrumental in establishing the association where we right now work, New Ventures) to gather bits of knowledge into how the segment has become up until this point, and what requirements to happen to expand the commonness and accomplishment of natural entrepreneurs in emerging markets in coming decades. We featured crafted by New Ventures explicitly, given our expert jobs and New Ventures' long-standing involvement with the market. Be that as it may, we likewise needed to include the bits of knowledge of others from accomplice associations who have been driving significant work right now.

The thought that private ventures can have positive ecological effects while tackling a benefit is never again radical. In any case, it was all the more so in the late 1990's, the point at which the spotless tech idea was simply entering the commercial center, and the possibility of earth helpful organizations was generally untested, particularly for financial specialists and assets. Indeed, even the humanitarian area had not yet been utilizing adventure charity as an idea.

When establishing in the late 1990s, a pioneer in the segment that subsidizes clean vitality organizations in emerging markets, this was some time before discussions included terms, for example, mixed worth, sway contributing, scale, open private associations, and triple primary concern, there was a great deal of disclosing to do and a ton of pushback. Not even the preservation bunches were altogether ready 10 years prior. A few players, as Eco Enterprises Fund and Verde Ventures, were simply starting to consider supporting business dares to advance preservation and jobs, and their underlying speculations were centered decisively around securing biodiversity.

It was right now the World Resources Institute chose to dispatch New Ventures, middle for natural undertaking concentrated on emerging markets. New Ventures was made to discover promising ecological speculation bargains and carry these arrangements to financial specialists, subsequently demonstrating that there was a pipeline of productive natural organizations in emerging markets prepared to develop. To test the idea, New Ventures held an underlying financial specialist discussion in Brazil in 2002, displaying organizations from around Latin America, which was a major achievement. New Ventures has assumed an original job, alongside a portion of these early assets, in quickening arrangements and bringing financial specialists right off the bat in the game, as of now executive of Enterprise for the Majority at the Inter-American Development Bank and a previous New Ventures chief.

"At the point when New Ventures developed on the scene, one of its radical new thoughts was to not to 'green' existing organizations, yet to really distinguish and choose organizations that set natural contemplations at the center of their business model," said Aram Kang, Global Network Officer at New Ventures. New Ventures started recognizing driving ecological businesses, furnishing them with tutoring and increasing speed administrations, and afterward displaying them to financial specialists. "The thought was to give organizations that were ready to develop with the vital specialized help administrations and afterward serve them up with a royal flair to financial specialists," clarified Virginia Barreiro, a previous New Ventures executive and Global Profit pro at the IFC. By making a strong record of speculation arrangements and triumphs, New Ventures meant to demonstrate that the putting resources into natural organizations were sound.

New Ventures was likewise one of the main go-betweens to take advantage of speculation capital in-nation. The program developed the idea of ecological putting resources into the six countries where it worked such as Brazil, China, Colombia, India, Indonesia, and Mexico and assembled financial specialists to see the best of these organizations at speculator discussions every year. Furthermore, these confined systems helped fabricate important nearby systems, New Ventures assisted with the production of a festival of ecological entrepreneurship with in-nation financial specialist gatherings by building a gathering of individuals who are learned and amped up for putting resources into natural enterprises. It is hard to envision when putting into ecological entrepreneurs was viewed as option and radical.

Since its beginning in 1999, New Ventures has assisted with encouraging over $230 million in speculation into the organizations it has worked with, and two of its portfolio organizations have held IPOs in the previous two years; each organization has been valued at a few 100 million dollars. Assets explicitly committed to putting resources into natural organizations inside emerging markets have propelled. In 2005, for instance, Strauss Investment Fund, a customary store in Brazil and an early member in the New Ventures Investor Forums, propelled VC III, a US$15 million investment finance committed exclusively to putting resources into natural enterprises. What's more, albeit ecological putting resources into emerging markets is not yet standard, numerous standard players are starting to pay heed and get drew in with the idea.

Ten years back, no banks were keen on ecotourism for instance, a private speculation finance that makes credits to little enterprises in zones of high biodiversity significance. It was entirely testing to work with any business neighborhood or worldwide banks. Even some multilateral and reciprocal benefactors, similar to IFC and OPIC are engaged with sway putting and attempting to join putting resources into practical organizations to additionally green monetary development enterprises. A significant impetus for the development of natural contributing will be the making of an away from of effect estimation principles, so speculators keen on making ecological advantages can quantify the accomplishment of their ventures.

The impact reporting investing standards (IRIS) developed by the global impact investing network (GIIN), has been attempting to give a typical language to announcing social and natural execution, including markers for vitality, practical horticulture, and water. This sort of framework is essential to the proceeded with improvement both natural and social speculation.

As ecological contributing has developed, all the more as of late so has the buzz and network around power contributing. While interests in social and natural organizations have formally existed since the Quakers, and increased a great deal of force during the 1960s, the expression power contributing was really begat under past years. The underlying definition was contributing with "ecological and social advantages." Although the natural and social missions that numerous associations were taking a stab at appear to combine right now sway contributing, there regularly is by all accounts a concentration inside the developing effect contributing industry on social effects.

Security of assets is frequently subject to the financial improvement of encompassing networks, and monetary development will keep on relying upon the accessibility of assets, for example, clean water, and air. Ecological and social cannot be decoupled; sway contributing ought to incorporate condition, and it is extremely unlikely you can discuss one without the other. In any case, as per an ongoing JP Morgan report, 58% of the institutional respondents in the effect contributing division recognized themselves as having an essentially social power objective, 34% distinguished as both "social and natural," and just 8% characterized themselves as simply ecological.

It's extremely about the attention on advertising based arrangements, regardless of whether it's to ensure nature or serve poor people. The distinction in scale does not keep us from being imaginative, taking a gander at the bottlenecks and having an incorporated way to deal with the two sides of effect contributing. For example, early ecological establishments are regularly reprimanded by concentrating solely on biodiversity preservation. In any case, a large number of these establishments have as of late fused a social part into their statements of purpose. Conservation international (CI) is one of these establishments. The entire part of giving individuals financial motivations for natural preservation is at the center of what CI does you cannot simply make park storehouses with equipped watchmen, this is not reasonable over the long-term. "You need to ensure the network is completely purchased in and that there are social and monetary advantages," remarks Jennifer Morris, who additionally is VP and overseeing chief of CI.

The zones of cover and regular difficulties looked by the natural and social venture networks give an away from to joint effort on advancement of pipeline, supply of capital and making of foundation. Albeit natural putting and entrepreneurship in emerging markets has experienced a change from an early idea to an expanding market over the previous decade, clear difficulties to more noteworthy development remain. We despite everything need to look at the main concern and address models that show investment funds, increment benefits, and increment advertise get to, however, many accept that the case has been made for whether "natural" organizations have financial reasonability. The discussion is not whether these organizations are reasonable, just like the case ten years back. We've seen that they create benefits, can develop, and are a decent business speculation.

Venture into ecological and social businesses is developing, numerous financial specialists are emptying capital into emerging markets, and GDP development paces of NV countries keep on developing. In any case, for ecological entrepreneurship to find a good pace, must be three conditions satisfied, as in every single other market: there must be hearty interest from speculators for a pipeline of natural ventures, a promising inventory of enterprises prepared for venture, and strong value-based framework to empower these ventures.

So as to feature the advancement of these three important conditions, Next billion will include a progression of articles throughout the following a year, notwithstanding this basic piece, to animate conversation around ecological entrepreneurship, with an emphasis on SMEs and emerging markets. A few writers will post month to month articles about developing the economic situations for ecological SMEs around these three principle points: supply (of organizations), request (with respect to speculation capital), and framework (e.g., trade stages and measurements).

Emerging economies are countries «with a quick pace of financial improvement and government approaches preferring monetary advancement and the appropriation of a free market system. Since the late 1980's, have transitioned from halfway wanted to showcase based monetary frameworks, submitting themselves (in fluctuating degrees) to reinforcing their market instruments through advancement, financial adjustment, and the consolation of private enterprises. Emerging economies represented 52% of the worldwide populace and 38% of the world GDP, twice their offer in 1990. Just about a fourth of the Fortune Global 500 firms are presently situated in the emerging markets, contrasted with just 4% in 1995. Emerging economies are estimated to indent up 56% of the expansion in worldwide GDP during the period 2011–2016, however, would be liable for just 13% of the expansion in worldwide obligation, supplanting the industrialized countries as the bedrock of the universal money related framework.

Emerging economies are much of the time credited with the presence of an energetic entrepreneurial class. The foundation and development of private entrepreneurial enterprises has extraordinarily quickened the progress of these countries from overwhelmingly state-focused economies to serious markets and has pushed the pace of their financial improvement. As per the 2012 Global Entrepreneurship Monitor (GEM) report, between 4% (in Russia) and 23% (in Chile) of the populace matured 18–64 in these countries is as of now associated with beginning period entrepreneurial movement. Entrepreneurial enterprises add to both monetary development and market change. They balance work misfortunes in the state-claimed and huge business segment, transform mechanical and showcase developments into financial yield, give a persistent wellspring of authoritative change and restoration, and ceaselessly reaffirm the job of market-based monetary trade. To put it plainly, as somewhere else around the globe, entrepreneurial exercises in emerging economies can be bridled to turn into a motor of development, advancement, and occupation formation.

New firm arrangement and advancement relies on the presence and appropriate working of an arrangement of formal and casual establishments that help entrepreneurship. To be sure, fabricating, and supporting a fitting institutional foundation for the advancement of high-yearning, development situated entrepreneurship is fundamental for the proceeded with financial and social improvement of emerging economies. Right now, we investigate how college understudies in nine emerging economies, spread across three worldwide districts, see their individual national institutional conditions as far as their idealness or in any case for the advancement of entrepreneurship.

Foundations are generally acknowledged frameworks of training, advances, and rules of social association which are normatively settled in a general public, so practices in opposition to such practices, innovations, and rules could be socially objected and even authorized to guarantee consistence. To put it plainly, organizations are the key political, social, and lawful standard procedures that oversee the lead of all monetary movement. Understudies of institutional hypothesis contend that all vital and monetary action is implanted in a social and regularizing setting, and that such a setting inspires associations to comply with social standards and desires so as to be agreed authenticity and backing. At the end of the day, institutional hypothesis manages the administrative, social, and social impacts, both formal and casual, that advance the endurance and authenticity of an association, instead of concentrating exclusively on its proficiency looking for conduct. It characterizes them into administrative, regulating, and subjective classes.

Administrative foundations are officially established laws and guidelines of a general public or country which are normally arranged and officially authorized to guarantee consistence. Regulating organizations are less formal yet similarly successful guidelines set up by expert and exchange bodies to institutionalize and control the direct of their individuals. Psychological establishments are generally held convictions and qualities that characterize what conduct in social collaborations are socially suitable, and these are disguised through living and developing in a network.

The institutional condition influences the speed and extent of new firm arrangement and resulting improvement by figuring out what is normatively passable, and along these lines characterizing and delimiting opportunity spaces. Further, by endorsing what is socially satisfactory, the institutional condition likewise impacts the way toward accomplishing psychological and political authenticity, in this manner expanding the odds of endurance for a beginning up. In the event that the institutional condition is seen as antagonistic to entrepreneurial exercises, hopeful entrepreneurs will be less propelled to take part in new pursuit development and enter rivalry.

Post-section, if the institutional condition is seen as dubious or threatening, entrepreneurs will be reluctant to contribute time, cash, and exertion into long-term ventures, in this way puzzling the development of their enterprises. To catch this impact, the idea of institutional readiness, conceptualized as the limit of the institutional condition to help little and-medium-sized enterprises' key activities (key collusion development).

the institutional condition in many emerging economies, including the main ones, on the whole known as the BRIC (Brazil, Russia, India, and China) countries, is commonly seen to be troublesome for entrepreneurial enterprises.

The administrative systems in a significant number of these countries are normally prohibitive and surely not helpful for new firm development. The expenses of establishing another firm, as far as the quantity of methodology, holding up time, and authority charges that a beginning up must bear before it can work legitimately, are very high, rearing defilement and impelling the rise of an immense «informal» economy. Casual organizations dependent on close to home associations and family relationship ties defeat the «voids» in the formal institutional foundation; subbing, supplementing, obliging, and in any event, contending with formal establishments.

Concerning the subjective mainstay of the institutional condition, information about how to dispatch or deal with a business might be missing and the help with statistical surveying and different business improvement exercises is as yet not broadly accessible in emerging economies. With respect to the regularizing condition, social standards, social mores, and mentalities to entrepreneurial businesses are very equivocal. On the move economies, for instance, the inheritance of communist belief system left a constant shame on entrepreneurship on account of the conventional relationship of private business action with profiteering and abuse. Individuals in some Latin American countries see entrepreneurship as having useful intrigue yet less status or deceivability. While independent ventures might be across the board in countries, for example, Mexico, and Korea, the longing to keep a business inside family control keep chiefs from taking their organizations open, along these lines restricting their potential for development and open impact.

Notwithstanding these expansive similitudes in the surface of the institutional texture, significant contrasts do exist over all the three elements of the institutional condition among emerging economies. The nine countries in our investigation embody these distinctions. On the administrative measurement, five of the nine countries in our example share the heritage of communism, which was described by cruel concealment of private business culture, dismissal for private property rights, and regulatory oversight of private enterprises by party-controlled organizations.

Concerning the intellectual measurement, the past communist economies generally set a high accentuation on the comprehensiveness and nature of their training frameworks, especially in the hard subjects, for example, science or designing, while India, Brazil, and Mexico are attempting to conquer their pilgrim inheritance of moderately lower levels of human advancement estimated by pointers, for example, proficiency or school enlistment. Concerning the standardizing measurement, other than chronicled heritages molding the national mind, social standards are inserted in particular strict customs, most remarkably Catholicism (Brazil, Mexico, and Hungary), Orthodox Christianity (Russia and Bulgaria), Lutheranism (Latvia), Hinduism (India), Buddhism (South Korea), and Confucianism (China). Every one of these aspects of the institutional condition clearly leaves its engraving on the national limit with respect to entrepreneurship.

This institutional heterogeneity underlies two parts of our exploration question about the favorability of the institutional condition for entrepreneurship in emerging economies across three geographic locales. As for territorial contrasts, look into in both universal business and entrepreneurship has shown a recharged enthusiasm for investigating the job and significance of spatial limits and geographic setting in financial action, including new pursuit arrangement. Exact research has archived that most firms will in general concentrate their deals inside their home district, and that speculators will in general hold their value riches in household resources.

Besides, territorial combination patterns prompted the development of exchanging coalitions, for example, the European Union (EU), NAFTA, and the ASEAN, driving in different degrees to the harmonization of the institutional structure for local financial movement. Geographic vicinity, shared history, and mass movements have likewise formed basic institutional recollections, qualities, convictions, and social mores. At the point when financial, segment, and socio-social factors inside an area cooperate in a considerate and self-strengthening way, they are probably going to make an institutional situation helpful for monetary action and entrepreneurial activities over the locale in general. In this way, we hope to discover contrasts between worldwide locales in the apparent positivity of the institutional system for the advancement of entrepreneurship.

A portion of the distinctions in their particular countries and locales' institutional profiles might be more notable than others. Globalization has been appeared to prompt the improvement of a bicultural identity among youngsters around the globe, joining their neighborhood personality with a character connected to worldwide culture, one that depends on independence, free market financial aspects, and popular government, and incorporates opportunity of decision, receptiveness to change, and resilience of contrasts. These global culture values are probably going to be related with a positive assessment of entrepreneurial activities. The degree to which a nation's occupants respect entrepreneurial action and worth inventive and creative thinking. In this manner, it is sensible to expect that the college understudies over the nine emerging economies may be more comparable than various in their assessment of the national regulating milieu for entrepreneurship.

Numerous specialists trust probably the most ideal approaches to improve financial conditions in emerging markets is to support entrepreneurs particularly those running private companies develop. These little, in many cases casual, firms incorporate dressmakers, eateries, auto fix shops, metal fabricators, cleaning administrations the rundown is immense and ever-evolving. The World Bank tallies around 400 million of them across Africa, Asia, and Latin America, where they make up about 60% of the employments and 40% of the GDP.

Bunches of individuals expect that it's entrance to back that they simply need cash. Something like 80% of the organizations needs access to credit. Also, without a doubt that is a significant requirement to development. You do require money. Be that as it may, you additionally need clients. You need to recognize or make a market, where individuals will really pay you cash in return for your contribution before the budgetary capital can be viably put resources into the business. You need to comprehend what various clients need or need, and how you're going to address those inclinations or take care of those issues.

Right, however, it's not ordinarily something individuals lead with when they come in to help businesses in emerging markets. Frequently when a global or NGO needs to help, it's simply, we must come in with cash. Cash will settle it. As of late, there's been a ton of incredible work on little firms and how to enable them to develop, however, it has would in general spotlight on either money or tasks. The promoting viewpoint has sort of been overlooked. Regularly, it's the manner by which a given showcasing mediation expands execution that offers the key bits of knowledge that we can use to sum up past the setting of an individual nation.

With the consistent improvement of speculations for development, business analysts have included work, capital, and innovation as contributions for the formation work. As of late, entrepreneurship has drawn a lot of consideration from scholastic analysts when they consider it as a significant factor influencing all of past variables in the formation work. Along these lines, entrepreneurship is the determinant for monetary development other than work, capital, and innovation. Nonetheless, researchers likewise contend that entrepreneurship benefits development just a nation has great establishments or administration.

This issue has prompted some past examinations on the impact of entrepreneurship on financial execution. Government approaches, instruments for entrepreneurial exercises, likewise get interests from scientists when various countries with various qualities follow extraordinary approaches to improve their entrepreneurship. Up to now, most of the investigations simply center around the instance of developed countries yet not developing ones where the governments likewise put forth attempt to advance entrepreneurial exercises.

Entrepreneurship is the main thrust for financial development when new businesses make greater business, rise formation, and acquaint developments with the economy. In this manner, entrepreneurial exercises have the positive relationship with financial development. Whether the economy will follow forward gainful or ineffective pattern primarily relies upon the stage a nation is in and the qualities it has. Therefore, it is fundamental for approach producers to have a blend of approaches to manage issues joblessness, salary imbalance, and macroeconomic troubles in the economy to make ready for development. To summarize, administration would have both an immediate and aberrant impact on financial development.

Other than work and capital (physical and human) contributions to the formation work for monetary development, innovation additionally makes an incredible commitment through the progression of advancement and profitability improvement. To measure the advancement of innovation, R&D consumptions and the number of licenses are great intermediaries for development. The financial needs to base on technology as exogenous variable to develop in the long-term, considers information spill overs and innovative substitution in the development procedure.

Despite the fact that the two models have gained tremendous ground in distinguishing factors for development, both neglected to make reference to entrepreneurship, the one deciding innovative innovation. Some past examinations have demonstrated the connections between financial development and entrepreneurship, yet their causality has not been examined at this point. The job of entrepreneurship just as advancement in the financial development and considers placing it into the development model because of the way that the presentation of advancement helps the improvement of items and gives opportunities for entrepreneurs to acquire benefits, which benefits development.

It is the challenge of entrepreneurs that drive the market procedure. The expansion in recently built up businesses and their presentation of imaginative innovations in the market is the establishment for the improvement of entrepreneurship. In this way, innovative development and the formation of new entrepreneurs are viewed as the main thrust of financial development. Thusly, entrepreneurship is an extra contribution to the formation work for monetary development on account of its cultivating advancement and advancing development in the economy. Entrepreneurs' embracing new formation procedures, reallocating assets, and differentiating items to contend with their opponents may shape the long-term monetary development. Entrepreneurship assumes the job of a factor for change, makes new thoughts in the economy, and invigorates monetary development through challenge. Entrepreneurship including the expansion of new advancements and new companies into the business sectors will help develop the economy.

Entrepreneurship exercises and monetary development have the positive relationship with one another. The interest side is connected opportunities an entrepreneur needs to state up, and the stockpile side spotlights on aptitudes also, assets of people in the populace. Whether this connection is positive or negative depends fair and square of entrepreneurship contrasted with its balance. All things considered, higher entrepreneurship rates mean higher development rates in the economy. New beginning up firms not just makes work opportunities inside their own organizations yet additionally increment work in different organizations. Entrepreneurs push development through advancement, consolidated assets, and serious weights. In any case, attributes of entrepreneurial exercises in every nation will drive the economy to beneficial or ineffective increases and the U-molded connection between entrepreneurial exercises furthermore, monetary execution exists thus.

Foundations are the determinants of entrepreneurship since entrepreneurs cannot build their exercises without the guide of establishments. History, culture, society, or governmental issues are various edges important to administration or foundations. A nation may have great administration as long as it improves its foundation through upgrading business condition, staying away from showcase disappointment, and constraining data asymmetry, which help draw in speculation and force advancement. While recognizing the effect of changes in foundation on development, monetary exhibition relies upon whether a nation's organization is appropriate or not and holds that the variety in establishment will impact all elements in different fields of the economy. It is confirmed that physical and human capital, innovation, speculation have a significant influence in financial advancement.

Notwithstanding, administration, and organization are the fundamental factors influencing these determinants. In this manner, in his exploration, enterprises to find qualities of foundation that carry beneficial outcomes to financial development. These qualities incorporate the implementation of the property rights to urge financial specialists to put resources into the nation, the restriction to the intensity of a gathering of elites or legislators on harming the property rights, and the acquaintance of good opportunities with all angles in the economy so every individual can gain admittance to assets and perform beneficial monetary exercises.

The improvement in showcase the board, physical, and human capital, and money related methodology will encourage straightforward organizations. Various procedures for monetary execution of a nation are contained measures to animate financial execution and measures to make it reasonable. While the momentary exhibition to touch off the economy depends on changes and goals, the long-term execution to improve development depends on an assortment of institutional approaches connected to exchange and money related progression, monetary control, serious monetary forms, and privatization just as deregulation. To invigorate the economy, the government needs to make a wise venture condition, improve physical, human, just as social capital, reinforce property rights, and lessen defilement, taxation rate, growth, and monetary flimsiness.

To support the economy, organizations are the guideline factors deciding exercises in the economy. There are three determinants of a nation's foundations: (1) world of politics identified with governmental organization, open administration, and laws, together with guidelines and approaches from the government, (2) monetary condition including the connections among money related intermediations, financial establishments, just as budgetary and capital market, and (3) entrepreneurial condition managing property rights, showcase disappointment, and social capital.

So as to push development in the economy, arrangement producers much of the time join different strategies to determine the issues of joblessness, pay imbalance, macroeconomic challenges, ecological contamination, and individuals' government assistance just as satisfaction. Development brings about higher pay per capita, utilization, and work in the economy. Nonetheless, development additionally prompts mechanical progression that causes work to lose positions to hardware. What's more, the expansion in salary will lessen pay disparity on account of the government's moving livelihoods from the rich to poor people.

It is the presentation of new innovation just as the moderate procedure of ability work improvement that raises untalented laborers' joblessness and brings down their wages. Nonetheless, disparity will be unsafe for development in light of the fact that the job of the entryways will decrease the viability of the measures structured by strategy creators. There is a negative connection between salary imbalance and financial development. The connection between the two is negative in poor countries, however, positive in rich ones.

Pay disparity is anything but a decent determinant for financial development as some past research despite everything finds the positive connection between them. Moreover, the higher salary imbalance is the higher open utilization in training gets, which has a transient negative impact in present moment and a long-term constructive outcome on monetary development. Hence, the connection among administration and financial development is immediate and circuitous, for the most part through its impacts on entrepreneurship. Regarding macroeconomic challenges, higher pay would prompt a more appeal, which prompts expansion and equalization of installment issues because of an expansion in imported merchandise. Right now, increment underway would take care of this issue and address people's issues. At the point when individuals become more extravagant and get advanced education, they will in general secure the earth more. The development in the economy requires more assets. This prompts the harm of the earth.

Subsequently, the connection between monetary development and condition is not clear. Their proposal to maintain a strategic distance from this issue is to improve logical information among individuals. Higher utilization, because of monetary development, likewise produces more significant levels of contamination and waste. On the off chance that the government can constrain the expenses of pay dispersion and natural issues, monetary development would help increment the degree of social government assistance and afterward satisfaction. In any case, the more individuals have, the more they need. In this way, individuals may not be happy with the expansion in utilization and their satisfaction and government assistance do not meet. Financial development would cause individuals to turn out to be increasingly materialistic, childish, and less mindful the general public and afterward social shades of malice would turn into a major issue. To advance monetary development, arrangement producers ought to have proper instruments to make the economy increasingly proficient. The government and market are reliant to one another in the financial exhibition. Government influences the economy through its strategies to empower instruction quality and give aptitude trainings to work. Government can likewise make financial aspects of scale and innovative externalities.

The government assumes a significant job in changing salary appropriation and presenting tax collection strategies. Markets need the government to perform suitably through lawful authorization. Monetary development relies upon productivity or innovation, the sparing rates, and the devaluation of capital. Be that as it may, these components are completely influenced by administration and foundations. Administration has impacts on speculation and entrepreneurship exercises through the social and business condition. To put it plainly, administration would have an immediate and circuitous impact on financial development.

Entrepreneurship has for some time been accepted to be a wellspring of financial development, yet the commitment of entrepreneurship has been watched diversely among emerging and developed countries. This exact investigation gives proof on the connection among entrepreneurship and financial development in 13 emerging countries from 2002 to 2013. The outcomes show that entrepreneurship truly assists with boosting the economy. The extent is moderately little with 0.9% expansion in GDP brought about by 1% expansion in entrepreneurship.

Notwithstanding, it merits seeing that so as to have a decent business condition, it needs a reasonable foundation. Thus, administration goes to the image as a key factor that guarantees the achievement of each entrepreneur. It very well may be comprehended that administration assumes a backhanded job yet a significant one to monetary execution. Understanding that reality, this examination puts forth an attempt to look at factors that influence entrepreneurship. True to form, entrepreneurship, and administration are emphatically identified with one another, yet for the instance of emerging countries, the relationship is upset.

Shockingly, the examination gives proof that better administration lessens entrepreneurship. A sensible clarification is that for emerging countries, casual independent work kind of business represents most of the absolute businesses; in this manner, a progressively sorted out and institutionalized administration implies stricter standards and guidelines and would demoralize new businesses' arrangement. Then again, government use has beneficial outcome on entrepreneurship true to form. There are three arrangement suggestions for emerging countries. To begin with, approaches should concentrate on fortifying General National Framework Conditions and advance undertaking improvement in the long-term.

These approaches should focus on firms with help with overseeing and financing. Diminishing administrative weights is additionally a decent method to empower entrepreneurship; in any case, the strategies that lessen passage hindrances may not be an answer for long-term improvement. The negative impact of administration on entrepreneurial exercises shows that guidelines can make contrasts in dissemination among formal and casual exercises; along these lines, the objective ought to be to lessen need entrepreneurship and upgrade existing little and medium-sized entrepreneurs.

Specific consideration ought to be paid to Intellectual Property Right. One of the inspirations for individuals to begin an appropriate business is giving their thoughts lawful assurance. Licensed innovation laws, for example, licenses, and copyrights are generally feeble in emerging countries, and this issue ought to be improved. Duty strategy likewise assumes a significant job. Lessening charge on salary of firms is a method for compensating their entrepreneurial exercises. A low degree of duty makes the business increasingly appealing and beneficial. Nonetheless, charge income gathered from firms is the primary wellspring of government salary and consumption, so this is a genuine test for strategy creators to adjust the expenses and advantages.

This connection directly to the second strategy ramifications through government use as following. Therefore, government consumption gives a gigantic lift to entrepreneurial exercises. By and by, spending shortfall can make potential vulnerabilities, making the fascination of capital from financial specialists increasingly troublesome and some individual feel too dangerous to even consider pursuing an entrepreneurial way. It is accepted that the conceivable arrangement ought to think about measures to adjust future incomes and consumption by slicing expensive projects to account for fundamental spending.

Under the situation, a sensible proposition is to concentrate on training framework since spending on human capital is viewed as an astute venture for what's to come. Thirdly, strategies ought to advance worldwide incorporation.

Along these lines, any arrangement that plans to help nearby businesses must consider the universal impacts. The two most significant applicable arrangements are exchange and movement approach. Firms cannot react to a globalized domain if the government keeps up guideline hindrances, so approaches that advance the versatility of merchandise, administrations, and capital ought to be executed. Coordinating can likewise give an entrance to outside innovation just as top notch work, two segments of the formation capacity, and this is regularly in type of FDI (Foreign direct investment). Hence, Vietnam can likewise follow the arrangement like other emerging countries when it is coordinating broadly into the world economy. By and large, the arrangement suggestions recommended by this examination offer explicit and sensible headings for strategy making thinking about attributes of emerging countries.

Chapter 6

GENDER ROLES

The world presently faces cultural difficulties in financial, physical, social, and ecological circles that should be handled and survive. Such difficulties incorporate worldwide downturn; fear mongering, a dangerous atmospheric deviation, joblessness, destitution, monetary imbalances, and other social ills. These issues have become so topical that they have developed such a great amount of disturbance in the open area and there is a developing worry into how arrangements might be found to a portion of these difficulties. One of such arrangements is the expanding mindfulness about entrepreneurship advancement and the jobs of entrepreneurs in the financial improvement of a country. Advancing entrepreneurship improvement in this manner will go far in tending to these apparent difficulties being experienced internationally.

Entrepreneurship is viewed as a critical segment during the time spent financial improvement and an entrepreneur is a term used to signify the inventive, present day mechanical business pioneer. This is a significant enormous lump of the populace whose financial possibilities are not appropriately tapped. A country that is resolved to help its economy must put resources into the entrepreneurial improvement of this gender who generally, are burdened with the job of home keeping. Entrepreneurship is the procedure whereby people become mindful of business proprietorship as a possibility for suitable other option, create thoughts for business, get familiar with the procedure of turning out to be entrepreneurs and attempt the commencement and advancement of business considers it to be the capacity to look for venture opportunities and set up an undertaking dependent on recognized opportunities.

It is a critical factor for social and financial development since it gives millions of openings for work, offers an assortment of purchaser products and ventures and by and large increments national success and intensity. It is not simply abilities securing for securing purpose, it is the acquisition of aptitudes and thoughts for making work for self furthermore, for other people. It prompts the improvement of little, medium and once in a while enormous scope businesses in light of imagination and advancement. The triumphs of these businesses thus help in building and developing the country. It additionally helps in diminishing neediness rate. Entrepreneurship in this manner grasps origination, realization, financing, information assortment and resemblance, profession development, arrangement proclamation, staff enlistment and direction, preparing thus on. It additionally includes the training by which an individual risks his time, cash, and exertion, look for change, reacts to it and enterprises it as an opportunity to build up the economy. An entrepreneur is in this way an individual who can distinguish and assess business opportunities and start proper activities for its prosperity; an individual who can change a thought into a business and expect all the risks related with such a business for benefit. For an entrepreneur to succeed he should have the craving, inspiration, energy, assurance, and duty to prevail despite seemingly insurmountable opposition.

An entrepreneur by and large chooses the item, secures the offices, and unites the work power, capital, and formation materials. On the off chance that the business succeeds, the entrepreneur receives the benefit or benefit. On the off chance that it fizzles, the person assumes the misfortune. They went on further to depict entrepreneurs as the individuals who bring thoughts from the universe of structures to the universe of the real world; the individuals who dream and never return to rest until their dreams become genuine. They are the individuals who start from pretty much nothing or nothing, to fabricate something from no place. They offer life to thoughts and make riches from nothing. They are the individuals who can without much of a stretch find the ability in others and outfit it to the greatest. In the event that our general public today is honored with numerous entrepreneurs, we will battle less with the issue of individuals who have gotten a greater amount of liabilities than resources; move away from the attitude of employment searchers to occupation and riches makers.

Thinking starts individuals into the area of thoughts; entrepreneurship includes positive and gainful reasoning, documentation, and assessment of same. Entrepreneurship flourishes with thoughts. Thoughts rule the world; the procedure of formation started with a thought and is continued by good thoughts. Cash streams toward thoughts. Entrepreneurship is dream-driven. The greater the fantasy, the better. It includes move making. Fruitful entrepreneurs talk less, think more, and act more. They find a way to complete their fantasies. It is opportunity-driven as opposed to asset driven. Opportunities exist yet some are too made.

It includes risk accepting. Each business has related risks. The individuals who are chance unwilling, may not prevail in business. It includes difficult work, abilities, information, and disposition. One requires information, difficult work, applicable aptitudes procurement, and the correct mentality to make remarkable outcomes and progress throughout everyday life. Entrepreneurship prompts work formation in this manner lessening joblessness; pay age and salary redistribution, along these lines lessening neediness; improves social attachment subsequently decreasing wrongdoing, prompts monetary development and eventually self-satisfaction and self-completion.

Truly, women are commonly seen in certain climes as homemakers' having little to do with economy or business particularly in Asian countries like Pakistan, India, and so forth. In any case, in countries like Nigeria, women are known to have supported financial exercises; a careless look at our different networks: provincial and urban, uncovers that women have built up themselves as mainstays of families' monetary prosperity by taking part in little, medium, and huge scope financial exercises through which numerous families are being supported. Women comprise a critical gathering in the economy of most sub-Saharan countries. However, their efficiency is obstructed by across the board disparity in access to training, business, medicinal services and profitable assets, for example, land also, credit.

This monetary significance of women is strengthened by numerous researchers who noticed that when women access improvement assets, their efficiency will rise and monetary improvement will be progressively quick. In fact, when women sit on dynamic bodies and take an interest in the structure of advancement programs, these projects will be progressively powerful since they will join women points of view which are all the more grasping. Women likewise have a method for seeing the world through an alternate focal point and thusly, do things any other way.

Entrepreneurs by and large are less than their male partners most particularly in individual and family enterprises. The overviews additionally uncovered that there is an enormous variety across countries. For instance, women possess less than 10% of enterprises in developing countries like Kenya, Morocco, Nigeria, Senegal, and Tanzania. Women are more outlandish than their male partners to possess businesses. They are for the most part found in family enterprises since it is a path for women to have the option to play out their double jobs of dealing with their business and simultaneously play out their local errands which are characteristically women' jobs.

Gender issues are vital in the thought of techniques for improving entrepreneurial advancement as a method for improving monetary development and improvement. These gender issues are significant on the grounds that the jobs played by women in national improvement cannot be overlooked, especially in Agriculture and in casual businesses. The world has come to acknowledge and acknowledge the irreplaceable job of women furthermore, their incredible potential, in advancing another financial request, which is quickening the pace of the monetary advancement. This aids in decreasing the hopeless outcomes of destitution on the planet, especially in the developing countries where 75% of world women live. It is assessed that women possessed businesses represent more than 33% everything being equal, and they are in the dominant part of businesses in the casual segment in African Countries.

In present day India, more women are taking up entrepreneurial exercises particularly in medium and little scope ventures. Indeed, even as a greater amount of their women are accepting training, they face the possibility of joblessness and self-business is subsequently observed as an answer for produce pay. This is a powerful technique to tackle the issue of provincial and urban poverty. Women strengthening will be up front in 2014 as additional organizations, networks, and countries put resources into women entrepreneurship. Referring to Global Entrepreneurial Monitor, there are 126 million women working new businesses and another 98 million in charge of built up ones, yet the world faces an enormous uniformity hole.

It is in just seven countries i.e., Panama, Thailand, Ghana, Ecuador, Nigeria, Mexico, and Uganda that women participate in businesses at rates equivalent to men's. In certain countries like Pakistan, they scarcely participate by any stretch of the imagination. In any event, when women are dynamic business proprietors, they do not come to their possibilities. In the U.S., women possess around 3 out of 10 American firms, yet utilize just 6% of the nation's workforce and record for scarcely 4% of business incomes. Another factor that makes gender issues significant in entrepreneurship improvement is that the capacity of women to formalize and develop their businesses to make occupations and to upgrade efficiency is hampered where legitimate and institutional obstructions influence people's ventures in an unexpected way.

Likewise, explore confirmations, uncovered that gender separation not just prevents women from arriving at their possibilities, it likewise lessens the development possibilities of the country in general. In decreasing the monetary possibilities of women, undertaking advancement, efficiency, and competiveness in the country are additionally unfavorably influenced. Gender disparity assumes a noteworthy job in representing poor development and neediness decrease execution. Gender disparity in instruction may restrain development.

Likewise, imbalances in access to land what's more, beneficial sources of info decrease horticultural profitability, speculation, and modernization. The legitimate what's more, administrative condition is additionally a compelling variable. Different elements including property rights, work laws, individual security, the exhibition of the legal executive, and the time and cost required to register, permit, and work a business all influence intensity and the dynamism of the private division. These ecological components influence women more than men. Laws and Customs obstruct women to a more noteworthy degree than men in getting credit, gainful data sources, instruction, preparing, and data expected to begin and work a business. For instance, women might be less capable than men to bear the cost of long and costly enlistment systems. Consequently, women might be more distraught than men in setting up and dealing with their ventures.

The imperatives that women face in running their businesses include adjusting work and family. Making sure about financing, that is, access to capital. Women face specific obstacles from an absence of insurance to unfair guidelines and imbued gender predisposition. Nascent businesses need backing to prosper and the estimation of coaches cannot be over-stressed. These guides or good examples fill in as consultants for understanding. Most women entrepreneurs do not have that help which clarifies why all around the globe they see less opportunities for entrepreneurship than men.

Likewise, women need Entrepreneurial Education. Winning business ideas are similarly prone to be considered at the kitchen table or in the commercial center yet specialists show that women question their abilities and dread disappointment more than men. Preparing can in this way furnish them with the certainty to oversee thoughts. Women Entrepreneurs are ordinarily crippled in the matter of arranging and running businesses, and there should be a help framework, for example, one that give entrepreneurial instruction to them to have the option to be furnished with important abilities to make them fruitful entrepreneurs.

Sometimes the family may cause the lady to feel blameworthy of disregarding family unit obligations in her quest for business commitments. Social Traditions may keep down a lady from wandering into her own business. Traditional wellspring of money like banks is hesitant to loan to women entrepreneurs particularly in the event that they do not have any male or family backing. This is particularly valid for lower pay females. Women do not have sufficient account or legitimate information to begin an enterprise. It is uncommon to discover women entrepreneurs whose spouses bolster their ventures where there are women enterprises; they are bound to remain in a family unit with different entrepreneurs. Women possess and oversee enterprises with relatives instead of doing it autonomously.

Different requirements incorporate absence of certainty, confidence, and absence of good examples. These undermine the fearlessness of women entrepreneurs. The requirements are debasement in the general public, access to fund, charge organization, dread of disappointment, absence of access to data and mechanical progression, unavailability to essential infrastructural offices, insufficient budgetary assets as banks give credit offices just to association with solid track records and great pledges. At the point when credit offices are given now and again, women are accepted to utilize the reserve to meet the prompt needs of their families or to improve their government assistance. Most women exercises are not referenced in national records. The nonappearance of information is frequently confused to imply that everything is great with women. It is basic to note that lacking information on gender strengthening related factors obstruct joining of women in entrepreneurship rehearses.

Emerging economy countries are constantly perplexing. On one hand, they are beginning later and frequently with fewer assets than progressively settled mechanical economies. Then again, they frequently have neglected cultural needs that can offer huge opportunities to organizations that position themselves appropriately. Regularly, those are organizations that have not yet been conceived. The abundance of opportunities and issues to settle are a bit of leeway, however, producing creative thoughts that go past the standard is not so natural. It tends to be difficult to persuade individuals that they can accomplish something other than what's expected. That is even hard in the United States, however, when you include the layer of rare assets and restricted capacity to bounce back for disappointment, that can achieve alert that restrains an endeavor's capacity to scale.

Entrepreneurs need to comprehend the setting where they are building, how to make things take a shot at alongside nothing for quite a while, and those they need to get income positive as fast as could be expected under the circumstances. In certain pieces of the reality where there are rank frameworks and strict and social hindrances, there are regularly more boundaries to passage for women to ascend in enterprises. Hence, the decision to be an entrepreneur is simpler it is regularly one of the main alternatives. That liberates women to wipe out the 99% of different things that they totally will never do or cannot do.

The best thing we can do is help make occupations on the grounds that these business sectors have not been taken advantage of; there is a gigantic opportunity to dispatch a business in any number of zones, since nothing is yet settled. Where there are more prominent difficulties, there are more prominent opportunities to really improve and think of one of a kind arrangement, to address difficulties that we haven't thought of. Numerous governments just as multilateral associations around the globe are perceiving that entrepreneurs are work makers and that there is an incredible thirst among the up and coming age of youngsters wherever to drive their own future. An ever increasing number of assets are being centered around this repressed interest. It is "the other insurgency," the entrepreneurship upheaval.

Countries must have a framework where individuals are permitted to have thoughts and execute. People can perceive what the issues are, yet would they say they are enabled to take care of those issues for themselves and their families, or their town, or past their town? In developing countries, individuals are heading out to Internet bistros and figuring out how to compose code. Out of nowhere, they are accomplishing work all around the globe. One of the extremely basic difficulties that women face is the absence of access to customary systems in instruction, preparing, financing contrasted with what's accessible with men. So women possessed businesses include discovered incredible opportunities inside helpful associations where they purchase and sell from one another.

They have perceived that while they are sitting tight for Walmart to find what they definitely know that their organizations offer the highest caliber, or speediest turnaround they are as of now working in an effective system with other women. They realize that in the event that they purchase what they need from one another, they speak to a conceivably enormous market in that spot. Each spot has an extraordinary social point of view that entrepreneurs can take advantage of and expand on to bring something new. Style is an extraordinary model. In the Middle East, women are beginning to provide food top of the line items to well-to-do Middle Eastern women. Dolce and Gabbana just presented an entire line intended for Muslim women, truly pursuing that top of the line advertises.

The excellence of being a lady in an emerging-advertise nation is that we're beginning to see colossal macroeconomic changes that not just make it simpler for financial speculators to come in, yet in addition for outsiders to come in and contribute. Frequently, there are amazing projects out there for entrepreneurship and mind-boggling opportunities yet there is a data hole. That data is not showcased to the individuals who need it so as to apply for an agreement or offer to an organization. So nobody gets the data, and opportunities pass. Governments have come to understand that they cannot in any way, shape or form meet their financial needs that is, giving enough government or mechanical occupations for youngsters without advancing entrepreneurship and an entrepreneurial attitude. These economies need to take into consideration advancement and entrepreneurship, else they fall flat.

For most entrepreneurs, their involvement in the government is not certain regardless of whether it's duties, administrative hindrances, permitting, or forms that are dark and troublesome. Limiting or dispensing with those obstructions makes a difference. In any case, governments additionally have a significant job in their capacity to associate, gather, and catalyze what goes on in the entrepreneurial world. Regularly it will be in organization with the private segment, by encouraging and boosting financial specialists or banks. They can get included legitimately by connecting private ventures through the acquirement procedure. In pretty much every nation, the single greatest acquisition source is the government. So if the government focuses on saving piece of that for independent companies that is an immense market.

Governments can add motivators like expense credits to expand speculation. They can advance soundness, IP rights, and value straightforwardness. Furthermore, they can concentrate on increasingly effective transportation that will help independent companies' capability to develop. In case you're a Colombian dairy cattle rancher who needs to pay four distinct dealers to move a cow to advertise, that eats into your capacity to scale. Transforming laws and arrangements to incorporate women will lift up women in emerging markets far quicker than has been the situation in the U.S. One of the essential reasons is that the worldwide economy is so powerful. Countries that are anxious to keep up their monetary development are exceptionally keen on having effective women in the workforce and in ensuring that those women have the essential instruction, but on the other hand are getting the kind of financing that will permit them to begin organizations and scale them up.

Chapter 7

OPPORTUNITIES FOR ENTREPRENEURS IN EMERGING MARKETS

From decades, the entrepreneurship and emerging markets ask about floods have met. Emerging markets are directly allowing a chance to see entrepreneurship in changed settings and structures, and the business parts are as often as possible indisputable from made countries, particularly those in the West, by strategy for culture, financial improvement and political associations. Emerging business division countries are never-endingly many-sided. From one point of view, they are starting later and much of the time with fewer resources than continuously settled present day economies. On in spite of what may be normal, they routinely have ignored social needs that can offer titanic opportunities to the associations that position themselves suitably. Oftentimes, those are the associations that have not yet been considered.

Various governments, similarly as multilateral relationship around the world, are seeing that entrepreneurs are work creators and that there is an unfathomable thirst among the best in class time of youths any place to drive their own future. A regularly expanding number of benefits are being based on this stifled intrigue, and it is the other disturbed called 'The Entrepreneurship Revolution.'

They have seen that while they are holding on for Walmart to discover what they unquestionably know, that their associations offer the most elevated gauge or quickest turnaround. They are starting at now working in a compelling framework with different women. They perceive what they need from each other and present a perhaps enormous market in that spot. Each spot has an exceptional social perspective that entrepreneurs can exploit and develop to bring something new. The greatness of being a woman in an emerging-feature country is that they are starting to see huge macroeconomic changes that not simply make it less difficult for money related examiners to come in yet furthermore for untouchables to come in and contribute.

Governments can add sparks like obligation credits to extend adventure. They can propel robustness, IP rights, and worth straightforwardness. Additionally, they can focus on progressively viable transportation that will help free enterprises' capacity to create. Countries that are on edge to keep up their money related improvement are incredibly enthusiastic about having productive women in the workforce and in guaranteeing that those women have the basic preparing just as getting the sort of sponsoring that will allow them to start associations and scale them up.

The emerging markets are known for its amassing inclination, and the organization business is rapidly developing. The ethnic social affairs are an entrepreneurial source both in emerging markets and among emerging business segment entrepreneurs in have markets. Assorted sensible central focuses may explain ethnic entrepreneurship in emerging markets, including institutional and business bundle hypotheses similarly as the benefit based view, in this way further our perception of entrepreneurship in emerging markets. We are looking forward and believing that the assessment on emerging markets and entrepreneurship will continue developing.

Numerous countries at various phases of improvement have perceived the significance of entrepreneurship in the economy. Entrepreneurship has been recognized as an important apparatus that improves work formation, lightens destitution, and encourages national monetary development. Countries with higher entrepreneurial exercises have consumed significant measures of human and material assets, and thusly experienced development. In any case, in emerging economies, just a chosen few endure the entrepreneurial procedure. A few entrepreneurs get by from fire up stage through to the built up stage, while others do not.

60% of South African private ventures bomb inside the initial five years of activity and over half of Nigerian businesses come up short with a comparative timespan. These figures have since expanded to 80% and 78%, individually. Continuing businesses in emerging economies is a titanic errand. Entrepreneurs experience different difficulties in their day by day exercises. These difficulties cannot all be settled simultaneously. They must be taken care of productively for the businesses to develop. Be that as it may, lamentably, just a chosen few can adapt to the difficulties and just a couple have been known to succeed.

Furthermore, the decision of two emerging economies in Africa, South Africa and Nigeria, is planned for understanding the significance of both merging and separating quirks in these two economies for entrepreneurship drive. South Africa and Nigeria are two countries of exceptionally high monetary pertinence in Africa and the globe. In spite of this, there are varieties in the fundamental entrepreneurship structure of the two countries. Entrepreneurs in Nigeria experience consistent force blackout, flimsy financial frameworks and money related establishments; and access to credit offices while their partners in South Africa appreciate stable power supply, they have very much controlled financial frameworks, and access to fund. It is in this way important to see how diversely the obstacles influence entrepreneurial exercises. Additionally, realizing what the entrepreneurs are facing would get them arranged and help limit the impacts of the difficulties.

Emerging economies are now and then alluded to as developing countries. They are countries with moderately low gross national product (GNP), low per capita pay, and low GDP when contrasted and the industrialized countries. Loads of entrepreneurial exercises occur at the casual part yet are not reflected in the national development record, for example, total national output, and GNP. In developing countries, the infrastructural offices, empowering condition and social qualities for entrepreneurship need bunches of progress.

Albeit entrepreneurial exercises are being empowered in emerging economies, poor usage arrangements and defilement has kept on dissolving the advantages that ought to have been gotten from entrepreneurship. For example, entrepreneurship instruction has been presented in schools, universities, and higher foundations. Hatching Centers and Entrepreneurship Clubs are additionally being built up to advance entrepreneurship. Many emerging economies have executed monetary change arrangements planned for reducing issues, for example, destitution, poor foundation, and overpopulation.

Be that as it may, the effects of such arrangements are yet to be felt at the grassroots. Thus, a large portion of the small and medium-sized enterprises (SMEs) set up by the entrepreneurs barely develop. SMEs establish most of businesses in numerous countries. By chance, there is nobody fundamental meaning of SMEs on the grounds that economies contrast and the real factors that exist change starting with one modern division then onto the next. Thus, the definition and grouping of SMEs differ from nation to another.

In certain countries, yearly turnover, fixed resource base, number of workers, and capital base are a portion of the criteria utilized in characterizing businesses as miniaturized scale, little, and medium enterprises. For example, in Nigeria, utilizing the quantity of representatives, SMEs are characterized as businesses having between 1–300 workers, however, in South Africa; SMEs are businesses having between 1–200 representatives.

Entrepreneurs set up business adventures essentially for different reasons. The force hypothesis contends that people direct entrepreneurial exercises due to individual thought processes, for example, self-satisfaction, riches, and freedom. The push hypothesis fights that people are driven into entrepreneurship by adverse outer powers, for example, joblessness, inadequate pay rates, and employment disappointment. Research discoveries show that people become entrepreneurs basically because of pull, then push factors. The business adventures, be that as it may, could begin as mice, gazelles, or elephants. The mice are smaller scale or independent companies, for example, the corner barbershops, and retail outlets with under 20 workers. Gazelles begin little, however, develop at a sensational rate.

Ventures are whose income twofold like clockwork, and are liable for 70% of every single new position. They are distinguished by their quick development, work making capacities, and deals volume. They can be retail shops, discount outlets, producing organizations, and administration organizations with staff quality of 20–500 representatives. Ultimately, the elephants are the enormous or huge companies, with in any event 500 laborers that frequently become multinationals. The businesses are purported on account of their sizes, development rates, staff quality, and number of branches, however, the two beginning up thought processes depict the business proprietors as way of life entrepreneurs and gazelle entrepreneurs.

The abundance of opportunities and issues to comprehend are a bit of leeway, however, creating imaginative thoughts that go past the model is not so natural. It very well may be difficult to persuade individuals that they can accomplish something else and novel, however, when you include the layer of rare assets and restricted capacity to bounce back for disappointment that realizes an alert that confines an enterprises capacity to scale. Entrepreneurs need to comprehend the setting where they are building, how to make things deal with beside nothing for quite a while, and those they need to get income positive as fast as could be allowed.

In certain pieces of the existence where there are standing frameworks and strict and social obstructions, there are regularly more hindrances to passage for ladies to ascend in organizations. In this way, the decision to be an entrepreneur is simpler; it is regularly one of the main choices. There is a huge opportunity to dispatch a business in any number of regions since nothing is yet dug in. Where there are more noteworthy difficulties, there are more noteworthy opportunities to improve and think of one of kind arrangements and to address difficulties that nobody has even idea of.

Frequently it will be in organization with the private area, by encouraging and boosting speculators or banks. They can get included straightforwardly by connecting independent ventures through the acquirement procedure. In pretty much every nation, the single greatest obtainment source is the government. So if the government resolves to save some portion of that for independent ventures, which will end up being a tremendous market. Governments can add motivators like duty credits to expand venture. They can advance solidness, IP rights, and value straightforwardness. What's more, they can concentrate on increasingly effective transportation that will help independent ventures' capability to develop. Countries that are anxious to keep up their financial development are exceptionally keen on having fruitful ladies in the workforce and in ensuring that those ladies have the essential training as well as getting the kind of subsidizing that will permit them to begin organizations and scale them up.

The emerging markets are known for its assembling aptitude, and the administration business is speedily developing. The ethnic gatherings are an entrepreneurial source both in emerging markets and among emerging business sector entrepreneurs in have markets. Diverse reasonable focal points may clarify ethnic entrepreneurship in emerging markets, including institutional and business bunch speculations just as the asset based view, thus further our comprehension of entrepreneurship in emerging markets. We are looking forward and trusting that the examination on emerging markets and entrepreneurship will keep on developing.

BIBLIOGRAPHY

1. Acemoglu, D., Autor, D., Hanson, G. H., & Price, B., (2016). Import competition and the great us employment sag of the 2000s. *Journal of Labor Economics, 34*(1), 141–198.
2. Acs, Z., Audretsch, D., & Strom, R., (2013). *Entrepreneurship, Growth, and Public Policy*. Cambridge: Cambridge University Press.
3. Acs, Z., Estrin, S., Mickiewicz, T., & Szerb, L., (2018). Entrepreneurship, institutional economics, and economic growth: An ecosystem perspective. *Small Business Economics*.
4. Alvaredo, B. F., Chancel, L., Piketty, T., Saez, E., & Zucman, G., (2017). Global inequality dynamics : New findings from WID. *World American Economic Review: Papers and Proceedings, 107*(5), 404–409.
5. Alvaredo, F., Atkinson, A. B., Piketty, T., & Saez, E., (2013). The top 1% in international and historical perspective. *Journal of Economic Perspectives, 27*(3), 3–20.
6. Anifowoshe, R., (2016). Controversial signposts of the alleged third term agenda. Olurode, L., (ed.), *A Third Term Agenda: To be or Not to be?* Lagos: Faculty of Social Sciences, University of Lagos.
7. Acs, Z., D. Audretsch, and R. Strom eds. (2013), Entrepreneurship, Growth and Public
8. Policy (pp. 219–248). Cambridge: Cambridge University Press.
9. Aulet, B., & Murray, F., (2013). *A Tale of Two Entrepreneurs: Understanding Differences in the Types of Entrepreneurship in the*

Economy. Research Report, Ewing Marion Kauffman Foundation.

10. Autio, E., & Fu, K., (2013). *Allocation of Effort into Informal Entrepreneurship: Contextual and Individual-Level Effects*. GEM Research Conference, Entrepreneurship, and Economic Development, Barcelona. Global Entrepreneurship Monitor.
11. Autor, D. H., Dorn, D., & Hanson, G. H., (2013). The China syndrome: Local labor market impacts of import competition in the United States. *American Economic Review, 103*(6), 2121–2168.
12. Autor, D. H., Dorn, D., Hanson, G. H., & Song, J., (2014). Trade adjustment: Worker-level evidence. *Quarterly Journal of Economics, 129*(4), 1799–1860.
13. Avnimelech, G., Zelekha, Y., & Sharabi, E., (2014). The effect of corruption on entrepreneurship in developed vs. non-developed countries. *International Journal of Entrepreneurial Behavior and Research, 20*, 237–262. https://doi.org/10.1108/IJEBR-10-2012-0121 (accessed on 8 April 2020).
14. Baliamoune-Lutz, M., (2015). Taxes and entrepreneurship in OECD countries. *Contemporary Economic Policy, 33*, 369–380. https://doi.org/10.1111/coep.2015.33.issue-2 (accessed on 8 April 2020).
15. Bloom, N., Draca, M., & Reenen, J. V., (2016). Trade induced technical change? The impact of Chinese import son innovation, it, and productivity. *Review of Economic Studies, 83*, 87–117.
16. Bottazzi, G., & Dindo, P., (2013). Globalizing knowledge: How technological openness affects output, spatial inequality, and welfare levels. *Journal of Regional Science, 53*(4), 631–655.
17. Chatterji, A., Glaeser, E., & Kerr, W., (2013). *Clusters of Entrepreneurship and Innovation*. NBER Working Paper Series, No. 19013, National Bureau of Economic Research.
18. Coulibaly, S., Erbao, C., & Mekongcho, T., (2018). Economic globalization, entrepreneurship, and development. *Technological Forecasting and Social Change, 127*, 271–280.
19. Dhahri, S., & Anis, O., (2018). Entrepreneurship contribution to the three pillars of sustainable development: What does the evidence really say? *World Development, 106*, 64–77.
20. Doran, J., McCarthy, N., & O'Connor, M., (2016). Entrepreneurship and employment growth across European regions. *Regional Studies, Regional Science, 3*, 121–128. https://doi.org/10.1080/21681376.2015

.1135406 (accessed on 8 April 2020).

21. Dreher, A., & Gassebner, M., (2013). Greasing the wheels? The impact of regulations and corruption on firm entry. *Public Choice, 155*, 413–432. https://doi.org/10.1007/s11127-011-9871-2 (accessed on 8 April 2020).

22. Dutta, N., & Sobel, R., (2016). Does corruption ever help entrepreneurship? *Small Business Economics, 47*, 179–199. https://doi.org/10.1007/s11187-016-9728-7 (accessed on 8 April 2020).

23. Fajgelbaum, P. D., & Khandelwal, A. K., (2016). Measuring the unequal gains from trade. *Quarterly Journal of Economics, 131*(3), 1113–1180.

24. Fatas, A., & Mihov, I., (2013). Policy volatility, institutions, and economic growth. *Review of Economic sand Statistics, 95*(2), 362–376.

25. Feenstra, R. C., Inklaar, R., & Timmer, M. P., (2015). The next generation of the Penn world table. *American Economic Review, 105*(10), 3150–3182. http://www.ggdc.net/pwt/ (accessed on 8 April 2020).

26. Ferreira, J. J., Fayolle, A., Fernandes, C., & Raposo, M., (2017). Effects of Schumpeterian and Kirznerian entrepreneurship on economic growth: Panel data evidence. *Entrepreneurship and Regional Development, 29*, 27–50. https://doi.org/10.1080/08985626.2016.1255431 (accessed on 8 April 2020).

27. Gebel, M., & Giesecke, J., (2016). Does deregulation help? The impact of employment protection reforms on youths' unemployment and temporary employment risks in Europe. *European Sociological Review, 32*(4), 486–500.

28. GEM, (2015). *GEM 2001–2014 APS Global Key Indicators*. Retrieved from: http://www.gemconsortium.org/data/sets (accessed on 8 April 2020).

29. Gianesini, G., Cubico, S., Favretto, G., & Leitao, J., (2018). Entrepreneurial competences: Comparing and contrasting models and taxonomies. In: *Entrepreneurship and the Industry Life Cycle* (pp. 13–32). https://doi.org/10.1007/978-3-319-89336-5 (accessed on 8 April 2020).

30. Gygli, S., Haelg, F., & Sturm, J. E., (2018). *The KOF Globalization Index-Revisited* (p. 439). KOF Working Papers.

31. Hampel-Milagrosa, A., Loewe, M., & Reeg, C., (2015). The entrepreneur makes a difference: Evidence on MSE upgrading factors from Egypt,

India, and the Philippines. *World Development, 66*, 118–130.

32. Jain, S. S. D., (2013). Institutional logic migration and industry evolution in emerging economies: The case of telephony in India. *Strategic Entrepreneurship Journal*, Special Issue 7.
33. Marcotte, C., (2013). Measuring entrepreneurship at the country level: A review and research agenda. *Entrepreneurship and Regional Development, 25*, 174–194. https://doi.org/10.1080/08985626.2012.710264 (accessed on 8 April 2020).
34. Marcotte, C., (2014). Entrepreneurship and innovation in emerging economies: Conceptual, methodological, and contextual issues. *International Journal of Entrepreneurial Behavior and Research, 20*, 42–65. https://doi.org/10.1108/IJEBR-09-2012-0089 (accessed on 8 April 2020).
35. Mariet, O. V., (2016). Financing village enterprises in rural Bangladesh: What determines nonfarm revenue growth? *International Journal of Development Issues, 15*, 76–94. https://doi.org/10.1108/IJDI-09-2015-0057 (accessed on 8 April 2020).
36. Nwokah, G. N., & Adiele, K. C., (2015). The socio-economic impact of globalization in Nigeria. *Journal of Economics and Sustainable Development, 6*(10), 238–247.
37. Olaison, L., & Meier, S. B., (2014). The abject of entrepreneurship: Failure, fiasco, fraud. *International Journal of Entrepreneurial Behavior and Research, 20*, 193–211. https://doi.org/10.1108/IJEBR-09-2013-0143 (accessed on 8 April 2020).
38. Prieger, J., Bampoky, C., Blanco, L., & Liu, A., (2016). Economic growth and the optimal level of entrepreneurship. *World Development, 82*, 95–109.
39. Sautet, F., (2013). Local and systemic entrepreneurship: Solving the puzzle of entrepreneurship and economic development. *Entrepreneurship Theory and Practice, 37*(2), 387–402.
40. Thurik, R. (2013), 'On Entrepreneurship, Economic Growth and Policy', in Z. Acs, D. Audretsch, and R. Strom (eds.), Entrepreneurship, Growth and Public Policy. Cambridge: Cambridge University Press, pp. 219-248.
41. Urbano, D., & Aparicio, S., (2016). Entrepreneurship capital types and economic growth: International evidence. *Technological Forecasting and Social Change, 102*, 34–44.

42. WB/IFC, (2013). *Doing Business 2013: Smarter Regulations for Small and Medium-Size Enterprises*. Washington DC: World Bank, International Finance Corporation.
43. WBES, (2013). *Informality.* World Bank Enterprise Surveys, Retrieved from: http://www.enterprisesurveys.org/data/exploreTopics/Informality (accessed on 8 April 2020).
44. World Bank, (2015). *Country and Lending Groups*. Retrieved from: http://data.worldbank.org/about/country-and-lending-groups#Low_income (accessed on 8 April 2020).
45. Xavier, S., Kelley, D., Kew, J., Herrington, M., & Vorderwülbecke, A., (2013). *Global Report 2012*. Global Entrepreneurship Monitor.
46. Yusuf, S., (2016). *Globalization and the Challenges for the Developing Countries*. World Bank Development Economic Research Group. Retrieved from: http://www.worldbank.org (accessed on 8 April 2020).
47. Zhang, Y., Yang, J., Tang, J., Au, K., & Xue, H., (2013). Prior experience and social class as moderators of the planning performance relationship in China's emerging economy. *Strategic Entrepreneurship Journal*, Special Issue 7.

INDEX

P

R

S

T

U

V

W